TOWARD A NEW PSYCHOLOGY:
The Miracle of the Mind

by Wilfred F. Garcia

DORRANCE
PUBLISHING CO
EST. 1920
PITTSBURGH, PENNSYLVANIA 15238

Dorrance Publishing Co
585 Alpha Drive, Suite 103
Pittsburg, PA 15238
Visit our website at www.dorrancebookstore.com

ISBN: 978-1-4809-2445-1
eISBN 978-1-4809-2215-0

CONTENTS

PREFACE

Hello. My name is Wilfred Francis Garcia. I have been nicknamed Fred, but Wilfred is okay too.

I have a Master of Science degree in clinical psychology, which involves a focus on the study of abnormal human behavior. This has also been my practice. I have worked primarily with seriously mentally ill people who occupy beds in psychiatric hospitals. Many also receive services through their community mental health centers or private practitioners. Although this is my practice, fundamentally, I am drawn to understanding the person or personality: to human understanding in whatever setting I am in. This interest pervades my daily existence.

Psychology, for those of you who do not know, is about the study of individual human behavior, as distinguished from sociology, which is more about how humans interact in groups. I titled this book *Toward a New Psychology* because of discoveries about our subconscious mind and mental illness that should provide everyone a better understanding of human behavior in general and mental illness in particular, which should also improve the treatment that is available for the mentally ill. I subtitled it *The Miracle of the Mind* because of the remarkable spirit world that comprises our mind, which is a rich inheritance from our God that is referenced in the doctrine that comprises my religion. Our minds are quite remarkable, which I think is aptly described in these pages. I am sure you will agree that our minds are miraculous.

This book is about psychology and religion. It has a broad scope. Its origins are in my personal struggle with a mental experience that we refer to as schizophrenia and what I have learned as a result of that struggle. It also reflects the knowledge that I have gained from a career devoted to human understanding and my lifelong indoctrination in Christianity: specifically, Catholicism. In reconciling the two—psychology and religion—I have been inspired to a greater understanding of humanity. It is these insights that I wish to share with the reader. I am not a theologian or a scholar, and I am not even well read, though I enjoy reading when I can.

Schizophrenia is one of the severe mental disorders along with delusional disorder, bipolar disorder (formerly manic-depressive disorder), major depressive disorder, and schizoaffective disorder. Schizoaffective disorder is a hybrid that includes either major depressive disorder or bipolar disorder as well as schizophrenia. One of the reasons they are called "severe" is because they are incapacitating to the extent that they affect social behavior, such as the ability to relate to other persons; work behavior, such as being able to perform a job effectively; and education, such as being able to apply oneself well in a school setting. People who receive a diagnosis of schizophrenia typically have gradual changes in behavior over time. Other people notice that they act differently, such as withdrawing from social settings, staying to themselves more, and not seeming to fit in as well. They may have unusual ideas, called schizotypal ideas, and act on them. The diagnosis results when these persons exhibit typical signs and symptoms that cause them difficulty relating to their world. They may distort events happening in their lives. I discuss these signs and symptoms in the next chapter, where I talk about schizophrenia and its cause.

I wrote this book out of a tremendous sense of responsibility because I expect that it will have a positive impact on millions of people who have a diagnosis of schizophrenia or who will meet the criteria over their lifetime. This will result from a better understanding of schizophrenia, which should lead to a better view of these people by society-at-large, improvement in treatment, and a better prognosis over the course of this disorder. I expect the ideas and findings contained herein will also have an impact on people who have other psychiatric disorders and human behavior in general. They address human behavior in a critical, revealing way that inherently challenges us all to change for the betterment of humanity. They are also very revealing about the state of humanity and how we got here, and they point to the vision of life that we can and were meant to have by our Creator.

My excitement about sharing these ideas is tempered by the knowledge of the path I feel that I should take to do so. Schizophrenia and other psychiatric disorders, as I have come to understand them, are most likely to occur within the family because it is within the family that we form bonds, develop patterns of relating, and become subject to other dynamics that will influence us for the rest of our lives. I have come to understand that there are various causes or routes to schizophrenia and various ways in which this disorder presents itself. I am most familiar about and most confident in speaking about mine, which should be an illuminating and, likely also, a classical, even if limited example, which should illustrate well for the reader some of the fundamental characteristics that are present in the development and maintenance of schizophrenia. Therefore, in order to describe this disorder in the clearest and most effective way—to provide a shining example that will be most helpful—I will need to disclose some of the dynamics within my family as I describe my personal struggle with schizophrenia. This will be a critical and revealing narrative of the most personal sort about me and my family that I would not do if I did not think it was of the utmost necessity. I will occasionally need to reveal other relationships also.

The ideas described in this book effectively provide an explanation for my own experience of schizophrenia, point the way to understanding other mental illnesses, and increase our understanding of human behavior. Initially, in regard to my experience of schizophrenia, they were hypotheses and theories, which were repeatedly tested and became explanations for me. They have been a part of my daily existence—I have lived and breathed them—and they have been developed and refined over time. They progressed beyond any hypotheses or theory in my integrative mental processes because they were necessary for my very survival. They have been put to the test in my mind's eye time and time again and have stood the test of considerable time while also developed and refined. When I became a student of psychology, they were subjected to as much scientific rigor as I encountered. They were in no case that I can recall effectively refuted by scientific findings but, rather, they have often been supported by them. This would include other explanations for schizophrenia than the predominant medical model view. Thus, I expect the scientific community to find agreement rather than disagreement with them over time, and I expect them to stand the test of time.

These ideas are presented broadly over the course of this book, which includes some significant corroboration or considerable supporting information that both the general public and those with a more scientific or psychology and related field persuasion will recognize as present or experienced by them in their respective lives. I have applied them to untold numbers of patients during psychological assessments in the psychiatric hospital where I work. When I entered the field, it seemed to me that contemporary psychological education singled out human behavior as unlike all else in being so complex as to be difficult to understand, explain, and predict. I can think of no instance in my assessments when I have had sufficient history and sample of behavior that I have not found the personality to be part of a coherent, understandable picture, even the most inscrutable personalities. It is possible to understand human behavior, which provides an explanation for it and which helps to predict it. I think the ideas presented in this book will help us all to understand and appreciate one another better, each in his or her own way. I hope that others will reap the immensurable enjoyment from this process and the added dimension to living that I have.

Psychology has many strategies to treat the afflictions of the human personality. I have always conceived such afflictions in the context of religion, intuitively, or inherently, which has been a general conceptualization that I have subjected people to, not in a judgmental way, but to understand better their course in living, for the insights that it brings. To say this another way, in assessing the personalities of various people, I have gathered information about their morality for what it may say about their spiritual lives and their afflictions or misfortunes. This has been an emphasis that I have always had because we need to make up for our mistakes in order to grow along spiritual lines, which is the way to personal growth, maturity, and happiness: qualities we all need. Alternatively, inconsiderate ways, imprudent living, and the like can encumber us psychologically and lead to mental and physical maladies.

The ideas in this book provide a clear explanation of the relationship between psychology and religion, which, I think, helps to bridge any gap in knowledge or understanding between them that existed previously. They make it clear, with unmistakable corroboration, how our transgressions, sins, faults, or wrongs cause us psychological problems that affect our relationship with God in a measurable, illuminating way that should motivate us to make positive changes in our lives. I hope and trust that the reader will be as impressed by and appreciate these findings to the same extent that I have. I could not believe that it would be otherwise.

I make reference in various sections of the book and most poignantly in chapter 11, "My Parents: Forces or Events That Influenced Their Behavior and Mine," to choices made by my parents during their lives that affected their personality and spiritual development, which affected their treatment of me and was relevant to my development of schizophrenia. These are events that many of us experience in life and that do not seem so impressive or significant, though we might also agree readily that they are mistakes. I have magnified these events in these pages to make it clear to the reader how such events, though they may not seem so impressive at first glance, are actually very significant. For example, with regard to mom and dad, I seek to make it crystal clear how they made complacent rather than rightful choices that affected the quality of their lives.

I point out how their choices affected their relationship with God and the Christian community, meaning also their spiritual lives and their capacity for enlightened thought, which is a rich heritage that God calls us to. It is as a result of consequences like these that parents may seek to limit their children. That is, the parental expectations are likely to be a reflection of their own achievement because that is what they know and what they are comfortable with. This can lead to problems if a child seeks a vibrant spiritual life that the parents cannot accept and the child does not acquiesce to the limits they impose. The ensuing mental opposition by the parent, parents, or significant others can lead to the disorder that we refer to as schizophrenia. I will show how it explains mine.

Chapter 12 speaks of early parental influences and family life. It highlights my immaturity and mistakes that I made during that time, while I was in the parental home, which may lead the reader to ask whether my attribution of the cause of my schizophrenia to parental shortcomings is correct or whether it could be something that I brought upon myself by my misbehavior. I did not begin hearing voices until 1981 (age 29), and it was after that when I acquired ideas about an awakening of the subconscious mind, subvocal speech, and mental opposition—concepts that I will explain in the next chapter on the cause of schizophrenia. Thus, it was not until about age thirty and afterward, gradually, that I began to acquire an understanding of the subconscious world and the forces that shaped my schizophrenia. For this reason, explanations of these influences on my life before then were made taking a retrospective or backward glance. Consequently, although the description of significant events in my life up to age thirty are sometimes notable, I have had to rely more on contemplation, parallels, analogy, inference, and supposition because I have no samples of subconscious events before then. Alternatively, I have rich examples since age thirty that support and corroborate many of my findings, which lend credence to my backward glance. Furthermore, I think all or most of the answers to the extraordinary findings described in this book lie within these pages or that the integrated findings explain them if we but consider them.

David Anders, a Catholic theologian who does book reviews for Eternal World Television Network (EWTN), was gracious enough to review my book. He sometimes questioned the extent that my ideas were supported by rigorous scientific methods, such as research and experimentation. My ideas are novel, unusual, and likely to be viewed as radical at first. They do not readily subject themselves to scientific methods because of the tremendous influence from the subconscious world. However, I have included pertinent data to support rich inferential information, have been able to establish some degree of corroboration, have found references to them in scripture, and describe my findings in a considerate way that enhances their credibility. In the final analysis, I think that I have subjected them to scientific rigor, the elements of which are described in these pages. The jury may still be out on whether science will support them. I have no question that they are reliable and valid.

I make a distinction in this book between the working and the professional class, expound on the merits of a college degree, measure progress in the accounting field, and talk of opportunities for social advancement. I draw parallels between the relative success or lack of success that my father and mother had in developing skills in these areas and the corresponding effect on their spiritual lives or capacity for enlightened thought, which, in turn, had an effect on the development of their language skills and intellect. Although my premise is subject to question, I provide rich examples to illustrate my point regarding their relative progress or lack of progress in these areas and explain clearly the relevance to my schizophrenia. However, these are not absolute but general distinctions that are not meant to undermine any class or group of people. I would not underestimate the ability of anyone to achieve enlightenment and genius in their respective capacities, whether members of the professional or trade class; the gifts endowed by their Creator; their mental capacity for mechanically oriented tasks; their capacity for great advancement within a technical field to become a leader, a manager, or someone who relates directly with professionals such as engineers and chief executive officers; their individual wills; and other capabilities. As a wise priest once told me in order to guide me on hearing my confession, "You can't capture the Holy Spirit."

This book focuses primarily on my course to schizophrenia and its cause or determinants. However, my deliberations over it have compelled me to ponder other courses to and determinants of schizophrenia and other mental disorders. In considering my younger brother George's schizophrenia and the many cases I have studied, some of which are documented in this book, I have come to more fully recognize that my experience, though likely a classical example, is but one of a number of courses to or determinants of schizophrenia. However, it is a most revealing example of the subconscious world, including how it relates to mental illness and human behavior. This knowledge of the subconscious should advance our understanding of normal and abnormal human behavior and the quality of treatment for the latter. This remarkable subconscious world is none other than our spirit life, a thrilling finding that is referenced with clarity in this manuscript.

PART I:

The Basis for Schizophrenia

CHAPTER 1:

SCHIZOPHRENIA: ITS CAUSE

The cause of schizophrenia has not been discovered. For many years, since the advent of medication to treat schizophrenia in the 1950s, the prevailing view was that schizophrenia was due to overstimulation in the limbic system of the brain, a part of the brain that is involved in regulation of strong emotion. This overstimulation was used to explain a cluster of symptoms seen in schizophrenia that are termed "positive symptoms" because the symptoms are regarded as abnormal and excessive in comparison to ordinary experience. These so-called positive symptoms of schizophrenia include hallucinations and delusions, which are posited as abnormal or distorted perceptions that can lead people to act in a way that is not in touch with the environment around them, sometimes in bizarre and dangerous ways; disorganized speech, the measurable product of thought disturbances and thought interference that makes it difficult for these persons to express their ideas in a direct and organized way; and other problems, such as agitation, irritation, and uncoordinated movements. This excess stimulation was attributed to overactivity of the neurotransmitter or nerve chemical dopamine, which has a tract of nerves that project to the limbic system in the brain (6)(12)(25).

This view about the cause of schizophrenia came about accidentally, when the scientific world discovered that a drug with strong sedating properties, Thorazine, was capable of alleviating the agitation seen in schizophrenia. One of the primary actions of Thorazine is to prevent one nerve from transmitting its message via dopamine to the next nerve by blocking the dopamine (e.g., dopamine-2 or D2) receptors on the receiving nerve: Thorazine is a dopamine antagonist (6). Subsequently, this drug and a number of others, termed neuroleptics, were used to target the purported excessive dopamine in the limbic system, thereby regulating it and alleviating the positive symptoms of schizophrenia (12). This view came to be known as the dopamine theory of schizophrenia (6)(12)(25). These findings were considered a scientific breakthrough, which allowed many of these hospitalized patients to live in the community again. They ushered in the community mental health centers movement during President John F. Kennedy's term, which was designed to provide the services these formerly hospitalized inpatients would require in their community and help them to remain there. Eventually, with advances in scientific knowledge and tools, such as radiographic and imaging technology that illustrated the structure and functioning of the brain, the dopamine mesolimbic pathway of the brain was identified as the relevant pathway for the overstimulation in the limbic system that was thought to produce positive symptoms of schizophrenia (6)(12)(25).

The scientific world, as a result of advances in technology, gradually recognized that the dopamine theory of schizophrenia was limited and incomplete (12). For example, in addition to positive symptoms of schizophrenia, negative and cognitive symptoms were identified. Negative symptoms pertain to the absence of normal behavior, such as being socially withdrawn, hardly saying anything, an absence of expression, and a lack of motivation to do anything (3) (4) (12). This cluster of regressed behavior is most often seen in people who do not achieve a very high level of academic, social, or functional skills before the onset of their mental illness (3) (4) (27). The cognitive symptoms include problems in such cognitive functions as attention, working memory, and executive functions, including problem solving, exercising judgment, and organizing and planning behavior (3) (4), (12). The mesocortical pathway, a dopamine tract of nerves that projects to the prefrontal cortex, has been identified and has been noted to be influential in these regards. Insufficient dopamine to this area of the brain has been associated with the negative and cognitive symptoms of schizophrenia (12), (25), (26). Imaging studies have shown a decrease in blood flow and glucose to this area of the brain and reduced brain size in the frontal and temporal lobes. These deficits have also been associated with the cognitive and negative symptoms (28, (29). Moreover, other neurotrans-

mitters have been implicated in schizophrenia, such as serotonin and gluta-
mate, either individually or by their effect on the dopamine neurotransmitter
system (12). Antipsychotic medications subsequent to the original medications have sought to target this broader array of symptoms of schizophrenia:
the positive, negative, and cognitive symptoms. What is the underlying reason for these chemical irregularities or imbalances as well as the reduced
blood flow, reduced glucose, and brain atrophy noted?

Demographic information provides strong evidence for a hereditary link
to schizophrenia. For example, the prevalence of schizophrenia in the general
population is much lower than it is for persons who have a parent or sibling
with schizophrenia, and it is higher for the identical twin than it is for the
fraternal twin of the sibling with schizophrenia. A diathesis-stress model has
also been posited (5). That is, many people are genetically predisposed to have
schizophrenia, meaning they have the genetic makeup researchers are trying
to discover, and environmental or other factors trigger the disorder to become
active, such as adverse events during the gestation period (e.g., malnutrition,
infection, or oxygen deficiency); traumatic events during their childhood; and
lack of nurturance and support. Some of these stressors are thought to impact
neuronal (nerve) development, such as the integrity of the nerve, its ability to
regulate neural transmitters, and the amount of neuronal connections, which
are events of biological and physiological significance that could have a bearing on the balance of neurotransmitters like dopamine (28), (29).

The genome project to map the human brain began in 1990 as a result
of technological advances pertinent to genetics and was declared as complete
initially in 2003. With these advances in technology, researchers sought to
identify the candidate genes for schizophrenia and their action. According
to pertinent literature, researchers have acquired the impression that schizophrenia is a heterogeneous disorder which is likely caused by not a few but
likely by hundreds of genes or genetic loci, each having a small effect. Furthermore, their advanced research methodology identified genes which they
think are or may be candidate genes for this disorder (3).

I have acquired knowledge that I expect to fill a missing link science
needs to explain schizophrenia. Instead of discounting either nature or nurture, such as heredity or the environment, I believe it helps to put them into
perspective. This I will elucidate in chapter 7, "Research on Genetics." Let
me begin by explaining my own experience, which I will make clearer over
the course of the discussion in this book.

The evidence I have gathered has led me to understand that the variety of schizophrenia I have experienced, which is just one course to the disorder, but an illuminating one, begins with and is due to the loss of mental support from significant other persons, an event that occurs primarily at a subconscious level. Additionally, in this variety, the person so affected also experiences mental antagonism from those significant persons and other people, which also occurs largely at a subconscious level. This loss of support and adversity makes it more difficult for people affected to succeed in their pursuits. They are more likely to experience problems in living and other forms of stress, which they may not be able to resolve. Consequently, they may become overwhelmed psychologically and begin to experience mental illness; more specifically, schizophrenia, as we have come to describe the signs and symptoms that they have. What actually happens that leads to these signs and symptoms of schizophrenia are influences from the subconscious mind as it is affected by antagonists, which causes it to become awakened in varying degrees, by which I mean more permeable or evident to the conscious mind, a very distracting influence that is not understood. Let me make this clearer.

Schizophrenia is most evidently present when a person's subconscious mind is awakened to the extent that the person so affected experiences what we refer to as auditory hallucinations—the phenomenon of hearing what I refer to as subvocal speech—which is the voices of other minds that most people cannot hear. For this phenomenon to occur, a person usually undergoes much stress and distress, like the sort that stems from serious problems or concerns that cannot be resolved and weigh heavily on that person, causing him continuous worry, much preoccupation, disturbed sleep, and the like, until, at some point, the subconscious mind or mental state begins to intrude on the conscious mind or mental state. Disturbed sleep over a period of time may be the key ingredient that eventually results in the conscious mind becoming permeable to the subconscious mind. The person begins hearing subvocal speech, which is an integral part of the transmission of thought. That is, we say every idea that we think or transmit to another person and vice versa: thought does not occur or transmit without the accompanying voice. We are not verbalizing with our mouths but with our minds.

These auditory hallucinations that the person so affected hears are the voices of other minds. Once the subconscious mind is awakened, the conscious mind seems to remain permeable to that influence in people who develop the disorder we refer to as schizophrenia. This is a most distracting influence because the two minds are not coordinated as to purpose or motivation in schizophrenia. It is as if the person is responding to two modes of existence at the same time: responding to interpersonal or environmental stimulation from the outside world, such as people speaking to him or in his vicinity, and responding to voices that his mind hears from the subconscious or spiritual world. Let me explain further why the awakening of the subconscious mind leads to schizophrenia.

When the subconscious mind begins intruding upon the conscious mind, the person experiencing this phenomenon has to attend to two different sources of stimulation that are not consonant with each other, which creates much distraction for that person. A look at the signs and symptoms of schizophrenia helps to understand this dual experience. One sign is referred to as inappropriate affect (affect being a reference to our emotional expressions), such as laughing in the middle of a conversation that is serious without any obvious external stimulation for the humor, which may puzzle the speaker. The most common explanation for this behavior has been that the person with schizophrenia was responding to intrusive stimulation at the time, such as auditory hallucinations (e.g., hearing "voices"), which is not a poor explanation at all. The idea that this person's subconscious mind was awakened allows for the more specific statement that he most likely heard the voice of another mind making a humorous statement.

Another example might be evidenced by this person exhibiting much discomfort in a social situation, to the extent that he leaves the room, and he later reports to a trusted friend or therapist that he could hear his very private thoughts being expressed out loud, which is a paranoid symptom or delusional idea observed in schizophrenia that is referred to as thought broadcasting. To expound on the idea that another mind can communicate to our mind at a subconscious level, which becomes a distraction to the person whose subconscious mind has been awakened, another mind can also become privy to the thoughts of an unwilling host and repeat them, an event that occurs at a subconscious level. When these subvocal statements are received by other people in the room, they act like a form of suggestion that may affect their expression and cause the affected person, who is able to hear the subvocal speech at a conscious level, to become very anxious. Still another example might have this person look away quickly or raise his hand to block a lewd image created by a statement made to him by the uninvited mind at a subconscious level, which intrudes upon his consciousness to result in the defensive response described, behavior that may appear very odd. In this instance, another mind most likely made a sexually suggestive statement that gave rise to the lewd image in order to make the affected person uncomfortable. These are but some brief examples of the distracting influences that a person who has had an awakening of his subconscious mind can have and why or how the distractions occur.

The hallucinations that are experienced by those people whose subconscious mind has been awakened, which are the voices of other minds, may contain paranoid content, such as preying on their vulnerabilities to make them think family members or co-workers are against them, plotting to do something to them, talking about them, and so forth. This can lead persons so affected to become angry without any apparent or outward cause. They may act in a hostile or dangerous manner or take other action that may indicate a need for psychiatric treatment. It is important to understand that a mind that is privy to another mind's every thought will become increasingly aware of the doubts, insecurities, vulnerabilities, and other weaknesses of the person whose mind he is affecting.

Another symptom of schizophrenia is inability to speak in a clear and organized fashion. This speech difficulty is referred to as thought disorder or thought disturbance. The person experiencing thought disorder may feel that his thoughts are being blocked; may have difficulty integrating the components of reasoning and speaking, such as accessing his memory, organizing his ideas while contemplating an issue or a response, and expressing his ideas clearly and concisely; and may tend to refrain from saying much due to the effects of the thought disorder, including a reduction of ideas. His speech difficulty may range from inefficiency in speaking, such as long, roundabout explanations and halting speech to ideas that are not connected well—a phenomenon referred to as loosening of associations or disjointed speech—and speech that is incoherent. The experience of thought disturbance is a further elaboration of how another mind can influence the mind which the perpetrator is opposing at a subconscious level. In this instance, another mind is seeking to suppress the affected person's reasoning and speaking ability, thereby creating the thought disturbance. When we access memory, we have to hear the idea that we are recalling, and another mind can seek to disrupt this process, slowing and interfering with reasoning, which has led to the coining of schizophrenic symptoms such as thought blocking.

Another mind can also influence the affected person's perception and feelings, which can cause that person's ideas and emotions to become overemphasized and distorted. Similarly, another mind can introduce alternative ideas that result in much ambivalence as the victim seeks to communicate. People subject to these influences sometimes report a feeling like a tight band around their head, which may describe tension produced by another mind. The combination of distracting influences from one or more antagonistic minds, such as subvocal speech and thought disturbances, can lead to another schizophrenic symptom referred to as disorganized behavior. The person experiencing such distraction may not be able to act in a coordinated way and may exhibit behaviors such as assuming a rigid posture, awkward staring, a lack of focus, walking aimlessly, frequently looking up, and occasionally hollering out at no one in particular.

I stated that the confirming experience for the syndrome that we refer to as schizophrenia is when the victim of interpersonal opposition begins hearing subvocal speech—the voices of other minds—which we refer to as auditory hallucinations. However, although most persons who receive the diagnosis of schizophrenia experience auditory hallucinations, not all do. My own experience was such that I did not begin to hear other minds regularly until my third schizophrenic episode. I had references from the television, which is the equivalent, but this happened briefly while I was watching television. Schizophrenia is a syndrome that gradually develops. The stress created by adversaries, both at a conscious and subconscious level, has such effects as augmenting the victim's emotional experience. As a result, he may interpret interpersonal events as relatively more malevolent or sinister than is common in ordinary experience, which may meet the criteria for the symptoms of schizophrenia that we refer to as paranoid or delusional ideas. Such stress can also cause the victim to have difficulty organizing his ideas so as to communicate effectively, which may have elements of the symptom of schizophrenia that we refer to as disorganized speech or meet those criteria.

These experiences are part of the same process that leads to the symptom of schizophrenia that we have referred to as auditory hallucinations: hearing other minds. They are caused by the mental adversaries. I am not certain why some people who appear to experience the syndrome that we refer to as schizophrenia do not hear subvocal speech. I could not say specifically whether some people who experience schizophrenic symptoms retain sufficient cognitive integrity that their subconscious minds are not awakened to the extent that they hear subvocal speech; that their cognitive integrity is gradually compromised until they begin hearing other minds; that their mental adversaries are relatively more silent; or that the permeability of their conscious mind to their subconscious mind remains subthreshhold as to subvocal speech for some other reason.

Schizophrenia, in my opinion, has historically been most likely to develop within the traditional family. It is often a dysfunctional or unhealthy pattern. Distinguishing features of the variety that I have experienced are the loss of mental support and mental opposition. From the moment of birth, we develop bonds with the significant other people in our lives, usually our parents, which occur at a conscious and subconscious level. At a subconscious level, particularly when the bonds are very healthy, we recognize their love, concern, aspirations for us, expectations, and other intimate ways. At a conscious level, in addition to such recognition, we develop effective if not intimate forms of communication with them in order to meet our needs, learn their expectations, and so forth. This relationship can become so close that we can literally recognize their guidance at an emotional level without them having to utter a word, consciously or subconsciously. I call this mental support. It is a binding and protective force that acts as a buffer or shield from outside forces—other people or other minds that might exploit or take advantage of us if given the chance. They are not able to penetrate this bond that develops within our families, and our parents have a natural alertness and motivation to see that it remains that way, because as they grow older and we mature, we will reciprocate this protective shield.

Once again, this distinguishing feature of the variety of schizophrenia that I have experienced is the loss of mental support. Amidst the structure of the family unit, a bond develops between children and parents that has a mental component, a psychological bond that shields and protects the child from outside forces—other minds that might exploit the mind of the child that lacks such support. Without such support, the child would become susceptible to being exploited, taken advantage of, and having a number of other negative experiences at the expense of other minds acting in an antagonistic fashion. These negative experiences can be of such significant proportions as to create ongoing distress that leads to schizophrenia. A necessary component of mine, as I have come to understand, is for a mind to become isolated from mental support, which comes from significant other people in our lives. I believe that mental support from one significant other person is sufficient to insulate the recipient from mental illness as I have experienced it: that it is sufficient for keeping other minds at bay. This is not a casual relationship but a very significant bond as is borne within the family, in a marriage, and the like. In the family unit, the mentoring and bonding usually comes from our parents if the nuclear family unit is intact.

Why would a parent decide not to bond with a child? My mother, despite all the love and affection, direction, and teaching that she gave me during my upbringing, for which I loved her dearly, also seemed to want to retain control over my ability to grow and develop into an independent and successful human being. Why would a mother want to do such a thing? I do not think that we have to look much further than human insecurity. A part of her did not want to let go. She had seven other children after me, her first, and I think that she was willing to let the rest go, but this was not so for me. She very actively strived to limit me in this way. It necessarily follows that such a decision demonstrates adjustment and personality problems within the parent, such as insecurity, jealousy, immaturity, and other acquired negative attributes that the parent has not overcome. For this reason, the child's unrestricted growth and development in such spheres as social, emotional, spiritual, and intellectual prowess would make the parent uncomfortable. Of course, I was very naïve about this phenomenon for many years, and it was most difficult to conceive my mother in this way, but I was eventually able to face this reality.

This decision by the parent to limit the child's growth and development has far-reaching implications for the child because it is a challenge to the child's growth and development along spiritual lines. To the extent that the child compromises his spiritual or Christian values and follows a lower standard to satisfy or appease the parent, he will necessarily encumber his mental life, which will have a detrimental effect on his ability to relate spiritually, meaning to the Christian community or people who are pursuing a vibrant spiritual life. An example of such a compromise might be for the child to enter into a dependency relationship with the parent, allowing the parent to make important decisions in his life in order to have the sense of security provided by the parent's support rather than to try to prevail along spiritual lines and face an epic struggle with the parent.

For another mind within the family to succeed in isolating the mind of the victim, and we are usually talking about the significant other persons who have the leading role in the success and survival of the family—the parents—

that mind needs to ensure that no other family member bonds effectively with the mind that he or she is seeking to isolate from mental support. This is a process of alienating the victim from other family members and other people who might become significant in the victim's life. At a subconscious level, the perpetrator (e.g., parent) tries to force mistakes by means of mental opposition that makes reasoning and decision-making slower and more difficult, introducing ideas that place the victim in so called "double binds" that create ambivalence or uncertainty, and evoking ideas from the victim that may not be received well by others. Similarly, at a conscious level, the perpetrator, guided by subconscious motivation, may introduce information or create situations that interfere with the victim's plans and success, which tends to compromise the victim's effectiveness and brings him criticism. The antagonistic mind will also seek to convince other family members and other significant people in the victim's life that they should not support the victim by means of a subconscious dialogue whereby the opposing mind exploits the inevitable mistakes that the victim makes. The visible effects on the life of the person affected are likely to be very undesirable and may include regular conflict with his other parent, jealous feelings from siblings, and serious mistakes brought about by opposition rather than support from the parent-perpetrator. Other family members who have come to feel alienated from the victim may also become antagonistic and contribute to this process.

The mind of a person who has become isolated from mental support, which is likely to be a gradual process, is less able to withstand stress than the mind of a person who has the protective mental support of one or more significant others. That mind lacks the protective shield that allows other minds to conduct their business and studies in an unencumbered way in many situations and to respond better in environments that are less conducive to concentration and studious work. Additionally, the person so affected is also subject to mental opposition that makes it more difficult to reason things out and that seeks to create adversity by influencing other people in the victim's environment. These disadvantages or handicaps make it difficult for the person whose mind is so affected to succeed and to thrive. An antagonistic mind or minds that have had such a relationship with the unwilling host mind are adept at creating social dynamics that make the hosted person feel inferior and intimidated, which are events that are not easily overcome. It is these sorts of events and experiences that lead to the stress and circumstances that begin the process toward schizophrenia for the person whose mind has become isolated from mental support and who has difficulty negotiating everyday life events successfully due to the corresponding mental opposition.

Can a mind that has mental support experience this phenomenon of an awakened subconscious or a similar subthreshold experience? Yes, I think so, but it would be more difficult. For example, such a person's sleep would not be as subject to disruption by an antagonistic mind. These persons would have mental support during times of stress that should help them to negotiate stress better than people who do not. In a pattern like that of persons who are addicted to alcohol or drugs, the accompanying stress could be sufficient to lead to an awakening of their subconscious mind or a similar subthreshold experience. The pattern is associated with regular binges that disrupt the sleep-wake cycle, much social conflict, and gradual isolation from society. It could be that addicted people who remain mentally supported are the ones who are likely to have a remission of their psychotic symptoms, such as the hallucinations, which is how we distinguish a psychotic disorder that is substance-induced from one that is primary, such as schizophrenia. That is, a psychotic experience that is brought about as a result of the substance use pattern is expected to resolve as the person becomes free of the effects of the substance. If the psychosis continues, then it is attributed to a primary mental disorder such as schizophrenia rather than to the effects of the substance or substances.

What about the idea that schizophrenia is primarily a family-based illness? This has been my experience, and in a traditional society, I think this would be so. However, with the greater instability that may occur from the proliferation of single-parent homes, homeless people, substance-use patterns, divisions within subcultural groups or their poor identification with society at large, and other variations to the traditional family and traditional living circumstances, there may be a wider range of situations in which a person does not bond with a significant other person or when those bonds are severed, compromised, or disrupted. The experience of schizophrenia I have had is liable to occur in any social, cultural, subcultural, or interpersonal context in which problems with bonding occur and the affected person begins to experience ongoing conflict that takes the form of mental opposition by an adversary or adversaries. This would be most likely when such adversaries become unwelcome mental opponents for an extended period, beyond the immediate argument or conflict, so that they become more than transitory unwelcome guests. These events are most likely to occur among people who have regular contact, whose lives are intertwined, and who are affected by one another's beliefs, actions, or behavior.

It may appear to some readers that I have put forth information in this chapter about my theory of schizophrenia as factual without a lot of explanation. In fact, I make all these statements out of firsthand experience and verification in ways that convinced me. I explained this in the preface, and I make remarks throughout the book supporting these inferences and findings. The idea that we hear every thought that we form and cannot communicate it without the accompanying voice of our minds may illustrate the point somewhat. Although I have come to recognize and validate this idea experientially over time, I acquired it originally from an introductory psychology book that was in use around the time I was working on my master's degree at Auburn University at Montgomery (AUM) in 1987-1988. It was text on such matters as sensation and perception, as I recall, which contained the idea that we hear our thinking (at a subconscious, inaudible level) when we process thought.

I do not hear my own thinking at a conscious level but very infrequently. I hear mental antagonists that say things at a subconscious level to undermine me. I also hear the voices of Christian or progressively minded persons who mildly admonish these antagonists. During the last 10 years, two peer professionals that I worked with died. I have since heard their voices admonishing one of my antagonists as a warning; one admonishment contained a mild note of despair or sorrow, regretful about having engaged in behavior that was not correct. Today, after a concern about my son, I heard his voice from another part of the country letting me know that he had previously given my sentiments consideration. This does not happen very often but was generated by his sensitivity to my concern. Those of you who do not hear the subconscious have untold instances such as that. Sometimes we sense these things, such as intuitively knowing that something is wrong or, conversely, feeling that everything is all right. These are subconscious experiences. I have had the experience of walking into a room with some preoccupation and have immediately heard the subconscious mind of someone in the room with a ready answer to my concern or have otherwise been in a room and had someone subconsciously respond to my thought with the voice of their mind. To reiterate, I have good reason to believe that we do not have an instance of thought, insight, or intuition without the accompanying voice.

I focus in this chapter on the nature of my schizophrenia as a rich, illustrative example of its cause with which I am intimately familiar. In retrospect, however, as I noted in the preface, I could not say that mine is the dominant cause or that the lack of bonding and corresponding antagonism that I have experienced are necessary ingredients. For example, I have formed the opinion in considering the many cases of schizophrenia which I have studied that some of these people could have developed schizophrenia as a result of alignment with a parent who experienced the disorder before them. What may happen in these cases is that the close bonds that the parent and child develop expose the child to the disorder in the parent. That is, these two individuals are bonded mentally; as a result, the child becomes subject to characteristics of the parent's brain, mental energy, and vacillations that are a part of the parent's schizophrenic process and cause the child to be vulnerable to it. This would most likely include naivety about the world; difficulty scrutinizing interpersonal relationships or viewing them accurately; ambivalence in regard to decision making, particularly when the parent is faced with mental opposition, including double binds; and periods when the child may not fit in well socially or feel a part of the social environment, quite possibly because the parent has lapsed into mental illness. These mental dynamics could become more a part of the offspring's personality over time, independent of the parent's psychological functioning. This explanation for schizophrenia in the offspring of a parent with the disorder would contrast with mine. It may provide an illustration of some of the variety of schizophrenia and its cause.

Another course to schizophrenia that I have noted in my clinical practice from studying individual cases and their family dynamics is behavior that goes against family norms and values, such as unscrupulous behavior that the parents and other family members cannot accept, which changes the nature of their relations. I discuss such a case in chapter 24, "Varieties of Schizophrenia within the Schizophrenia Spectrum." These individuals neglected to heed parental teaching and direction, for example, and proceeded to commit serious transgressions that were unacceptable to their parents and other family members. They may be remorseful yet find that they cannot resume their place or standing within family life until they have atoned for their transgressions, an immediate irreconcilable difference which can lead to the ongoing distress that precipitates schizophrenia. If these persons are not immediately remorseful and continue the pattern instead, such as persons with antisocial characteristics, they may alienate and encounter criticism not only from their family, but also from their community, which can eventually create sufficient instability to precipitate schizophrenia. In both of these examples, the nature of their schizophrenia may be such that they do not encounter mental opposition from their family but do so from unfriendly persons in their environment, although it is also possible they have antagonized a family member to the extent of experiencing such mental opposition from family also, particularly in the latter example. My schizophrenia is distinguished from these by the nature of the parental influences before the onset of schizophrenia.

CHAPTER 2:

MORE ABOUT MENTAL OPPOSITION

My lifelong struggle with schizophrenia led me to gradually understand that I have not formed a permanent bond with a significant other person, such as a parent. I make reference to efforts of significant other persons in my life to prevent such bonds from forming as well as to the inception of those bonds in a former romantic relationship. I would also like to point out that my typical mental state is usually serene and unfettered with worry, which provides me the mentality to do studious work. This typical mental state, I think, comes from applying myself to meet the demands of my job and to do conscientious work. It could perhaps be termed the Judeo-Christian work-ethic mentality.

I felt initially that the reasons for the mental opposition I acquired were due to such factors as insecurity and jealousy. However, I have gradually come to a broader understanding of my mental opponents through a theory or hypothesis that has been answered in the same way time and time again. It is a concept that has far- reaching implications for humanity, the various cultures that we are a part of daily, and people such as me, who have not bonded permanently with a significant other and must contend with antagonistic minds on an ongoing basis. I should point out that I do have temporary significant bonds in various settings that act to shield me in the same way that a permanent bond with a significant other does, an example being several of my graduate school teachers with whom I communicated intimately during my graduate school studies, whose mental support provided the ambient culture for me to read and absorb well the material. I have also had such relationships in my work and have a culture there that is conducive to doing good work. However, let me continue with the discussion on mental opposition.

I have had a charming time with my sister Conchita in the past only to watch her do an about face to present an obstacle course that is obviously meant to trip me up, creating conflict or controversy that leads me to lose my composure and result in the discord that detracts from my mental well being, like being pulled down a few notches. This is a common tactic by many people in many settings. It is often an ingenuous tactic, such as direct repeated opposition, regardless of the issue. That is, predictably, if you say yea to an idea, they say nay; if you say nay, they say yea. The problem is that unless these situations are managed expertly, you are apt to make a mistake that upsets your mental integrity. At other times, when faced with such adversity from someone regularly, this antagonism becomes more of a mental struggle, and it can be an ongoing thing. In these instances, it actually feels as if your mind is being drained; it feels as if some of your mental energy is being sucked right out. Your work may be slowed, or you may have to take more frequent breaks while you study and get less accomplished. At a subconscious level, opposing minds also try every tactic they can to upset your mental integrity, which can be a daylong struggle. They are relatively successful in that it is a constant process of adjusting your mental set and learning how to manage the various obstacles they present, both in purely a mental sense by introducing content that makes you anxious because you do not have a satisfactory response or by affecting others in your environment to act in a way that causes you problems, and in other ways.

I could not understand why my mother and my sister Conchita, when they were provided the opportunity to have a wonderful life in Tuscaloosa if only they would be willing to work together for our mutual good and advancement, continued to employ these various forms of opposition, or why a co-worker could repeatedly act in such an insensitive way. I recognized that changing one's ways, admitting one's mistakes, and learning a better way is not easy. However, beyond that, I eventually came to recognize that one of the primary reasons these people do not change their pattern of behavior so easily is that they are gaining access to your mental life: your mind, if you will. That is what the strong mental opposition is about, whereby you feel a loss of energy; they are pulling mental energy from you, which makes their mental task easier.

That is also the ongoing effort of the mental antagonist. She is seeking to distract you by presenting doubt and hesitation in your thinking that creates anxiety and indecision; she is seeking to create a window to access your mental energy or better, to rankle you and upset your mental state so that she can have a more sustained period of access to your mind or soul, a synonym for mind that I will discuss in chapter 4, "The Spiritual World."

Once again, that is the motivation of the mental antagonist who is communicating with other people in your environment at a subconscious level in an effort to create an obstacle for you. That person is not only seeking to slow you down due to feelings such as jealousy or a desire to win out or be on top, that person is seeking to force a mistake that will upset your mental or spiritual integrity—to cause you to commit what may be a relatively minor fault or sin that will upset your mental integrity for a period of time to her gain—because when that happens, she has access to it. Essentially, what seems to happen in all these occasions is that the antagonist is responsible for your loss of mental integrity by successfully permeating your protective shield. Similarly, the co-worker who repeatedly says nay when you say yea, who gets you frustrated and defensive and causes you to lose your mental composure, gets access to your mind or soul in compromising that serene mental state so that you no longer feel that you can think as clearly or very well at all. It took me many years to conceptualize and establish this idea, which draws a lot from inference, but I have become more comfortable and assured about it over time. I can provide other support that helps to corroborate it.

I read an article in The Tuscaloosa News a long time ago on school behavior. One of the Tuscaloosa area teachers or principals commented that the main problem they were seeing in the schools at that time was noise, which interfered with the atmosphere necessary for studious work. I thought at the time and think now that this is part of the same thing. I have sat in my office with a perfect mental state for writing a report and have had to contend with repeated noise that disturbed the mental state that is necessary for reasoned, considered thinking, after which my mental state became compromised. These are situations wherein the organizational leadership has to support the atmosphere for studious thinking and learning and where the noise factor is designed to facilitate the efforts of people who have not struggled to acquire the sort of mental life necessary for insightful reasoning to acquire it from others: they are on the attack.

I have had to do a number of behavioral analyses in my work for the purpose of devising contingency management plans for individuals with behavior problems in order to bring about behavior change or other assessments designed to give treatment teams, of which I have often been a member, a better understanding of the client in order to guide her treatment. In doing so, I have observed persons who exhibit a pattern of negative attention seeking that seems to be very rewarding to them. The pattern may include loud cursing, taunting, hostility, threats, complaining, sexually inappropriate behavior, abusive language, horseplay, hitting, and similar behaviors that upset the milieu of a ward or living area. In these instances, I have been trained to ask, "What is maintaining this behavior?" Although there may be a variety of explanations, depending on the person who exhibits the behavior and the person who it is directed to, I think that it may often, or at least sometimes, represent the antisocial behavior of a person who is matching wits with an authority figure, trying to get the better of the authority figure in order to enhance her mental life by gaining access to the authority's mental life. To be specific, when successful in this endeavor, the reasoning ability of the antagonist is enhanced by being able to access more fully the mental life of the mind she is opposing: the antagonist's mind is illuminated in this way. This is a pervasive influence across society at large. I have become aware of this phenomenon in various ways.

I made a decision to transition from accounting to psychology and took coursework towards a master's degree in clinical psychology in 1987 and 1988. Throughout that time, I had mental opposition from a family member who opposed this pursuit of higher education. At the same time, I had some relatively concrete evidence that the family member was benefitting from mentally opposing me. That is, I came to recognize this person's writing style as very similar to my own. By opposing me mentally and gaining access to my subconscious mind, this family member began to exhibit a writing style that I recognized as my own. To reduce room for doubt, I have noted similar phenomena in working relationships when the antagonism from a perpetrator is relatively long, a sort of copycat syndrome. For example, you recognize their writing style, reasoning, thought patterns, and expressions as very similar to yours, almost unmistakably so. You may also recognize that it is not a very good fit with their general style. This is in contrast to the mentoring effects from Christian people with loving concern, such as a parent, teacher, or elder in your church or your work, who help you to tap, organize, and express your ideas cogently. In the vernacular of the subconscious, what these mental foes are doing is referred to as robbing or stealing, and the unwelcome perpetrator is referred to as a robber.

Thus, what I am saying is that an opposing mind is not only able to be privy to your thoughts and influence your environment, an opposing mind can gain access to your mental ability by various tactics aimed at compromising your mental life or mental integrity. This appears to be a primary reason why it is difficult to persuade an opposing mind to discontinue an antagonistic attitude. The mind who has become accustomed to robbing insight is like a child who would have to struggle by applying herself to learning daily in order to acquire the mental life or reasoning capacity that would help her to, not only become successful, but to maintain a present level of functioning that has been achieved by a lifelong pattern of mental cheating. There are many variations to this pattern, such as people who are capable mentally but also rely on absconding insight like I have just mentioned.

My impression has been that these people may have gained a more limited mental ability, such as an acquired status that consists of quick, intuitive thinking rather than more reasoned judgment. It is like proceeding within an acquired status without having to think about things very much, seemingly a swift, intuitive mind, but limited in capacity to take that knowledge and apply it. Effectively, people in society who act in such a fashion have acquired a lazy streak. They have engaged in mental cheating at a subconscious level throughout their lives in order to achieve their status and are not willing to undergo the process of change that is necessary for them to discontinue their parasitic role. That would lead them to be insecure at first, until they become comfortable with their more considerate behavior. My impression is that their tactics apply to robbing any mind that has acquired the vibrant, unencumbered mental life that allows for higher order reasoning within society-at-large, not just minds that have experienced problems in bonding. However, these tactics are likely to be more disturbing or harder to overcome for the mind that lacks support, and especially so if the opposing mind were to take the form of a permanent oppositional resident, a relationship that tends to involve significant other persons whose personality functioning has become maladaptive to that extent.

Chapter 3:

More About Subvocal Speech

The subconscious mind and subconscious world are dimensions of our existence that we do not know much about because we do not have firsthand knowledge about them, as a general rule. I believe that they are a most essential facet of our existence. This subconscious world is governed by communication that we do not hear externally. It may consist of our own thinking and contemplation. Every thought that we have, intuition, moment of insight or understanding, and the memory components that we use as we integrate our ideas have an accompanying language counterpart that we do not hear externally. This speech that is not audible to the person who has never had an awakening of the subconscious mind, which is referred to here as subvocal speech, may also consist of subconscious communication with other people. We have the capacity to communicate subconsciously with significant other people that we engage daily. This occurs by means of a medium that works alongside our conscious thinking and planning, which is an integral part of it and which helps us to organize and prepare for what is to come so that events go smoothly. Its effectiveness is governed by the cohesiveness of the groups or units that we are a part of, so that it helps to explain both successful organizations and systemic problems, depending on the ability of the members to work together. To look for examples, one may consider great productions, such as *The Sound of Music*, where the cast seemed to all work well together, or a fractious meeting where nothing was accomplished in several hours because the members were not able to reach agreement on anything.

There are ample examples of the influence of subvocal speech in our individual relationships. This may be seen in mentoring by an older sibling, a parent, a good friend, a teacher, a coach, and others who become our leaders and special mentors for a time. They become our role models: people who we listen to and who guide us consciously and subconsciously, who we seek to emulate, and who sometimes literally seem to talk through us. We feel comfortable when they are guiding us. This intimate communication is so special that we may become like them as we achieve mastery over their teachings and go on with our lives. Particularly among siblings and between parents and children but also between other people, this can become a fairly permanent communication that has been established from a social reinforcement system or values with which we have become indoctrinated. We continue to have communication with them, and they also speak through us. Some of the great family traditions, such as a family of lawyers and a family with a military tradition, illustrate this intimate communication that includes well developed patterns of responding in various situations and helps to explain the success enjoyed by its members. They can be summoned to be there with us in spirit when we need them, in varying degrees, to some extent, depending on their significance in our lives and our interdependence. This bond is likely to remain strong if we have ongoing contact with them to rekindle our relations. Great football traditions and special peer groups embody these characteristics. We always seem to be at our best among these people or within these groups, which help us to overcome our insecurities. This is due to the group leaders who have helped to forge harmony that is supported at a conscious and subconscious level.

There are also plenty of examples of conflict-riddled relations in which we encounter adversity and opposition that has a subconscious component. For example, a peer group may form a coalition that excludes a newcomer who has a different value system. The newcomer may try to be friendly but find little opportunity to be a part of the group. The person may report later to a parent that he was unable to "get a word in edgewise." This control mechanism by the adversarial group or coalition is facilitated by subconscious maneuverings so that it may become necessary to interrupt in order to make a point or assert oneself.

Terms such as "our personalities clash" may describe the tension of competition between people with different value systems who do not accept the other. In these relations, the person encountering opposition from the other may have much difficulty forming and expressing good responses due to subconscious blocking by the other. In systemic problems, an entire organization may not be progressive in its management and operations so that efforts by well meaning individuals are constantly being thwarted by members who would like to maintain the status quo. One may experience much difficulty communicating in these situations because the group is not interested in hearing what that member has to say and can create a subconscious atmosphere of disharmony. One may find oneself stammering to get words out initially due to the opposing forces. There may also be considerable discord at a conscious level due to distractions that are coordinated at a subconscious level by group members.

CHAPTER 4:

THE SPIRITUAL WORLD

The late Robert W. Lundin wrote about the birth of psychology in ancient Greece in his textbook, *Theories and Systems of Psychology* (17). He noted that the ancient Greek scholars were naturalists who believed in what they could observe, sense and quantify and drew a comparison to 20th century psychologists who reduced behavior to observable phenomena. In fact, he noted that Aristotle has been referred to as the first behaviorist. Though famous Greek scholars such as Socrates, Plato, and Aristotle made reference to the psyche, or form as opposed to substance, and mental events such as reasoning, their thought did not appear to consider the mind as a spiritual substance that functioned separately from the body. Lundin wrote that with the emergence of Christian thought and theological psychology, the mind came to be viewed as independent from the body and synonymous with the soul or spirit world. He referred to this change in emphasis from naturalism as the mind route or rise of the spirit so that philosophy, which introduced psychology, now had to contend with a non-physical world that could not be seen, felt, or grasped very well: the unobserved, spiritual world. In reference to the word pneuma, which appears to have originated with the Greeks and to have been transformed within religious theology, this concept of mind was described by one of my professors as a consciousness that extends beyond us, such as a medium for thinking and communication that has no bounds. Lundin noted that this dichotomous view of man, the physical and mental, came to be known as dualism or the mind and body problem. Lundin stated that over time, philosophy gradually stopped placing so much emphasis on the mind as akin to the soul or spirit, though it has continued to be viewed as separate from physical, observable phenomena. Alternatively, when placed in such a historical context, references to the mind as the soul appear to be consistent with Christian views and with Catholicism, as I understand it.

Catholicism teaches us that Jesus Christ was God in the form of a man. Jesus, or God, when he died, left the world the gift of the Holy Spirit, a medium by which we could have special communion with him and with one another. In order to have this intimate communion, he called us to be a royal priesthood: a people set apart. In other words, he said that we could have access to this guiding force if we followed Christian ways: if we followed his teachings in order to become more perfect individuals. By developing our spiritual life, we would have greater access to this special communion. This was his gift to the world. The structure to realize this gift is present in our church system, which seeks to indoctrinate us in Christian teachings so that we may learn to lead more perfect lives. These Christian teachings are the education we are called to practice through learning that often entails trials and tribulations. In this process of learning to practice Christian ways, in the agony of our trials and tribulations to become more Christian in our daily affairs, we gain access to spiritual guidance. This guidance of which I speak of here, in addition to any direct engagement with these Christian people, direct teaching, or conscious guidance that we may seek out during difficult times, also can occur at a subconscious level, essentially mentoring, which we may be little aware of early in our Christian growth. It can come directly from God, which we may refer to as divine inspiration—we hear the voice of God—or from any follower of Jesus Christ, such as from the Christian community. Intuitively, as a result of engaging us during our daily lives, these members of our community of Christians hear our plea and become our guiding source and inspiration; they become that light in the darkness that comes about when we struggle along a faithful journey. I should add that these individuals act as positive influences on any lives they touch.

The mind, or soul, in order to have greater access to communion with other Christians, or anyone with a God presence who recognizes the divine guidance in her life, must become free of the things that encumber it. We call these transgression or faults "sin," such as the those listed in the Ten Commandments, including failing to honor our mother and father, coveting our neighbor's goods, lying, stealing, and killing. In Catholicism, we distinguish the more serious sins as mortal sins, because they significantly interfere with our ability to access God's grace (or communication with one another through the medium of the Holy Spirit), and lesser sins as venial sins, which only temporarily obstruct our spiritual life, such as driving without sufficient caution. The point is that when we limit our subconscious communication or spiritual life by encumbering our minds with faults, we become less open-minded and thereby lose access to the most vital communication possible, that of a people directing us toward God's plan and God himself. We have a more limited communication of those who think like us, who would prefer to keep things as they are, who would control events for selfish reasons, and who are jealous of their neighbors for the success their neighbors have gained. On the other hand, if we become ever more perfect by practicing Christian principles and gaining greater mastery of them in living, then we have greater access to the holy spirit of God, which is a medium of communication with one another and with God. We become more enlightened individuals as a result. Though we may not have thought much about it, we have all been witnesses to groups that were filled with "spirit" or social spark and individuals who seemed alive with joy and very intimate in their communication with us. These would be individuals who had gained access to this intimate form of communication that is mediated by the Holy Spirit: by God.

The Bible is filled with references to what we must do to gain access to this Holy Communion that also spells the difference between true success, joy, and intimacy in our lives and a less enlightened existence. I recall in the Epistle of James where he speaks of the need to begin our weeping, a period of darkness in our lives that is necessary to atone for our past mistakes and thereby become worthy of God's presence, meaning the presence of the Holy Ghost, that intimate medium of communication that will make such a difference in daily living. I have always felt that half the battle is knowing what to do. Imagine the confidence and positive feelings from knowing what to do, such as from daily direction in living by means of intimate communication. That is the mark of a successful people: a people set apart.

A good example, speaking in general terms, would be the upper-middle class of society, who are very successful in living, enjoying a high standard of living. They and their children are welcome in our schools, at parent-teacher meetings, and other social occasions for their social warmth and leadership, helping us to set a higher standard and to work more cohesively. Alcoholics Anonymous self-help groups, which were founded to help alcoholic men and women overcome their alcoholism, provides an excellent, practical illustration of the period of weeping that we who have fallen in the way of sin that blemishes our soul must experience to broaden our spiritual life. By working twelve steps, they make amends for their wrongs in order to remain sober. They agree to lead their lives more correctly, following spiritual principles, in order to maintain their sobriety. Over time, many report that they come in contact with a guiding force in their lives that they refer to as God. This experience and growth they report is a source of immensurable joy. Alcoholics Anonymous groups were meant to be a bridge back to society for people who have crushed their ability to be very sociable by the obstruction of their spiritual life.

One observation is that the communion of saints that Jesus Christ said we could have access to by becoming a holy people is the communication or voice of minds that goes on at a subconscious level as well as conscious dialogue. That is, the communication he spoke about, at a subconscious level, is the same medium as that of the patient with a diagnosis of schizophrenia. It is the "voice of minds" heard when the subconscious is awakened by repeated disturbed sleep, a sort of twilight mental state that makes one susceptible to hearing subvocal speech. They are both the medium of minds speaking to one another. The difference lies in the quality of the experience. The Christian person tends to be confident, positive, and considerate from the growth and maturity she is gaining as she seeks to follow Christian ways in daily living. Her mind is not likely to be encumbered by the conflicts of sin. This mental state helps her to receive daily affirmation, enlightenment, and direction from other Christians at a conscious and subconscious level—the communion of saints that Jesus spoke about.

The schizophrenic experience is that of a mind in a state of discord from a lack of sleep. We have all experienced sluggish thinking and mild irritation after a poor night's sleep. It is a struggle to reason things well, meaning that our subconscious mind is having difficulty accessing memory and integrating our ideas. At times, we literally have to make our plans "out loud" because our minds are not working efficiently. We should also consider the reason for the lack of sleep. These people have been encountering adversity at a subconscious level that is responsible for their disturbed sleep and distress, such as their disturbing "auditory hallucinations" or the intense adversity that places their minds and body, their metabolism, in the so-called "fight or flight" syndrome. They are unable to relax. These voices, then, usually are not those of other enlightened minds; rather, they are adversarial voices that may be scary and create feelings of fright and paranoia. These voices or other minds have access to the subconscious thinking of the person having the schizophrenic experience and are in a position to prey on her vulnerabilities. For example, a classical symptom of schizophrenia is a voice or voices repeating the "mentally ill" person's thoughts or commenting about that person's environment in a way that can make the victim feel very anxious and fearful. Thus, there can be a very significant difference in the quality of our subconscious communication, which also has conscious parallels. If not at first, over time, the mentally ill person will also report the experience of hearing "good voices." This would most likely be the subconscious communication of virtuous people, such as those who are practicing Christian values: more enlightened minds whose mental support provides the mentally ill some relief.

David Anders, the Catholic theologian who reviewed the book, had these comments about this chapter: "(Fred), the doctrine of salvation you articulate is essentially Pelagian … (It is) not necessary to atone for past faults to become worthy of God's presence … (This is) not Catholic doctrine." David also said, "The doctrine of the communion of saints you articulate is not Catholic."

My response to David is that my comments about the path back to God ought to be uniquely Catholic because there are ample scriptural references to it. One example that I provided of God's redeeming grace was that of the alcoholic who makes amends for his transgressions by leading a principled life. A biblical parallel can be seen in the Epistle of James. Saint James asks sinful man to submit to God, cleanse his hands, and begin a period of mourning. From a psychological standpoint, it is my opinion that what we refer to as an endogenous depression, meaning a depressed state that seems internal to us rather than the result of undesirable events in our lives, can be a depression of the spirit. We can be on a Christian path, yet we may feel mentally bland, dull, and "not happy" because we have to gradually be redeemed by the grace of God's holy spirit, which is directing our journey back to God. This emerging awareness and growing wisdom is our solace during this period of sadness.

My doctrine of the communion of saints simply gets at the miracle of the communication of minds that I have become aware of through my ever-growing awareness of communication between people at a subconscious level and how it can transcend space and time. I have always had Christian mentors in my life, who have been my source of inspiration during times of trouble. As my subconscious mind became awakened, I began to recognize their guidance more directly by hearing their minds.

CHAPTER 5:

MORE ABOUT THE SPIRITUAL WORLD

The spiritual world is a phenomenon that is presently guiding and affecting all of our lives. Our world is governed by spiritual laws. God does not micromanage us. He gives us a free will to choose whom we will listen to and the direction that we will take in life. However, our choices have a definite impact on our lives, which are governed by spiritual laws or God. He is definitely in control of our world. We do not reach our lot in life by making a big mistake that was not our fault. God loves us unconditionally, and he is both loving and merciful. He gives each and every one of us the opportunity to make up for mistakes that we did not truly mean and to change our course. He is unmistakably fair with us. But he is also the God of an eye for an eye and a tooth for a tooth. We will repay each and every mistake, whether it is occurring at a conscious or subconscious level. Like the proverb says, we may hide our transgressions from other people, but God counts each one; we cannot hide from him.

Our warnings often come not directly from God but from other Christians: enlightened minds that speak to us at a conscious and subconscious level. The conscious may be more nonverbal, yet we get a strong sense of their disapproval, and their subconscious support for their nonverbal message may well make their message clear and unmistakable, yet we may still decide not to listen to it. These enlightened minds do not seem at all upset or controversial. We may actually enjoy their company, manner, proficiency, and other admirable qualities of such remarkable people. At some point, often after repeated warnings, we find our lives changed somehow, in an undesirable way. This is the spiritual law that I speak of. God let us exercise our free will, and we made poor choices instead of good ones, so we eventually had to answer for them. It was not a big mistake. We had ample opportunity and direction to change our course but we decided not to. Thus, we may find ourselves in limbo for a while, prisoners of sorts, unable to change our lot in life right away, because God wishes it so.

I think a classical example may be illustrated by a girl who wants to be perfect in every way: to prepare herself for her husband, listen to her parents, and be faithful. She devotes all her time and energy toward this end, refines herself, becomes skilled at homemaking, and goes to college, where she learns a useful profession that will get her by well and be an asset to her family when the time comes. She listens very well consciously and subconsciously, except in one area. She considers herself important and excludes some people as lesser somehow. She lacks a basic humility that is necessary to grow closer to God. To illustrate the point, let us say that she loses her virginity upon meeting a guy who she wanted so badly that she was enticed to use cocaine with him, which lowered her threshold for saying no. She later learns the hard way that he is not truly interested in her and that he is not the sort of guy that she would want to spend her life with. Had she shown the humility to be more inclusive, God, perhaps through the Christian community, would have made her wiser about such things, and he would have given her the grace to maintain her virginity so that she could become privy to the gifts of a virgin in Holy Matrimony. All is not lost. God will enlighten her if she seeks the truth. She will have the opportunity to change her ways, and he will give her the opportunity to regain all that she has lost, in due time. I believe that God works in just that way.

I make these comments to emphasize this spiritual aspect of our lives that has such a profound bearing on the people we become. Those enlightened minds did not become so by chance. They were thoughtful in living and made the right choices, through the guidance and inspiration of God and the vast Christian community. They listened well and did not make costly mistakes. If they did, they recognized them and changed their course in living.

I was born into a Catholic family and was raised to be a Christian. Catholicism and Christianity are inclusive religions going back to the time of Jesus Christ as exemplified by the ministry and message of the apostle

Paul to the Gentiles. Jesus' ministry reached out beyond the Hebrews, God's chosen people in the Old Testament, to all peoples. He was not only the Deliverer of the Hebrews but of all the human race. Thus, while I am speaking about Christianity as the spiritual life that is sanctioned by God, in the spirit of the New Testament of Jesus Christ, I am not excluding anyone seeking the spirit of truth.

David Anders remarked, "This whole chapter in problematic from the point of view of Catholic doctrine. God is not 'eye for eye' in Catholic theology. We believe in grace, not karma. Free will is required to cooperate with grace, but the grace of justification comes to us unbidden and without our merits." David referred me to paragraph 1987 in the Catholic catechism (and following), which reads, "The grace of the Holy Spirit has the power to justify us, that is, to cleanse us from our sins and to communicate to us 'the righteousness of God through faith in Jesus Christ' and through Baptism (21)." Karma, according to my American Heritage Dictionary (2), is the Hindu or Buddhist belief that our conduct and actions determine our destiny.

My response to David is that in reading paragraph 1987 of the Catholic catechism (21), I discern that the cleansing of our sins by the Holy Spirit can be a gradual process during which, through his direction, we become reconciled with God and with our neighbor. It makes sense that the Holy Spirit, the great teacher, will help us to recognize and make up for our mistakes as he leads us on a path to greater perfection. Scripture has it that if we make a transgression against someone, we should be reconciled with that person to receive the sacrament of Holy Communion. Without such reconciliation, many sinners would have difficulty appreciating the victory over sin represented by their baptism or entry into a life with Christ. From a psychological standpoint, I think that it is uniquely human to feel that we have to make up for our sins to feel wholesome again. Similarly, I think our community will hold us accountable for our wrongdoings against its members and refrain from welcoming us until we have made up for our wrongs. Subconsciously, our neighbors, church community, and those whom we have wronged can size us up quickly and tell whether we have changed our ways.

Chapter 6:

In Defense of My Views: Responses to Critical Questions

I will round out the first five chapters on "The Basis for Schizophrenia" with my response to several questions about the book put to me by colleagues in psychology. They had a number of questions regarding the support or corroboration that I could provide for seminal ideas that might be challenged by the psychological community and others, including ideas for which there are existing alternative or competing views. My responses to some of these questions are enumerated below.

1. "Fred, a review of the literature on hallucinations could provide alternative explanations to your ideas about people communicating 'mind to mind' by means of subvocal speech. What support could you provide to show that this is actually so? How do you know that this is not simply the workings of your human mind, such as memories or thought patterns that are stirred?"

I think the body of ideas contained in this book provides various support and corroboration to answer these and similar questions and that they represent authentic discoveries about the human mind that will be supported by the existing body of scientific knowledge, religious doctrine, and everyday human experience. Recently, in meeting my everyday needs, I had the occasion of having a number of engagements with someone whom I would describe as an enlightened mind. Following these engagements, I would hear this person's supportive voice throughout the day, sometimes directly intervening with helpful advice about my line of work, professional responsibilities, and work agenda or duties, generating a positive and confident attitude. She spurred me to have a successful day filled with human compassion and understanding balanced with alertness to my professional responsibilities. I have similarly sensed the beneficial influence in my work from other progressively-minded persons—considerate people who have my best interests at heart—at a somewhat reduced level, after engaging them in various personal engagements away from the office, like a community of friends. I may have a keener sense of these experiences than most people due to my awakened subconscious mind, but I feel they are a facet of everyday living that all of us have encountered and should all have some awareness of. I have made similar statements about the mentoring from teachers and professionals in my work.

2. **"Fred, how would you corroborate the idea that someone can be an unwelcome guest or 'inhabit' another mind?"**

My previous comments about the very close and intimate communication with an enlightened mind was testament to more that just a casual relationship. Out of her love and concern for me, this person became privy to my thoughts and experiences that day and intervened to affect me and those in my environment in a positive way. I was greeted warmly throughout the day by friends, casual acquaintances, and strangers by means of her intercession for me and their recognition of her. My clients similarly benefitted from her gentle manner and understanding, which provided us a beneficial atmosphere for our engagements. I would ascribe these events to a warm embrace from an elevated member of the Christian community, but I would also ascribe this potential to any spiritual and loving person. In fact, I have had such a relationship with a person or persons who did not recognize at the time their closeness to Jesus Christ or their nearness to sharing in a blissful relationship with their Heavenly Father, which they had earned as a result of a lifelong career of thoughtful consideration and devotion to their family, friends, other professionals with whom they worked, and their clientele. Of course, I am talking about very welcome guests who communicated with me at a subconscious level.

I have also had regular contact with people in my life who have not earned such a good lot in life and who may harbor bitter feelings, spite, and anger due to their less fortunate circumstances or towards someone whom they consider to be more fortunate than they have been. These people have not learned rightful paths in human relations that will benefit them in the long run. They would exploit another mind to the extent that they are able to, or they would seek to challenge, compromise, and limit another mind to the extent that they could out of insecurity, jealousy, or a desire to prevail over that person, such as in their professional work. These are some of the makings for a relatively permanent unwelcome guest who would seek to undermine you at a subconscious level, such as for the length of time that your lives are intertwined. These remarks have parallel biblical references. For example, the Bible has passages about people who were possessed by a devil, whose evil spirits Jesus and his disciples "cast out." Similarly, the apostle Paul spoke of having to contend with three devils all the time.

3. **"Fred, what support could you give to the idea that people can subconsciously communicate with people they don't know?**

I have answered this question in the previous comments about an enlightened mind who subconsciously influenced those around me to greet me warmly and kindly, which included pedestrians on foot that I passed and other drivers. I have progressed in my awareness of such relationships to the extent that I was able to recognize her influence upon them and the source of their camaraderie with me. Usually, those whom I encounter, except for the more enlightened people who are not easy to fool on a spiritual realm, are put on the defensive by my mental opponent(s), may be unsure or skeptical about me, and may feel a need to question me or my motives before reaching a decision to greet or welcome me as someone that measures up to their standards. It is not so often that I have a guardian saint, guardian angel, or another enlightened mind to light my path.

My colleagues asked me another question that may be of pertinence to the reader, especially for people who have experienced schizophrenia or their relatives. I will list it as question 4.

4. "Fred, how is it that people who report auditory hallucinations experience them as alien at the same time as typically acknowledging that they are from within themselves?"

I think that it is the nature of auditory hallucinations that at times they seem to emanate from an object in the environment, such as a person or thing, and sometimes they seem to be experienced as an internal voice within one's mind, though they are in each case the voice of other minds. Another explanation, which subsumes some of the comment in the previous sentence, is that the voice of an enduring opponent who has a hold on you mentally, who is an unwelcome guest, would be experienced internally because that is the position he or she has in order to be privy to your every thought, whereas the voices of some other people, such as those heard at a public place, would be external to the voice hearer because their mind is not inhabiting you but, rather, it remains external to you. I have only more recently begun to hear my own thoughts as a voice, occasionally, which would certainly be an internal experience, but I am not aware that many people hear their own voice. They may hear or listen to their mind or their thoughts, but, once again, I do not think that this is experienced as a voice. There appears to be a common understanding that people who report the experience of auditory hallucinations in the form of a voice are hearing a voice or voices other than their own. I can also say with relative certainty that people diagnosed with schizophrenia, such as people who have had an awakening of their subconscious mind and have begun experiencing auditory hallucinations, are hearing the voices of other minds primarily or principally as regards schizophrenia because that is the nature of this so-called mental disorder. I think my discussion of the nature of its symptoms, such as the distraction from having to respond to two sources of stimulation that are not coordinated, attests to this.

This experience is tricky at times. I have observed that both mental adversaries and people who are aligned with me mentally have communicated their subconscious message by means of objects in the environment, particularly birds and trains, using such objects to make it seem as if their voice or message were coming from them, so that the source seems external to you when, in fact, it is not. I also hear subconscious messages, not as a voice but, rather, more like an implanted thought from a person who was once aligned with me mentally, meaning also that she was a permanent guest or resident during that time, for a year or so. The cue for her messages is a train whistle, and she appears to use one of my mental residents, with whom I have a relationship similar to the one I had with her, to communicate or implant her message. This form of communication apparently is acceptable to them both. It is okay with me, also.

One of my colleagues asked me, "How do you know that this is not simply a psychotic experience that you are having?" and "Are you saying that your discoveries about an awakened subconscious and hearing subvocal speech mean that schizophrenia is not actually a mental illness—something that heretofore has been explained by many authorities on the subject as not grounded in reality or in science?"

I am first of all saying that what we have heretofore referred to as the mental disorder schizophrenia, one of the severe mental disorders or mental illnesses, is an experience that occurs within the spirit world or mental life. It would be considered a subconscious experience in regard to the auditory hallucinations because we do not generally hear the voices of other minds, although it may no longer be a subconscious experience for persons who acquire a diagnosis of schizophrenia if that also means that their subconscious mind has become awakened, a process that appears to occur gradually. They are hearing the voices of other minds, which is within the realm of the spirit world or mental life. Other symptoms of schizophrenia, such as paranoid thoughts, also appear to be influenced by subconscious experiences or forces, such as mental opponents, as I have explained. I would also say that schizophrenia follows scientific principles or scientific laws and that if our technology were sufficiently advanced, we could perform scientific experiments to prove it. The preponderance of the ideas in this book provides a measure of proof for it, in my opinion, using common sense reasoning and judgment.

The experience that we refer to as schizophrenia might be considered a mental illness to the extent that it is not understood and managed by the victim, because it tends to result in a misinterpretation of reality that can have very dire consequences for the victim. For example, people who experience paranoid symptoms may feel their lives are in peril and act in self defense. They may feel compelled to follow a biblical path in an impulsive or unthoughtful way before they acquire a mature faith and a thorough understanding of biblical scripture or God's intended meaning. They may have other problems in relating to their environment as a result of the adversarial schizophrenia experience. It is my hope that the ideas contained in this book will help people with the diagnosis of schizophrenia to understand and manage their experience successfully, as I have. It has added a dimension to my life that has enriched it, but, as I have explained to the reader, it can be a tricky experience at times, such as when an adversary fools you or gets the better of you.

My colleagues also asked me this question, "Fred, your idea that a person can rob another person's mind is an interesting one. How might this occur?"

I became aware of this phenomenon later than the phenomenon of the mental adversary who seeks to prevail over you and to limit your advancement by opposing you subconsciously. It appears that the natural sequence of events at inception is for the mental adversary to seek to prevail over you first and seek to rob you second, and this latter finding appears to be harder to corroborate. Over time, during close interaction with adversaries, such as observing them in our interpersonal interactions, I regularly observed their mental struggle with me and their efforts to outwit me in numerous ways. What became apparent during those times they prevailed, which I have learned to manage without excessive worry and concern, is that I lost a degree of cognitive integrity that I need to engage in thoughtful reasoning and meditation and they behaved as if they had been enlightened. Gradually, I have become convinced that they become privy to my mentality in varying degrees at those times. Originally, these people may have opposed another person in order to prevent their advancement, and in the process, they became aware that when they upset that person's cognitive integrity, they gained access to the person's consciousness, such as becoming privy to their state of mind for thinking and reasoning: their intelligence, if you will. This seems akin to robbing people of their reasoning ability, to the robber's gain.

Dr. John Toppins, a former Director of Psychology at Bryce Hospital and now the Director of Psychology at Taylor Hardin Secure Medical Facility (THSMF), the forensic hospital for the criminally insane in Tuscaloosa, Alabama, asked me a similar question. I provided him indirect corroboration of various sorts that supported this idea, like I provided above. For example, I described the mental antagonist during my work on the master's degree in clinical psychology whose writing style, in my opinion, was unmistakably mine, like a copycat syndrome. I have noted this phenomenon in other persons with whom I have associated for periods of time. What eventually became clearer to me in observing their written language was that more than a copycat syndrome, their analytical thinking resembled mine. I eventually came to the conclusion that some of these individuals were mental adversaries because, over time, they were able to learn my reasoning patterns, such as my analytical thinking style, from repeatedly accessing my consciousness, as if they were able to trace my thought patterns again and again until they became a part of theirs.

The attitude of these opponents varies considerably. Some seem to recognize what they are doing and set limits on the extent to which they exploit you. For example, they may refrain from taking further advantage of you when your reasoning capacity is compromised by a mistake, which may be partly motivated to avoid more dire spiritual consequences, an aspect of the spiritual world or spiritual laws that they may have learned to respect. Other mental adversaries are relatively more immature and inconsiderate. They may seek to undermine you constantly, to their gain, and if they do not prevail, they may exhibit subconscious tantrums of sorts. At these times, I can feel the anger and agitation that is directed to me, palpably. It has literally shaken my head while I have been lying in bed. When they prevail over you, they may not be as considerate as an adversary who exercises more maturity and consideration.

I think that the process of being enlightened may provide some support for the idea that someone can rob you of your reasoning or gain access to it. I have been mentored by significant other people throughout my life, such as teachers, supervisors, and church leaders. In mentoring me, they have infused me with mental energy; enlightened my mind to a clear recollection of the relevant information, sometimes directly by the voice of their minds; and provided me the ambient culture to organize and describe ideas, similarly facilitating my insight. In a similar vein, during my freshman year in college, I was beginning to share in a spiritual life with a girlfriend who was making a difference in my studies. The beginning of some spiritual union was augmenting my academic aptitude. Thus, the finding that desirable people in your life can increase your mental and reasoning capacity by means of mentoring, enlightenment, and spiritual union provides some indirect support for the idea that a mental adversary who accesses your mind, seeking to undermine you at a subconscious level, can also benefit at a reasoning level by such access. Incidentally, I describe in chapter 22, "The Spirit World, Revisited" a different sort of mental robbing. For example, I describe how a group can become privy to your ideas at a subconscious level during a meeting and seek to undermine them in various ways.

CHAPTER 7:

RESEARCH ON GENETICS

Several drafts of this manuscript had been completed by the time I submitted it for review by two psychologists. Subsequently, I responded to their review points and began considering publication in earnest. I anticipated one additional intervening step. I wanted a religious body or person schooled in Catholicism to review the book to ensure that nothing I had said would be considered to be offensive or inconsistent in regard to my Catholic faith.

It so happened that at just that time, I became engaged in a discussion with Dr. Lee Mallory, my supervisor at the time and the Director of Psychology at Bryce Hospital—a discussion about the case of a person who had a disorganized-type schizophrenia, effectively a long-standing regressed form of schizophrenia, and whether a diagnosis of dementia would be appropriate in these instances. Dementia entails a permanent decline in intellect due to injury or disease, which can be progressive, depending on the physical process. As part of our consideration, he submitted relevant literature on the subject for me to read. In reviewing these articles and their underlying references, I became aware of the medical world's emphasis and progress in finding a genetic basis for schizophrenia. For example, page 103 of the *Diagnostic and Statistical Manual of Mental Disorders, Fifth Edition* (DSM-5), copyright 2013, which is published by the American Psychiatric Association, describes risk and prognostic factors for schizophrenia. In the subsection for genetic and physiological factors, it begins, "There is a strong contribution for genetic factors in determining risk for schizophrenia, although most individuals who have been diagnosed with schizophrenia have no family history of psychosis ...." It goes on to note that risk alleles or genetic loci for schizophrenia have been identified (3) (Risk alleles are discussed subsequently in this chapter).

The genome project—that is, the quest to map the human DNA sequence—did not begin until 1990. I graduated in clinical psychology from AUM in 1988. I remember that in my Advanced General Psychology class, Dr. Susan Dudley, who had a strong background in physiology, was very interested in research on genetic and biological factors in psychology. She informed the class that schizophrenia can be distinguished by the nature of its onset. For example, she said that a reactive case would be one that has a clear precipitating event and a sudden onset. She noted that such events are likely to be related to a specific situation in the person's life, which is subject to change and thus would carry a good prognosis, relatively speaking. Alternatively, process schizophrenia would describe a person who has likely had a slow or gradual onset and who has experienced a chronic course, about whom someone might say, "Albert has always been that way." She posited that the reactive cases may be environmentally related, whereas the process cases may be related to genetics and have a biological basis, although they could be precipitated by an environmental event, which seems a reference to the diathesis-stress model (5). That is, certain people have a diathesis or disposition to experience schizophrenia. They have a vulnerability to it, which can be brought on by stress.

Dr. Dudley also informed us that the negative symptoms of schizophrenia, such as the absence of emotional expression, minimal speech, and lack of motivation, which are evident in these cases, have been correlated with brain deterioration or brain damage based on radiographic techniques and autopsies of people who have exhibited negative symptoms. She said that what could happen when there has been such deterioration or cell loss is that neurons (nerve cells) have shifted from their normal route and directed their firing to neurons they were not intended to affect, resulting in abnormal behavior. She also pointed out that the cell loss from brain deterioration tends to result in gliosis, such as an excessive accumulation of glial cells that normally support, protect, and repair neurons, which is another complicating factor. Dr. Dudley posited that these people may have a genetic basis for their schizophrenic disorder, such as a genetically determined nervous system life.

Many or most of them would probably fit her process schizophrenia model and the case of disorganized schizophrenia that Dr. Mallory and I discussed.

Dr. Dudley said further that we know some disorders to be biologically based, such as disorders involving balances of neurotransmitters, in which regard she used bipolar disorder as an example. She noted that our central nervous system is comprised of competing systems, such as the opposition of the sympathetic and parasympathetic branches of the autonomic nervous system, the former promoting action-oriented activities and the latter promoting restful activities. She made reference specifically to the competing inhibitory and excitatory functions within the reticular activating system of the brain, where there are two sets of neurotransmitters involved. When these neurotransmitters are out of balance, we may be too aroused or too depressed. Thus, activation could lead to a bipolar-manic swing and inactivation to a bipolar-depressive swing (bipolar disorder was formerly referred to as manic-depressive disorder). The dopamine theory of schizophrenia, of which I have spoken of earlier, presumes such a biologically-based neurotransmitter imbalance.

Dr. Dudley was scientifically and research oriented. She prided herself in staying abreast of the literature in her field. Thus, I expect that her discourse conferred upon the class a good sample of the relative state of knowledge of the genetic and physiological influences in psychology at the time. Her comments encompassed genetic and environmental explanations for schizophrenia. For my part, I viewed my schizophrenic experience as a reactive one and my brother George's as a process one. My impressions then were that Dr. Dudley's ideas were more a theory than an absolute. I had great respect for her as a rigorous scientist-teacher that could well support anything that she said. I did not discount her comments at all and felt that they could very well have a place in the conceptions of mine and George's schizophrenia that I had acquired. But I was also confident that heredity and biology would not supplant those ideas, which were evident to me and corroborated in various ways on a daily basis.

I have been to numerous in-service presentations at Bryce Hospital for psychology and psychiatry staff, and I have attended a few conferences focused on a variety of pertinent psychological subjects. I have also pursued self study in new, developing, or pertinent psychological areas. My continuing education has had a strong clinical emphasis, though I consider myself to be scientifically minded. I did not become aware until recently of the emphasis in the medical-scientific community on finding the genes involved in schizophrenia, and, as a corollary, I was also not aware of the relative success of that research. When it came to my attention, I sought to understand it better so that I could properly integrate those findings in this book.

I am sorry that I am not a molecular biologist, a biochemist, or in possession of a degree in a field that would allow me to fully grasp and consider the current state of knowledge about the genetic basis for schizophrenia so that I could evaluate in a critical way how it may complement my findings. I tried to do educate myself sufficiently well to do just that but found the knowledge that I would have to acquire too broad and complex for me to reach that level of competence without a more rigorous program of study. Feeling that time was of the essence for a variety or reasons, a sufficient one being the findings contained in this book, I decided to proceed without such understanding.

My appraisal of this research (1) indicated to me that the human genome, that is, the 22 chromosomes plus the male or female sex chromosome to make 23 chromosomes, which are contained in the nuclei of the cells in our body, has now been mapped. We actually have 22 pairs of homologous chromosomes referred to as autosomes, one member of the pair coming from our father and one member of the pair coming from our mother. They match up with one another during our lifetime by aligning along their complementary genes, which are essentially in the same location. In addition, we have a sex chromosome from each parent that line up with one another, of which the sex chromosome from our father determines our gender.

These chromosomes are essentially strands of deoxyribonucleic acid (DNA), which are the master copy of genetic material that determine our structure and encode proteins to carry out cellular functions throughout our lives. The genes are the functional unit of the DNA strands or the chromosomes. They are responsible for coding proteins, as directed by the DNA, to carry out cellular functions. There appear to be some 30,000 genes of varying size within our chromosomes, which themselves vary in size. The genes consist of a strand of DNA, which exists in the form of a double helix or spiral and within the strands, up and down the whole strand, are 4 nitrogenous bases that are repeated: adenine, which always pairs with guanine, and cytosine, which always pairs with thymine. If one pictures a spiraled ladder, the rungs of each ladder would consist of part adenine and part guanine or part cytosine and part thymine. These nitrogenous bases are the rungs of the chromosomal strands or DNA, and a section of that strand makes up a particular gene. Genes can vary in size from 1,000 of these nitrogen base pairs or ladder rungs to more than half a million base pairs for a large gene, with the average gene consisting of some 27,000 base pairs.

Okay, so how do we determine that schizophrenia is a genetic disorder? The very basic understanding of this process I acquired is that, apparently, our human chromosomes are essentially very similar, meaning that the sequence of nitrogenous bases, the rungs of the ladder, are very similar. Thus, when we learn something about one gene, we are learning about the function of that gene for all the human race. Furthermore, there is also much similarity within the genetic material of the plant and animal kingdom, which means that we can also learn much about the function of our genes from mutations carried out intentionally on plant and animal species. Thus, we have not only mapped the entire human genome or set of chromosomes, but we have been developing a database on the function of our genes. Okay, so let us say that in tracing a family tree, the parents, who are now deceased, produced six offspring, all living, and two of those offspring have suffered from schizophrenia. As I understand it, it would be possible to take a sample of blood cells for each sibling and determine the genetic makeup of each, then compare those genes in order to determine whether there are any differences between the genes of the siblings as well as the part of the human body or body function implicated by those differences, such as genes that are pertinent to neural functions, affecting the central nervous system, meaning the brain or a certain part of the brain.

This information, as I understand it, would come from variations in the sequence of the nitrogenous bases that we spoke of previously and from other exceptions to the expected sequences noted within that person's DNA. These are findings that appear to account for our heterogeneity as a human race. In particular, you would note whether the two siblings who have experienced schizophrenia had a mutation that was not present in the other siblings and whether the mutation occurred in an area that would be relevant to schizophrenia. These mutations could have been present and unexpressed within the parental chromosomes or could have occurred during the exchange of genetic material that takes place during meiosis and passes to the offspring. Recall that meiosis is a cell event that is unique to the reproductive phase, after which the paired chromosomes divide to become gametes (sperm and eggs). Consequently, if such differences are identified, that particular genetic location or area on that chromosome, including such relevant information as the nitrogen-base sequence giving rise to the mutation, would represent the relevant genetic information or code that is implicated in schizophrenia. That allele, meaning the genes at that genetic locus for the offspring that developed schizophrenia, would be considered a "risk allele." Another way of saying this is that the expression of genetic material within that gene has been implicated in schizophrenia.

The medical-scientific community has established such risk alleles or candidate genes by studying family trees (30). They have also established risk alleles by studying specific ethnic groups or specific populations (7), such as determining specific regions or sites on specific chromosomes that are implicated in schizophrenia using the plethora of scientific methods and scientific tools at their disposal and the ever-growing knowledge of the human genome. To date, scientists have not been able to study the DNA of people in whatever stage of development they are in or even those who have developed the syndrome "schizophrenia" and say that these persons have this genetic variation or that genetic variation that caused them to acquire this disorder. The reason, according to the scientific community, is that schizophrenia, like some developmental events in an organism's life that determine the organism's structure and function, is a complex event that is determined by a host of genes or risk alleles (3), (7), (9). Effectively, one genetic mutation or risk allele explains only a small part of the variance for the disorder. In order to acquire it, one would need to inherit a sufficient number of these risk alleles for the disorder to be expressed. Because we have not identified all the genes or risk alleles implicated in schizophrenia to date, we cannot look at a person's genetic material and say, for example, he acquired such percentage of risk alleles for developing schizophrenia. In fact, a comprehensive study published in March 2015 (9) found that past research relating to candidate genes for schizophrenia did not support a genetic basis for schizophrenia due to problems in the experimental designs, such as insufficient design rigor and inadequate power in regard to sample sizes. It did not discount heritability and our enhanced understanding of biology with respect to schizophrenia resulting from the research while pointing to the need for better experimental designs.

The research on a genetic basis for schizophrenia, as I mentioned, requires someone with a background in fields like molecular biology or biochemistry to fully understand, evaluate, and reach informed opinions about it, in my estimation. It seemed sufficiently complex as to require more than a basic understanding in those fields and likely advanced knowledge and know-how, such as that which might be acquired by pursuing a degree in such fields. However, having reviewed and considered it in a general way, with some reading to understand it better, about which I have commented in this chapter, I believe that my understanding is sufficient to provide some perspective or opinion.

I begin this second part of this chapter by considering differences between the rate of schizophrenia in the general population and the rate in families in which a member has schizophrenia. These comparisons provide support for the view that schizophrenia is a genetic disorder, for which I provide an alternative view. Subsequently, I discuss several adoption studies and consider pertinent identical twin data while seeking to provide a balanced view of genetic and non-genetic factors before providing my opinion. The remainder of the chapter describes case studies that support a non-genetic basis for schizophrenia. I finish the chapter by drawing a parallel to bipolar disorder and substance use disorders.

The latest figures on heredity reveal that whereas the lifetime prevalence for schizophrenia in the general population is 0.5 to 1 percent, it jumps to 13 percent if a parent has it, 15 percent if a fraternal twin has it, and 40 percent or more if an identical twin has it, which seems to be fairly compelling evidence for a strong genetic basis for schizophrenia (3), (5), (27). Could there be another explanation other than genetic factors to account for the increased rate of schizophrenia when a family member is affected? The influence from the unconscious may provide us another explanation. Previously, I described the bonding that occurs between a parent and a child and between that child and other significant people in his life, such as a sibling or a future spouse. Furthermore, I described how those bonds act like a protective shield that insulates the child from people who psychologically oppose him for some reason. Unfortunately, as I previously mentioned, that psychological bonding between a child and a significant other person in the child's life, such as a parent or a sibling, could also subject the child to the vulnerabilities of the mind that he has bonded with, such as mental illness.

I think this may be a primary reason for the higher incidence of schizophrenia in families, a finding which, in my estimation, is also pertinent for other psychiatric disorders, such as bipolar disorder. This is not a genetic basis but a psychological basis for schizophrenia. The difference in the concordance rates for fraternal and identical twins could be explained by the apparent tendency of identical twins to be raised closer together. These inferences are consistent with my impressions about the nature of subconscious influences, such as the family of lawyers or the family with a strong military tradition that I described in chapter 3, "More About Subvocal Speech," only this is a family with a strain of schizophrenia. What appears to happen is that the significant other family member, in his manifestation of love, concern, and consideration that is part of the bonding process, exposes the affected family member to his vulnerability to schizophrenia.

Adoption studies are another area where heritability for schizophrenia has been considered. One such study is the Kety et al. (1968) study in Denmark, a country that keeps demographic records of its citizens, which provide the data necessary to carry out longitudinal family studies. In the Kety study, there was a high incidence of schizophrenia in relatives (parents or siblings) of children who were adopted and later developed schizophrenia, whereas the incidence of schizophrenia in their adoptive families was no different than the rate in the general population (15). These data provide a strong argument for a genetic component, particularly because schizophrenia within the adoptive family was ruled out. However, researchers or educators have pointed out that those results lacked sufficient support. For example, they note that of the 34 adopted children with a diagnosis of schizophrenia who were a part of the research study group, only one of their relatives had schizophrenia. The affected relatives of eight other children had diagnoses of schizotypal personality, borderline personality, or uncertain schizophrenia. Thus, support from this study for heredity as the cause for schizophrenia was viewed by some researchers as absent (5). It also seems noteworthy that 25 of these adopted children who developed schizophrenia did not have relatives who had a disorder within the schizophrenia spectrum.

Heston (1966) conducted another schizophrenia adoption study. In this study, 17% of children whose mothers experienced schizophrenia and who were given up for adoption within 2 weeks of birth later developed schizophrenia, whereas children whose mothers did not experience schizophrenia, who were given up for adoption, did not go on to develop schizophrenia (14). These findings appear to provide strong support for a genetic component. However, the study pointed out that emotional disorders were common among the children whose mothers were diagnosed with schizophrenia regardless of whether they developed schizophrenia, many had a substance-use disorder, and their histories were rife with arrests for antisocial crimes. These data, without further information, indicate that environmental factors could have had a bearing on their risk for and development of schizophrenia.

Bennet (2003) cited a more recent study by Tienari, et al. (2000), which studied children who were adopted and whose biological mothers either did or did not have a diagnosis of schizophrenia. Their findings show that even though the adopted children who had a mother diagnosed with schizophrenia were four times more likely to acquire it themselves, only those who were adopted into families where a communication disorder prevailed were at risk; adopted children with biological mothers who were diagnosed with schizophrenia were not at greater risk than adopted children with biological mothers who were not diagnosed with schizophrenia as long as a communication disorder was not present in the adoptive family. This was viewed as supportive of the diathesis-stress model; that is, of a genetic disposition rather than a genetic cause.

The DSM-5 notes that most persons who experience schizophrenia do not have a family history of this disorder (p.103) (3), an observation that appears to cast doubt on whether schizophrenia is a genetic disorder or exclusively so. Furthermore, when there is a family history of the disorder, the relationship is not fully explained by genetics. For example, because identical twins have the same genetic makeup, both twins would develop schizophrenia if it were strictly a genetic disorder. However, the concordance rate for schizophrenia in monozygotic twins is not 100% but between 35% and 58% (6). This finding raises the question, "If schizophrenia is a genetic disorder, why is it that the concordance rate for identical twins is not 100%, considering that they have the same genetic makeup?" From a genetic viewpoint, the plausible answer could be a division or area of genetics termed "epigenetics." That is, differences in the environmental influences on identical twins as they grow up and mature affect certain genes to become active or inactive, resulting in genetic differences between the twins (24). Thus, epigenetics appear to add complexity to previous statements about differences on specific genes or sequences of base pairs within genes determining risk for schizophrenia or risk alleles. That is, epigenetics appear to add the variable of whether or to what extent the genetic material is "turned on" or "turned off" as relevant to the phenotype—the expression of the genotype. Incidentally, these findings appear to be consistent with the diathesis-stress model for schizophrenia that has been developed, which posits that persons have a diathesis or vulnerability to schizophrenia, which expression or lack of expression is a function of stress (5) in the environment of living and learning.

Bennett (2003) points out that despite the fact that schizophrenia is more commonly observed in families, we cannot assume that it has a genetic basis (5). In fact, there are a number of non-genetic prognostic factors or factors that increase the risk for schizophrenia, including growing up in an urban environment, adverse events during the gestation period or at the time of birth, drug use, childhood trauma, belonging to some minority ethnic groups, and various other sources of stress people encounter in living (3), (5), (28). Although it might be convenient to incorporate these environmental influences into a diathesis-stress model, Bennett points out that the diathesis-stress model views the diathesis or biological cause as the primary one and places stress or psychological factors as secondary without considering they could stand alone. Similarly, Spear et al. (1988) note that a genetic diathesis is not always suggested by the diathesis-stress model; the disposition to schizophrenia can result strictly from environmental effects, such as a fetal virus (22).

My impression from the insights that I have gathered about subconscious life or the spiritual world, including the astonishing ways that our minds can affect one another, sometimes in consistent and ongoing ways, is that schizophrenia is primarily a psychological phenomenon. I think that other people will also arrive at this conclusion as they acquire these insights. I start with my own example, which is I attribute to oppositional forces and which is well explained. I follow with two examples at the end of chapter 1: children who are bonded to a family member with schizophrenia, and children who have violated a family norm and must atone for their transgressions before they can regain the good graces of their family. My brother George's schizophrenia I attribute to instability that resulted from inconsistent parental direction and insufficient development of a reference group, and I describe several cases where the global brain or cognition—mild mental deficiency—led to overwhelming psychological effects that precipitated and maintained schizophrenia. In all these cases, the factors precipitating schizophrenia may have had an epigenetic effect, but not the other way around. Also, these varieties of schizophrenia would not have resulted from specific genes or risk alleles.

I note previously in this chapter that mental bonding may serve to explain the higher incidence in families, which may also explain some adoption cases. The Kety et al. study initially appeared to support heritability but did not in retrospect. The Heston study also appeared to support heritability; but findings of emotional, substance use, and personality problems in these children, without further study, suggested that family dysfunction could have created sufficient instability for a host of other problems and could have been a breeding ground for mental illness. The Tienari study was deemed supportive of the diathesis-stress model, but the presumption of that model that biological factors are the diathesis or primary influence is subject to qualification, as noted by Bennett and Spear et al. (above). Paul Bennett notes further in his book, Abnormal and Clinical Psychology: An Introductory Textbook (2003), that a child's disposition, whether due entirely to genetics or also to the fetal and early rearing environment, can also influence the adoptive family's rearing of the child, particularly in cases of children who exhibit problematic behavior. He says that "as a result, separated children may experience both a common genetic heritage and a common family background, despite their separation (p.19)" (5).

Let's consider my own experience. I think that I acquired it primarily for the reasons that I have mentioned, such as the lack of bonding with a significant other and the subconscious opposition that presented significant obstacles in many important areas of my life, such as my academic performance, intellectual growth, spiritual well being, and social success. It was shortcomings in these areas and mistakes that led to the stress or distress that precipitated schizophrenia. Even so, I think this process is made clearer by describing my basic personality, the challenges I faced, and my adjustment or response to those challenges.

I believe that my basic personality pattern sheds light on my experience of schizophrenia at different times in my life. My first instance of schizophrenia occurred when I did not succeed in my course of study in college and could not think of a viable alternative, about which I was not very resourceful. Although I did not know my personality very well at the time, I think that it reflects what are sometimes referred to as obsessive-compulsive personality characteristics. I am a high achiever with strong values who strives for perfection and I am not very satisfied with mediocrity. These personality attributes help to explain my difficulty finding an alternative course of study that was satisfactory to me when I did not make the grades to get into medical school. In addition, the liberal ideas of the time and a drug such as marijuana did not help, probably because I was more idealistic than practical then. Due to my immature faith and idealistic nature, such liberal ideas and the heady drug that I found marijuana to be presented a challenge to my spiritual life that became a distracting influence. I believe that these events and my personality created something of an identity crisis for me.

I finally had to be practical and settle for accounting. During the most stressful times in accounting, I became more meticulous and more of a perfectionist in my work, which suffered as to time constraints due to my inability to be more practical. This appears to represent an obsessive-compulsive personality feature—a coping pattern to avoid the anxiety from decisions that are perceived as less scrupulous and thus anxiety provoking. In psychology, we refer to these obsessive-compulsive personality features as the glue that holds the personality together. We were able to spot these persons in our Psychological Assessment Services Department at Bryce Hospital by their time-consuming behavior, such as the amount of time they required to complete a personality test, answer questions, and so forth. There appears to be a representative group of these persons with the disorder schizophrenia, which seems to be a product of their personality functioning. I could not say without a study of their histories if they also had not bonded with a significant other, which might help to explain why they used perfectionism as a coping pattern to avoid anxiety. This anxiety was described by Sigmund Freud as an emanating from the punishing superego, essentially parental influences. I describe it similarly as antagonistic minds that exact perfection from the host-victim by introducing doubt that is the source of anxiety when that person tries to be more flexible. Unfortunately, these poor or rigid coping patterns eventually lead to such inefficiency that stress increases and these persons may eventually have a psychotic break.

My impression is that this increasing stress is a period of very high emotionality and perceived adversity, much like the "fight or flight" syndrome, when our metabolism is very active. I have always thought that this would explain the overactivity of dopaminergic action in the limbic system of the brain, which Dr. Dudley portrayed as an emotional center. I think similar personality characteristics may be present in a number of individuals who experience schizophrenia during the critical period of time when they are making the transition from living with their parents to becoming independent and self supporting; that is, a number of persons in this subgroup may be idealistic and experience an identity crisis. They are not able to see their way in society right away, if ever.

What about my brother George's schizophrenia? What would be an alternative explanation to genetics for it? I recall reading a paragraph that George wrote to my parents when he was around six years old. If my memory serves me well, it was written in the back of a picture of his Holy Communion that my mother had. What impressed me was how thoughtful his comments were. Although he was likely mentored by my parents, I questioned whether I had such ability at that age. I cannot help but think that if he had not been uprooted from the mentoring and traditions that were facets of his daily life in Cuba, he would have become successful at the endeavor or occupation of his choice. Alternatively, his response to the changed circumstances in the United States suggested to me that he needed support more than me.

My brother George, in my opinion, was not a high achiever like I was, or as independent-minded; he was more of a follower, not so driven or ambitious. He needed the direction or mentoring from a significant other to see his way clearly. When we came to the States in October or November 1960, he was in the second grade and I was in the third. During that time, he typically followed me, his older brother by one year. At that age, we could have passed for identical twins and surely for fraternal twins. People had difficulty telling us apart. George did not fare very well in school after losing the support that he had in Cuba. He needed to regain that support in the States but did not. He might have gotten it from me, but we did not seem to bond in that way, which might have helped us both. We had a falling out of sorts before he entered the fifth grade, which did not help. He might have received mentoring from my parents that would have directed his paths to satisfactory adjustment and worthwhile pursuits, but he apparently did not receive it, which I speak more about in later chapters. He was a different personality when he was no longer grounded in a solid foundation of support and direction, which can make a difference in whether someone like him is successful and thrives or has problems in living. I know that personality type well because I have observed these persons in case histories from time to time. The following describes his personality without the beneficial influence of such support and direction, in my opinion. I think these personality changes reflected the framework for the negative symptoms of schizophrenia that he exhibited.

George was easily led by his peer group. He was suggestible. His actions were liable to be condoned and desirable if he had support from scrupulous people, but they could just as well become whimsical, impulsive, and antisocial if he was among friends who engaged in juvenile delinquency, sometimes just for "kicks." Thus, he was liable to engage in a range of behaviors that were sometimes incongruous, such as participating in sociable, desirable activities among some peers but apt to act somewhat "wildly" among other peers. This attitude led him to get in some trouble in junior high school and high school. Unfortunately, events such as these affected his social development and likely also his academic and intellectual development, an area where he already appeared to be struggling, which made it relatively more difficult for him to acquire and practice the social skills that he needed to get along well socially. His underdeveloped social skills, then, had an effect on his self image and emotional adjustment, beyond the effects of negative publicity.

What other attributes described my brother? If you asked those who knew him to tell you what George was like premorbidly, before he became mentally ill, but after the setbacks that I described, they would probably tell you that he was fairly quiet and shy. They might say that he was friendly and fun-loving but did not say much. From what I gathered about him, he probably liked to get "high," play and listen to rock and hard rock music, and have a romantic time with a girl. He tended to be rather innocent, fairly naïve, and easily swayed. He was not academically inclined, did not have a storehouse of ideas, was not very knowledgeable, and had simple views. He most likely fit in within his peer group due to such group dynamics as consideration and concern from some, which would have helped him to gain acceptance; similar counter-cultural interests or activities, including the music of the times; years of familiarity contributing to their mutual understanding of one another; modeling influences; and other peer group benefits. However, beyond enjoyment and a sense of belonging, I am not aware that George had any serious, long-ranging plans that provided him direction beyond this phase in his life. His personality functioning and level of adjustment then, without someone to direct him and steady his way, in my opinion, were a breeding ground for some further and more serious adjustment problems than those he had faced already, if not mental illness. He had gradually begun to exhibit a range of behaviors that simulated the negative and cognitive symptoms of schizophrenia in an attenuated form.

George's schizophrenia was altogether different than mine. I feel that he did not have adequate mentoring and direction after our relations deteriorated, but I do not think that George had to contend with oppositional forces like I did. Rather, as I discuss in later pages, I think that he was aligned with my parents and was directed in ways that were meant to undermine me. Although he obviously heard "voices," judging from some of his unusual expressions and behavior, negative and cognitive symptoms of schizophrenia were dominant, seemingly from the start. For example, if you tried to engage him in a conversation, you would likely be met with an "Uh huh" sort of acknowledgement, and you could expect regular interruptions with odd comments like, "How about the Allman Brothers?" or "Willie Garcia!" a mention of dad with a big smile. He would not say anything for long periods of time. If he broke the silence, he was apt to make brief statements like, "Ana Maria is pretty cool, isn't she?" speaking of his younger sister, or "How about Johnny Nodine on lead guitar?" referring to her husband. He would pace back and forth for long periods of time. Eventually, his penchant for cigarettes dominated his thinking. He did not seem very interested or motivated to do much but would usually go along with whatever you planned for him, particularly if he could smoke. He, of course, liked music and most likely liked good food and snacks. He appeared rather disheveled, such as burn holes on his clothing, discolored teeth, and a not-quite-clean face at times. It is my impression that George exhibited this form of regressed behavior from the onset of his schizophrenic disorder around age 18 until his untimely death at age 27.

George did not appear to be very cognitively stimulated once he began to experience schizophrenia. He did not seem to have many ideas or very much to say. This can result from an absence of other stimulating activities that help us acquire a storehouse of daily ideas, which make us more productive speakers, such as reading the newspaper, watching interesting or informative television programs, engaging other people we know regularly in a conversation, and becoming a part of various groups, such as those at work, church, or in the neighborhood. These activities and interests have corresponding neural exchanges, which stimulate our brains to recall, recollect, and reason. Thus, you would expect the brains of people who do not engage in these activities to be less active or stimulated. George did not appear to engage in the higher-order thinking processes that typically involve the frontal lobes, such as reasoning, planning, and executing behavior. Others in the family felt that he was lazy because he never seemed to participate in constructive activities that would have helped him to fit in. He really did not do much at all. He did not have a basic plan that showed satisfactory judgment. He was driven to do those things that he enjoyed, which were often indulgences that did not reflect good judgment in the overall scheme of things. Regardless, he did not employ skilled reasoning processes. He seemed rather thoughtless, which was often mirrored in his lack of emotional expression. Consequently, he needed daily supervision and direction.

There is a body of research indicating that the incidence of schizophrenia is greater for children growing up in urban settings (3). In my 25 years of clinical practice at Bryce Hospital, I have found that an inpatient hospital setting can be sufficiently stressful as to produce and maintain symptoms of schizophrenia or psychosis. The common thread that I have found is low intellectual functioning and other conditions that are associated with limited stress tolerance, such as persons who have suffered a head injury. That is, I have learned over the years that such persons can have difficulty tolerating the hospital environment, particularly in some of our more restrictive wards or programs. Those conditions can lead to and maintain a paranoid distortion of reality. It can cause them to have active paranoid or psychotic symptoms.

Some years ago, I treated an alcoholic who had a history of alcohol withdrawal seizures. He was not raised in an intellectually stimulating environment, and his schooling was limited. He had a good work history, but he had done semi-skilled labor. After talking to him, it seemed likely that his intellect had been reduced by his years of drinking. He had also reached a point where he needed some support in living. He was no longer able to manage the requirements of independent living, which had become too stressful for him. Before he was admitted to Bryce Hospital (for a second time), his source of community support dwindled, he began drinking again, and he became paranoid. He was admitted to THSMF before his transfer to a closed ward on the second floor of the Behavioral Rehabilitation Unit (BRU), a long-term unit at the former Bryce Hospital (in July 2014, the University of Alabama acquired our property and we moved into a new, state-of-the-art hospital in Tuscaloosa). Later, he was moved to an open ward on the first floor of BRU, where I received him.

This man was very ornery and distrustful on that first occasion when we met. He mistook my benign statements, applying unintended meanings to them. He misunderstood and distorted them in a paranoid way. It was necessary for me to go over each one slowly in very simple terms due to his limited comprehension. Over several meetings and after several engagements in his living area, I was able to gain his confidence and had no further problems of this sort, but some of his treatment providers did. I spoke to them about his limited ability to understand material that was not limited in scope and provided simply and repeatedly until he obviously understood it. During our engagements, he made reports to me of mistreatment at THSMF and the second floor of BRU, where he was initially, statements which were highly unlikely. In reviewing his THSMF records, I learned that the events he reported to me had been listed as a problem on his treatment plan there. I was also able to determine that his reports about mistreatment on the second floor of BRU were of a similar sort. The problem seemed to be that these relatively more confining living areas, which were more likely to house unstable and volatile patients, created sufficient stress for him that he was psychologically overwhelmed and distorted events in those living areas. He did not have that problem when we moved him to the first floor of BRU, a relatively less congested, less confining, and calmer living area housing a more stable patient population where I provided him supportive therapy, which he needed initially to dispel his fears.

When I was working with a female population on the second floor of BRU at Bryce Hospital approximately nine years ago, I treated a young girl who impressed me by her kind and considerate manner. She had diagnoses of Schizophrenia and Mild Intellectual Disability. I do not remember the events that precipitated her admission. However, it became apparent to me in working with her that the second floor was sufficiently stressful for her as to maintain symptoms of her mental illness, thereby providing an obstruction to her placement. She would become indignant by her interpretation of events in her living area, which would elicit angry comments from her that probably had a paranoid flavor. I expressed these concerns to our staff members in order to increase their understanding of her behavior. We were able to get her out of the hospital fairly quickly, which may have been engineered by means of successful family outings. Effectively, whether intellectual deficiency is developmental or acquired as a result of undesirable events, such as a head injury or alcoholism, these persons are susceptible to experiencing environments as sufficiently stressful that it precipitates paranoid ideas and delusional thinking from them. Their low intelligence seems to prevent them from using reasoning processes to become comfortable in some living environments and other settings. Their corresponding unremitting distress can precipitate and maintain mental illness (e.g., a psychotic condition), which sometimes can be remedied by supportive intervention.

We have a group of disorders that was referred to in the *Diagnostic and Statistical Manual of Mental Disorders, Fourth Edition, Text Revision* (*DSM-4-TR*) as dementias (4). This same group of disorders is referred to in the *DSM-5* as neurocognitive disorders (NCDs) (3). According to *DSM-5*, "the NCD category encompasses the group of disorders in which the primary clinical deficit is in cognitive function, and that are acquired rather than developmental." These are often disorders for which there is a known cause that can be identified by an underlying physical or disease process, such as the Alzheimer's type dementia. For Alzheimer's dementia, there is a decline in memory and one or more cognitive functions, such as language comprehension or language expression. There is a strong genetic or heritable causative factor, but genetics is not exclusively the route to acquiring this form of dementia, which is incurable to date and gradually progresses to death. For example, *DSM-5* notes that the strongest risk for Alzheimer's disease is simply age and that risk can be influenced by vascular factors. It notes from U. S. census data that an estimated 7% of people between the ages of 65 and 74 acquire Alzheimer's disease, which increases to 53% for the 75 to 84 age group, and the estimated risk is 40% for those who are 85-years-old and over.

When I was working in the Psychological Assessments Services (PAS) Unit at the former Bryce Hospital between 1990 and 1999, we regularly assessed elderly patients who had experienced a dementia process which became sufficiently complicated that they had to enter the hospital. Dementia of the Alzheimer's Type was the most common, by far. My father acquired it around 1990. I had become so familiar with it that I was able to tell mom a step-by-step progression, more or less, and how to treat it. A complicated form of dementia requiring hospitalization occurs when, as a part of the disease process causing the cognitive decline, the victim manifests psychological and behavioral problems that present a danger to himself or someone else. The problems of persons with Alzheimer's-type dementia gradually become broad in range, such as confusion that can necessitate limit setting or supervision, examples of which would be drawing large amounts of money from a bank account or forgetfulness about the significance of "red light" signals when driving. These persons can also begin to exhibit behavior problems, as noted. For example, the demented person may have auditory or visual hallucinations, become suspicious or paranoid in regard to the actions of family members, neighbors, or other people in his environment, and resort to such actions as wandering away from home, displaying angry emotions, and striking someone.

I was informed while I was working in PAS that visual hallucinations may often have an "organic" or neurological basis, such as the chemical effects from alcohol or the effects from the cause of the dementia disease process. Such learning was useful because it helped to distinguish them from the auditory hallucinations that predominate in the disorder schizophrenia or to recognize the reasons they may have been present. Bizarre experiences of all sorts may not be unusual for people who experience a progressive and terminal neurological decline of the sort that is observed in progressive dementias and other disorders, such as AIDS. These may well be largely explained by physiological or neurological effects. What about the auditory hallucinations?

Dementia of the Alzheimer's Type, as an example of a dementia, does not seem to be very exclusive. That is, it can affect people from all walks of life, such as elderly people with good family backgrounds who impress as conservative and who may have been well adjusted all their lives. Auditory hallucinations, as I have explained, are the voices of other minds. Considering the unusual events that people experience during a progressive course of dementia, such as confusion, disorientation, changes in sleeping habits, and the like, it does not seem very unusual that their distress may reach such proportions as to result in an awakening of their subconscious mind sufficient to hear the voices of other minds. This phenomenon would likely not have occurred if they had not experienced impairment in their cognitive integrity, in their brain, which made them more pervious to various forms of stress. Besides auditory hallucinations, they can have misperceptions and suspicion that spring from their changing brain capacity and altered perceptions.

What about the auditory hallucinations of these persons, are they benign or malevolent? They are certainly not merely benign as they may entertain persecutory ideas about other persons, an event that hallucinations can promote. An example of the interaction of confusion and auditory hallucinations that comes to mind is represented by an elderly demented patient who we treated at Bryce Hospital in the early to mid-nineties. She began "hearing voices," believed there were persons in the attic of her home, and began to poke the ceiling with a rod. Thus, it appears that a deteriorating brain disease process can make those affected more susceptible to stress, causing their cognitive integrity to become compromised or less supported and making them more pervious to psychological influences. Of course, the predominant view at present would likely attribute the hallucinatory experience of these persons to the effects of their brain impairment on their neuroanatomy and neurochemistry.

The limited studies that I reviewed regarding "research on genetics" included a family that had genetically acquired a disposition for a neurocognitive disorder, a dementia (30). The researchers found that before the onset of this dementia, which was a middle-age event, many of the affected family members experienced what the researchers referred to as a behavioral syndrome or behavior disinhibition: personality changes. Broadly classified, this syndrome included features of schizophrenia and depression as well as addiction problems, delinquency, and other socially aberrant behaviors, such as sexual indiscretions. Thus, there may be some speculation that, like the neurocognitive disorder, schizophrenia in these family members could have been genetically predetermined. On reviewing this data, my impression was that the process that eventually led to their dementia made them vulnerable to the behavior disinhibition earlier in life described by the researchers. One explanation, for example, could be that the changing brain made them more vulnerable to subconscious influences, such as less able to screen out those influences, or it affected their discernment. They became more subject to stress and less able to inhibit their impulses. We treated a patient at Bryce Hospital some years ago who was afflicted with the neurocognitive disorder Huntingdon's chorea. He had similar behavioral problems earlier in life before the signs or symptoms of Huntingdon's disease became notable. This, I think, is a common finding.

I have previously made reference to mention in the *DSM-5* on the strong contribution to schizophrenia from genetics. The *DSM-5* also mentions that risk alleles for bipolar disorder have been identified. I am not as familiar with bipolar disorder as with schizophrenia because I have not experienced it personally. I have treated a number of patients with bipolar disorder, reviewed their histories, and met some of their family members. Some of our clients with this disorder have had repeated hospitalizations. Their disorders have been very difficult for them to manage in the community. Their seeming lack of control during its active phase has led to such out-of-control and sometimes egregious behavior that they are reluctant to return to the community environment and decompensate (become actively mentally ill) during efforts to make such plans. I like to think that it is treatable with specialized cognitive-behavior therapy as an adjunct to their psychiatric medications and the insights from persons who have successfully treated their disorder and published their treatment plans. I am only aware of one instance when a person with bipolar features was able to stop her medications, and it was based on a report from her family. She was the sister of one of our clients. During a conference with her family that she attended, her mother indicated that she had been able to do without her medication after building a structured program that was rewarding to her. That is an exception that does not appear to be supported by literature I have read on the subject. For example, one such resource noted that the clients with bipolar disorder that do best over the course of their lifetime are those who comply in taking their medication and manage to avoid hospitalization (10).

I mention in the preface that my findings have implications for other mental disorders. My impressions about bipolar disorder are not well corroborated. They are largely inferential from knowledge gained by empirical means, such as observation, reviews of histories, testing, individual therapy, annual assessments, and meetings with families. These impressions have been that these family members may be bonded strongly and that these bonds likely provide one explanation for the disorder, such as in the offspring, a feature that may be captured in the statement, "She is just like her mother" or "She is just like her father." To elaborate a bit, if one parent has bipolar disorder and the other does not, and the child only bonds with the parent that does not have the disorder, then the child would not be expected to acquire the disorder, and vice versa. My inference in the positive cases is that the child is acquiring the bipolar features from the mental or psychological energy of the parent with the disorder. But I have also observed cases of bipolar disorder that seemed to arise following very traumatic events in these people's lives. For example, some appeared to have committed indiscretions of various sorts that likely alienated significant other persons in their lives or which could have had a profound effect on their psychological well being, including their alignment with their community and their significant others. Thus, such events could have had the effect of compromising a protective shield formed by means of psychological bonding (or their cognitive integrity), which they would somehow have to aright to become impervious to psychological influences that underlie their mania.

Another area where genetics is thought to have a strong influence is substance use disorders. Although it has not been my intention to broaden the scope of this book to consider how the ideas contained in it will affect that population, I believe that substance addiction falls within the body of ideas that I have introduced. That is, I think that psychological influences such as personality factors, familial bonding, and subconscious influences along with the environment of social reinforcement and social learning will help to explain the conditions that precipitate and maintain substance use patterns. This is not to undermine the insights about mental disorders that we may gain from research on genetics.

PART II:

Schizophrenia, My Story

CHAPTER 8:

A CHAPTER IN TUSCALOOSA

I consider myself to be a schizophrenic sort of guy. I say this because I have had an awakening of the subconscious mind: I hear subvocal speech. Although this is a regular occurrence, it is not like walking into a room and becoming privy to the personal thoughts of everyone or anyone in the room. It is a much more selective experience than that. That is, while I am around significant other persons, and persons who are part of my everyday life, such as co-workers, and at other times when they are not present, I will sometimes hear their voice or voices. This is not a trite experience, because the content tends to be something these persons mean to communicate, whether friendly or unfriendly, so that it usually makes an impression on me. It can be tricky, because they mean to exert an influence on my thinking and behavior, so that I have to use my own reasoning ability to judge how to use that information. Also, we are not always progressive, so that someone who is subconsciously friendly today may not be so tomorrow, and you may learn this the hard way if she has gained your trust and you rely on her. Over time, you come to know the people that you can count on, those that you can usually count on, and those that are not supportive but antagonistic, as a general rule.

I am not starting my story at the beginning, and I should say that it was a long process to become skilled at meetings life's daily demands with an awakened subconscious and the distractions it can bring. This would include such aspects of this subconscious experience as understanding the motivation of the people whose voices I hear, to hear their voices clearly, and to understand the layers of subconscious opposition that I face. For example, you can have subconscious opposition from your immediate environment—the people that you come in contact with daily; at the same time, family members may be unwelcome subconscious residents that are privy to your thoughts and communication with others, but you may not be aware of this because they may be silent for the most part; and different family members may be the unwelcome residents at different times. Family members may also communicate subconsciously with people in your present circumstances whom they have never met to facilitate those people's opposition by alerting them to your thoughts or motivation and in other ways, which—I have come to understand—is a further violation of the sanctity of mental life. Essentially, family members become so invested in limiting you that they violate another boundary by including non-family members in an alliance against you.

I will describe the events that brought me to this understanding. I do not consider myself very different from anyone else who has struggled with schizophrenia. I think that I was very fortunate in regard to my circumstances and relationships, including very good mentoring that together with a strong spiritual foundation, learning, and hard work helped me to weather storms and continue to pursue goals despite significant setbacks. Let me begin with the chapter here in Tuscaloosa, Alabama.

I had "detached with love" from my family before coming to Tuscaloosa, the title (*Detaching with Love*) on an Alanon booklet that I read while a counselor in Montgomery, Alabama, where I worked at a 30-day intensive treatment program for people addicted to alcohol and drugs. For those of you who are not familiar with Alanon, it is the educational and supportive group for the family of the alcoholic person. This substance use counselor job began as my practicum in 1988 on the way to earning a Master of Science degree in clinical psychology from Auburn University at Montgomery (AUM) while winding down and transitioning from a private practice in accounting, a business where I shared expenses with my father. This detachment took place over the year that I was working on my master's degree and was meant to be primarily from the people that still resided in the family home: my father, my mother, and my sister Conchita, who is two years younger than me. I felt that this would be in our best interests because of patterns in our relations that I felt were unhealthy and that were reinforced by the frequency of our engagements. I took the position of always trying to be kind and considerate while, at the same time, being somewhat assertive in letting them know in a nice way that I wanted to lead my own life and did not want to be very involved in family life at that time. Actually, I was very involved in school and my practicum and had little time for much else.

This detachment continued in Tuscaloosa with considerable success. I was fortunate enough to be hired on April 30, 1990, for a position in the Psychology Department at Bryce Hospital by the Director of Psychology, Violet Perney. My father died from Alzheimer's disease in 1998. My mother and sister continued to live in the family home until 2004, when they relocated to the home of my brother Raymond and his family in Miami. This was a well planned decision brought about by mom's difficulty keeping up an older home that was larger than she needed. My sister Conchita, who lived with her, could provide some assistance but needed supervision and guidance due to a closed head injury that she suffered in an automobile accident in the fall of 1973 during her first year in college. Although she retains much of her intellectual ability, she has difficulty in cognitive functions such as short-term memory and reasoning functions related to organizing, planning, and executing well-considered goals. For example, she could not cook a meal because she could not organize it and plan it and because she might leave the kitchen and become involved in another activity.

Socially, Conchita was at that time liable to say just about anything without taking note of the social context or situation, what we refer to as social blunders that can be very embarrassing. She was often energetic, but her everyday decisions were less considered or modulated than before the accident: she tended to be more impulsive or somewhat rash in regard to everyday decisions. She remained very religious and indoctrinated in the strong Catholic tradition that was a part of her upbringing, which were central and prominent aspects of her daily life. She also retained strong future aspirations, but these seemed to become frustrated over time, such as difficulty staying abreast of her schoolwork on returning to college. Similarly, although she dated and had involvement in relationships, her cognitive deficits carried a degree of dependency and less mature thinking that made it difficult for her to find the right suitor. Over time, she seemed to view her former educational and romantic goals as less reachable. She dwelt on these matters much like someone leading a fantasy life that was not expected to come to pass with great certainty. Her life became centered on events and relationships past and present, primarily her vast extended family, which was to be expected as she lived primarily with mom and dad, who were the hub of a very large family-of-origin (they had nine children) and a large extended family.

Conchita, though compromised by her head injury, retained some unusual capabilities: special qualities that are not only a part of her personality, but also an outgrowth of the love she received from her family, which was to a large extent reciprocal, because she was and is an attractive, charming person. These attributes that define her are also a legacy from the wonderful peer group that she had been a part of, who were another force that shaped her personality. When I divorced in 1984, I took the opportunity of doing things with her frequently, at first to spend some time with her and provide her some entertainment, but subsequently because we always had a lot of fun. This was much like dating a sister in a non-sexual, romantic way, because we would go to football games, movies, out to eat, for a refreshment, to a restaurant-bar, dancing, and the like, at times among mutual friends, whom we would greet. During these times, she was most charming and sweet, and I would be amazed at her sensitivity, considering her head injury, which would all but be forgotten. She also has a special ability to charm the elderly, which has been one of her penchants from my observations of her life at the family home in an old neighborhood where she was acquainted with many elderly people. I have been frustrated with her over some of her shenanigans towards me (which I will explain later, as there are two sides to her behavior) and then have been amazed by her about face on engaging an elderly person and watching her exude such warmth and charm as to cheer and enliven the elderly—a very special quality indeed. She also has the heart of a child and has a love affair with many of her nieces and nephews.

In 2005, I learned from my brother Raymond, in whose home mom and Conchita had been living, that his family was experiencing some adjustment problems in living with my mother and Conchita and that he had been talking to my sister Ana Maria about the possibility of mom and Conchita relocating to Baton Rouge, Louisiana, to live with her and her family. This was the most plausible alternative because Ana Maria and mom were very close, Conchita had lived with Ana Maria and her family for six or seven years before dad died, during which time Ana Maria and her husband John spearheaded Conchita's rehabilitation efforts, and mom and Conchita had visited them for a month during the previous year, meaning that they had some idea about what life would be like in Baton Rouge with Ana Maria, John, and their four daughters. Thus, this seemed like a very good alternative for mom and Conchita. However, on learning of these plans, and after giving the matter some consideration, I decided to give my mother the option of relocating to Tuscaloosa in order to live with me. I based this decision on the strong Catholic community here in Tuscaloosa; the size of the town and accessibility of its resources, which I felt that mom would find to her liking; the potential resources available through the University of Alabama, which might benefit Conchita; and the friendliness of the townspeople here.

When I approached my mother about these plans and the reasons I thought that she and Conchita may like Tuscaloosa, I also established certain conditions, which I emphasized several times so that they would be clear. A primary condition was that Conchita would be willing to listen to or work with me. It had been about 20 years since I had lived with mom and Conchita. In the past, I had not been able to live with or around Conchita very well because, like my mother, she tried to limit my behavior, and this, I feel certain, was at least partly related to her insecurities following her accident. That is, I figured into her scheme of things, considering her dependency needs. We could have a wonderful time together, when our behavior would be coordinated much like peas in a pod; then, much like the example with the elderly, she would do an about face and become a stumbling block—a veritable obstacle course that would require very careful maneuvering to avoid becoming entangled in some controversy that would displace my focus and energy. This obstacle would usually take the form of subconscious opposition, like that I will mention later in this chapter regarding household chores. It could also take the form of conscious comments emanating from her subconscious motivation in order to outwit me, such as creating a dilemma that would make it difficult for me to respond effectively.

I told mom that it was not my intention to sacrifice my life for Conchita—that I have a life of my own. At the same time, I expressed my opinion that Tuscaloosa provided a good reintegration opportunity for Conchita and that I could facilitate that as long as she and Conchita were willing to work with me. During visits with mom and Conchita in Montgomery after dad's death, I had become aware that Conchita was very dependent on mom, who did not discourage this relationship. At times, this seemed a loving role they both played, bantering with one another. Conchita, for her part, seems capable of a lot more, which she has shown when so motivated, such as when she is interested in someone that she has met and feels a need to assert herself, and in similar situations. Due to my awareness of this relationship, I stressed to mom the importance of structuring relations with Conchita in such a way as to encourage Conchita's independence. Mom can be difficult to pin down about such things. She may discount them and leave you feeling like you did not make an impression. But I was sure to do so, and she agreed. And, somewhat to my surprise and pleasure, because I felt they might be comfortable in Tuscaloosa, mom accepted my offer.

We rented a home in an older neighborhood that was fairly much like the one mom and Conchita were used to in Montgomery. The street to our home was off a main street and made a circle that comprised the second and third blocks from the main street, within which was our home, which provided a natural walking track away from traffic and added safety from its sequestered nature and the familiarity gained with neighbors of such close proximity, in addition to it being a friendly neighborhood. It was not long before Conchita and mom got to know a number of the neighbors who they made friends with and visited. They also became involved in three different church groups that met once a month for lunch and specific group functions related to meeting the needs of the church or the group members, so that it was not long before they also made friends within the church community who were the object of regular calls and whom they would greet and socialize with on Sundays after church.

My mother I refer to as a lady's lady because she always made girlfriends easily. One might have never guessed this side of her without seeing her in action because she was always the homemaker in the home caring for nine children. Dad seemed to make all the decisions, she seemed rather passive and submissive to him and even to her children's wishes in many respects, and she always seemed the rather timid wife in the background socially. She grew up in the bosom of a large, extended, Catholic family in her native Cuba. She was the only girl of four children, and she was very close to her parents, particularly her father. She attended Catholic schools for girls, had many girlfriends, and was active socially amidst this social circle of friends and relatives, enjoying life so much that she seemingly did not give much thought to courtship. She did not marry until the age of thirty, which was quite late for her culture and her eligibility, I would think, and then seemingly only due to dad's persistence.

One need only spend time with mom to recognize her social capabilities. At age eighty-five, within a short while, she had made a circle of friends that she could call on when she had a need and was enjoying herself in Tuscaloosa.

She soon learned the Tuscaloosa area that she frequented and was accessing it by car. She retained a sharp memory and very good social judgment. She was also a good and careful driver during her stay. She had a healthy curiosity about people and was a very entertaining storyteller, qualities that are very illuminating about her interests and the sort of person that she was in her native Cuba. She had unending stories about her life there and the people she knew, which was the material for her interesting stories that captured the imagination. At eighty-five, she was still not a homebody, I learned; she liked to get out and do things. And this gets me back to my comment that she was a girls' girl: socially resourceful and entertaining, a lot of fun to be with, and socially sensitive and adept in her own way.

Conchita, for her part, enjoyed mom's company and became a part of the same social group, and not just as mom's daughter, but in her own right, despite some disability that is not entirely unnoticed and corresponding dependency, because she also has a healthy curiosity about people and can be endearing, as I have noted. That is, within this nucleus of friends that they were making, there existed some potential for her to develop a more independent social life. Alternatively, she sometimes gave the impression, if in an indirect or subtle way, that she was here because mom chose to come here and somewhat concerned, unsure about the prospects of becoming stuck in Tuscaloosa.

The game plan. I quickly developed a game plan, which was not reactive, as I had thought about our initial needs. This plan was formed alongside the developments previously mentioned (or preceded them)—the neighborhood friendships and church groups that I previously mentioned. We rented a three bedroom, one bathroom home that mom fell in love with. The front entrance led through the living room to a hall that accessed a spacious kitchen on the right, with a small bedroom and the side door at that end, and a hallway to the left that accessed a bathroom, a master bedroom that was large enough to accommodate Conchita and mom (they wanted it that way), and another room where I slept. The smaller room at the end of the kitchen by the side door became the den, the guest bedroom, and my study, but I soon made it my bedroom and study for convenience and privacy because I kept late hours related to my profession. At that point, mom decided that she would not mind additional privacy and moved into the room I vacated.

The first issue at hand was dining. I had learned from vacationing with mom and Conchita at our Destin, Florida, beach condominium, a time-sharing unit that we own for about the third week in September, that if I want to have good, nutritious meals, which I need due to the amount of energy that I require daily to meet life's responsibilities, then I have to plan them or they will be up in the air, because mom was not really up to doing that and Conchita either. Alternatively, mom had been studious about her cooking, was fairly much a gourmet cook, and was capable of preparing a delicious supper daily if I planned it and bought the groceries. Thus, every Sunday, I wrote our menu for the week and bought the necessary groceries. Mom, who owned her own car, eventually became comfortable driving to the grocery store and was able to help me out with the shopping during the week.

I know that mom liked her job. For one, she is somewhat of an epicure. She is particular about food, which she likes to be prepared a certain way, and she likes to eat good food. For another, she knew that she was needed, that this was her role, and she was thankful for the responsibility at her very senior age. Then there was Conchita. We quickly got her enrolled in piano lessons every Tuesday afternoon due to the good fortune of having a piano teacher within the neighborhood circle, about half of a block away, a kind-hearted person who soon became a friend of mom and Conchita along with her daughter. Her daughter was a few years younger than Conchita yet more mature and a good influence on Conchita, whose ideas can be capricious. The fact that mom and Conchita were now living with me made them and Conchita's rehabilitation my responsibility, as I saw it, because I was the one who spent each day with them and was in the best position to understand their needs. I got as much information as I could from my brother Raymond about his and his family's experiences with them in Miami and both talked to and read material sent by my sister Ana Maria related to Conchita's activities and responsibilities during her time with her and her family in Baton Rouge. Beyond that, I used my intuition, in which regard the sixteen years that I had spent in the field of human behavior, which included special populations like Conchita, was an asset.

The immediate answer became obvious to me because it was staring me right in the face. I would put in a day of work, part of a long day considering that I had ample responsibilities at work and at home, and I would have the peace, serenity, and integrity that comes when one applies his skills to one's responsibilities in a considerate way that leads to greater success at life, which I have come to recognize in my pursuits as the Judeo-Christian work ethic. While socializing with Conchita and mom, taking a walk around the block with them, greeting neighbors, dining, and so forth, I would often come to the keen realization that Conchita had very little structure or responsibilities during the day, had lived that way for some time, and, thus, had grown at least somewhat accustomed to such a lifestyle—bantering with mom, seeking mom out about what to do, participating in shared activities with mom, and so forth. This is not to say that she was particularly enamored with her lifestyle or did not aspire for more. In fact, she was taking an antidepressant and had little enthusiasm and drive on awakening some mornings, but out of habit, she had grown accustomed to this pattern of daily living.

I soon noticed that Conchita did not seem to recognize or share in the work ethic that is a part of most people's lives—whether a homemaker, mother, wife, husband, or breadwinner—and that she lacked the sense of maturity and responsibility that comes from such a tradition. She also did not defer to my lead, prompting, and efforts to mentor her. Perhaps she did not recognize this sense of direction that I tried to give her, but my impression was that she ignored it. Beyond that, she played the game that I presume she learned from mom, who also played it, though much more subtly or expertly than Conchita, of being mindful that I did not retain my mental well being and did not integrate and bond well with the neighbors, in keeping with her and mom's motives for me. This behavior occurs across all settings, such as church, the neighborhood, and family. It is like a reaction formation, to use a term coined by Sigmund Freud to describe a subconscious defense mechanism. Essentially, it is like putting up a front that everything is all right when it is not, such as smiling when you are actually angry. We would greet the public as if everything was all right. However, there was no harmony to this engagement, which was actually mediated by a subconscious battle, so that we came across visibly as awkward; and it was my impression that the public eventually came to recognize this, was practically forced to take sides, and, therefore, our joint relationships did not grow and develop as they should have, with a real sense of intimacy and wholesomeness. Of course, it upset me to learn that beyond failing to respond to my direction, she and mom would continue to be disrespectful in the way that I just mentioned—that I would have to contend with such immaturity—and I am speaking about Conchita here, because I would not use the same words to describe relations with mom.

Getting back to difficulty changing habits, I felt that one thing that I could do for Conchita was to provide her a greater sense of responsibility:

of the work ethic. As I said earlier, it was a natural result, because mom was not capable of keeping house, and it required time that I could devote to other activities if I could recruit Conchita's help. We initially considered a housekeeper, which did not work out, and this seemed a way for Conchita to earn her keep, so to speak. Conchita was not very keen on the idea from the beginning, but one admirable quality that she has is that she will listen to good advice, even though part of her resists it, and she can also be persuaded by impressing upon her when she should do something out of a sense of fair play because to do otherwise would be neglecting to do her part. The goal as I saw it, which I explained to her, was for her to become a skilled homemaker: a veritable asset that would be appreciated by anyone that she lives with. This goal, in my opinion, was also consistent with her goals, judging from remarks that she made about family members such as, "I am just a burden," and her capability to be attractive to potential suitors when she should want to. Thus, I began by assigning her one household task to do daily. I would provide her training on Saturday mornings and develop specific instructions for her to follow on her own later, usually including mom in the plan so that she could be available for coaching or directions if necessary.

Shortly after this undertaking, I learned a lot about Conchita that I did not know. I soon became aware that Conchita did not like housework very much and gradually it seemed to me that she felt that she was too important for it, as if to do it went against the special class that she saw herself as belonging to. I had not realized how particular she is about such things as clothing and cosmetics. She is very particular about her wardrobe, which is an attribute that she acquired from her peer group, I am sure, and which is a desirable attribute, in general. This extends to her cosmetics, furniture, and other things. Mom also liked nice things but had simpler tastes and tended to be more practical. Conchita has more difficulty assessing her needs and is swayed more emotionally, tending to buy excessively and impulsively for that reason. I want to mention here that part of the reason that I did not know Conchita very well then—I feel that I know her better now—I attribute to schizophrenia. Although this aspect of my personality was not quite evident to anyone during my upbringing, I feel that it has been a lifelong pattern. I would compare this childhood schizophrenia to a milder form of autism, because the oppositional behavior that one encounters makes it more difficult to relate to, absorb, and notice one's environment. Whereas a parent can help each child to recognize what her siblings are like, a parent can similarly strive to keep that from a child, and it is a fact, I am sure, that people like me who experience features of schizophrenia during their childhood are naïve about their world for that reason.

Conchita's repugnance for housework due to lack of practice and feelings about doing something that's not suitable for her class did not serve her well in this instance, in my opinion, and I explained that to her. I pointed out that her niece, who is doing well financially, assumed that responsibility along with raising children because it helped her family to live more comfortably at that early stage of her marriage, even though she at first did not like this suggestion by her husband and also felt unsure if it was right for her, or so I have been told and have gathered. I also pointed out to her that if she ever hires someone to do this for her, she will have the skills, will be better able to delegate those household chores, and will know whether they are carried out properly. In other words, I pointed out, a refined woman who hires a housekeeper is not worth her salt quite as much if she is naïve about how to delegate and supervise those duties. Therefore, she will likely be respected less by her servants, who will be more able to take advantage of her for that reason.

Conchita and I set off on this endeavor with another obstacle, myasthenia gravis, which we were not aware of until she became acutely ill some three and a half years later, though I feel relatively certain that she was already afflicted, because she often complained of feeling tired. Laboratory work did not reveal significant findings. The nurse practitioner who we saw at Indian Rivers Mental Health Center felt that her head injury could have been a contributing factor to her lack of energy as could depression, including some effects that are termed "pseudodementia" due to the dulling of cognition from depression. I felt that her lifestyle could also have been a contributing factor and that strategic plans for her could have helped to alleviate her depression and improve her energy level. If we had been aware of the signs and symptoms of myasthenia gravis, we would have eventually recognized them because Conchita reported or experienced other signs and symptoms. However, because we were not familiar with it, it was difficult to recognize this syndrome, particularly due to a number of confounding factors.

Myasthenia gravis can be a formidable obstacle. I cannot describe the severity of Conchita's condition at the time. I would judge that if she had been willing to give it the effort required, our endeavor should have worked for a time, considering other things that she did or was able to do, such as audiovisual aerobics exercises at home, chores at a group home, and water aerobics at the YMCA during the six months before she became acutely ill. Even so, she scared me when I noticed that she did not seem capable of pacing herself and would overdo it and exhaust herself, which led to closer supervision and coaching and the inclusion of rest periods in the instructions to her so that she would not overdo it. I had a constant vigil about this and have also noted that Conchita is capable of learning new tasks and skills when she is motivated to do so. However, in this endeavor with Conchita, I also had to contend with resistance from her in the nature of passive aggression. I had encountered it from her regularly 20 years earlier, and at times it becomes outright ridiculous, like someone acting outright dumb. I apologize for saying this about her, but it really stands out in relief when you recognize her full pattern of behavior and what she is capable of. I am intimately acquainted with it in my work.

Passive aggression, essentially, occurs when a person fails to perform according to her capability or a recognized standard, not because that person lacks the skills, but due to her motivation not to do so. It is passive because that individual is expressing her anger, dissatisfaction, or other strong feelings indirectly by not performing according to the expected standard. A classical example might be illustrated by the traditional housewife, who, displeased by her husband's actions that day, forgets to prepare supper timely, knowing that her husband will be disappointed. It is a psychological defense mechanism that occurs at a subconscious level, reflecting subconscious motivation and protecting the person from knowingly doing something that is wrong. It would be more desirable if the person could communicate her feelings directly in an assertive way, which may be more typical of a modern marriage in the case in point, but it may require some basic changes if the person's motive for the behavior cannot be justified, such as the motivation that I ascribe to my sister's behavior.

Effectively, I worked very hard at this endeavor from August 2005 until Conchita was placed in a group home around April 2008 and had partial success. Typically, Conchita devised her defenses to make my work difficult. I tried to remain upbeat, lively, and pleasant throughout the coaching, making it difficult for her not to respond, and she would think of every trick in the book to trip me up. This is like asking somebody to do something for you when she does not want to do it, and by the end of the activity, it is hard to feel entirely at peace, even if you have not made any mistakes, which can happen and then tend to create emotional conflict, so that you feel a need to be away from that person for a time until you can regain a sense of well-being. Conchita became skilled at washing the dishes, which was her nightly duty; she learned to sweep and mop the kitchen satisfactorily in our initial home, which we rented for about a year before someone purchased it at a higher price than our offer; and she did similarly at the home across the street from it that we rented during the next three years. As to the other duties, such as cleaning the bathroom or dusting and arranging her room to be orderly, she did not make much progress toward doing those tasks independently. She continued to need a lot of coaching and would not always do those chores satisfactorily.

Conchita tested in the Low Average range of intelligence on the Verbal Scale of the Wechsler Adult Intelligence Scale-III during that period, which is equivalent to performing at a junior high school level on language skills that include subtests measuring word knowledge, abstract reasoning, and comprehension of a variety of cultural events. I mention this to complement my general inferences about her ability in contrast to her variable motivation and how it affected the performance that she demonstrated at any given time.

Conchita saw a female therapist at Indian Rivers Mental Health Center (IRMHC) in July 2006, around the time that we moved across the street. She told the therapist that she wanted to experience less frustration with her life— I presume due to deficits related to her head injury and attendant problems— and she also expressed an interest in a schedule of activities. The therapist suggested that she look in the "Today" section of *The Tuscaloosa News* and the church bulletin for things to do, planned a referral to a social work case manager who could help her plan activities on a regular basis, and said that she would enroll Conchita in their Partial Hospitalization Program (PHP) or day treatment program, a forum to learn new skills, to have recreational activities, and to learn about resources or ways to continue her life in the community. Conchita had some transitory enthusiasm about this endeavor, but it did not persist. She did not pursue the therapist's suggestions to my knowledge, and her desire to see a therapist seemed to subside. Although one might say that her low initiative could have been a function of her head injury, I have noticed that when Conchita is impressed, she can focus on that subject very persistently, so much that she does not fail to mention it several times daily. Although she might have done much more, the effects from medication that she was prescribed during this same period proved to be extraordinary.

Conchita's medication during this period included an increase in her antidepressant and a small dose of a newer antipsychotic medication, Abilify. These adjustments to her medication were meant to lift her mood and increase her energy level in the morning, but the effects of the Abilify resembled mania. She was a bundle of energy, walking everywhere, becoming hot as a result and needing to shower and change several times daily; doing chores into the night, then awakening early and starting over; and using so much energy that she was constantly eating. She liked plants and would brighten the home with a plant or two, but now there were plants everywhere, and her room was disorderly—plants, books, and clothes all over the place. Whereas previously one could reason with her, she became more adamant and resisted our advice. She returned to her former self several weeks after we reverted back to her former medication regimen, meaning that she was sleeping throughout the night, that she was not overly invested in various activities, and that she was not disorderly, although her room tends to become disorderly over time. The good that came out of this was that even though Conchita did not qualify for the PHP, her therapist was able to place her in a day program that teaches social and independent living skills, which she initially began attending once per week and eventually attended twice weekly.

Conchita was skeptical about her day program and expressed various complaints about it from time to time, but what I noticed was that she was more energetic and livelier on returning, at least some of the time, which indicated to me that she was benefiting from the structure and responsibility. I visited with her one day and noticed that she had lively banter with a male friend that she made, of whom she often spoke. However, she did not seem very motivated to apply herself to the general program of learning social and independent living skills that were offered, seemingly viewing that part of the program as too elementary and unnecessary; and she also did not seem to make an effort to make friends with other students, about which I formed the impression that she did not really want to fit into the program very well. If she had been properly motivated, she might have done much more. For example, she is an avid piano player, and they had a piano, meaning that she could have taken her music and played the piano daily. Also, she has artistic talent and has enjoyed learning about and practicing that skill in the past, but she did not want to take her artwork and apply herself to it, even though the program had good facilities for her to do that. Similarly, she did not want to develop her program at home or take the initiative to become more independent socially or in other aspects of her life.

Conchita experienced another dramatic behavior change around April 2007. She began to become aggravated easily and would make rude or impertinent comments to mom like, "I can't hear you! Come here if you want to tell me something!" At times, her comments were outright ridiculous. For example, she did not have much in the way of responsibilities, and washing the evening dishes was one way that she could help, but she began stating, "Do you all expect me to do this by myself? Am I going to get any help? I am being worked like a dog!" Her usual concerns became amplified and were complemented by her actions. This behavior pattern was mediated by anxiety together with some lack of understanding and distortion that seemed to be brought about by her ongoing distressful feelings. She was constantly concerned about hair in the bathroom, which she was constantly picking up. During walks around the block, she would insist that mom and I not walk over the darker spots on the street, which she identified as car oil. Similarly, she became afraid that something bad was going to happen to her at the day program, about which I talked to the director and to her therapist in order to be sure that her concerns were not justified and to reassure her.

Conchita tended to be very loud and vocal and to resist mom's and my direction during this same period. One frequent concern was about her future. She would state, "Where are you all going to put me?! I have a right to know about my future!" This, I think, was a concern that she developed on her own at this point of her stay in Tuscaloosa, although it is possible that we had discussed her future. At any rate, I would explain to her that she was comfortable in the home of her family at the time and that she has a loving family that would not neglect her but that we could not predict the future and had no certain plans, so that, to that extent, she would need to have faith. I would also tell her that we were striving to make her more independent and self supporting so that she would be more capable in the future, which might help her improve her circumstances. Nevertheless, these concerns would resurface periodically. One night, mostly from mom's astute observations, because it had gotten past me, though it had been right under my nose, I realized that she was having symptoms of menopause, the most obvious indicator being the so-called hot flashes. She would get very hot, very easily and would have to turn on a fan when mom and I found the room temperature to be comfortable. The menopause experience was causing her to experience her typical concerns more intensely. Her condition ameliorated considerably after we took her to Capstone Medical Center and she was prescribed estrogen and progesterone prophylactic therapy.

I began planning for Conchita's and mom's departure considerably before the end of our next lease period, which was July 31, 2008. This was a process and a decision that I had come to gradually, after considering all that was involved in our relations and in keeping with the agreement that I had initially made with mom. For one, it became obvious that Conchita was not going to make a sincere effort to further her rehabilitation here in Tuscaloosa, at least not at the time. I felt that she had had ample opportunity but had not shown the motivation to do so. I was prepared to give her the necessary guidance and direction, but it became obvious that she was not going to follow my direction. Where did mom fit into the scheme of things? Mom did not support me in my efforts to direct Conchita, which was evident in her failure to give verbal (oral) and nonverbal support or tacit approval to my efforts when it was obvious that she could have. She also did not follow my lead in matters that I think anyone in circumstances similar to mine would have expected, considering that she was living with me and I had ultimate responsibility for her and Conchita. At one point, mom and Conchita embarked on their own program, as if we were living under the same roof but separate lives, more or less like their lives in Montgomery after dad died, before the responsibilities of maintaining the family home and overseeing day to day affairs for herself and Conchita became too challenging for mom, only now I was managing things and seeing to it that their needs were met.

I would not have minded at all and would have supported mom and Conchita's efforts if it had been part of a mutually agreed upon, coordinated plan wherein we had decided to live together yet have separate, independent lives. That is a healthy relationship wherein the mutual understanding also results in emotional support from the other family members, which serves to give all concerned direction and helps everyone to thrive, but such was not the nature of this undertaking. It failed to satisfy the importance of Conchita demonstrating progress toward becoming more independent minded and progress toward rehabilitative efforts that had been made available to her, which would have shown self determination. Similarly, it failed to satisfy the requirement that my mother accept and support this course for Conchita, relinquishing the relationship they had had for a more vital one that required her to place more trust in me and Conchita. No, I recognized right away that if I ignored this development, I would also be ignoring the changes from them that I had mandated for us to have a life together here in Tuscaloosa—changes that would require our relations to be based on mutual trust and respect for each other and that would not have limited or encumbered one another in any way. In effect, I would have been allowing them to become more reliant on me, and I was not so naïve as to think that it would not be limiting. I knew full well what this next move from them would mean for me, and I communicated clearly to them that it could not be so. Although I have not spoken about what such actions meant in terms of my mental life or theirs, for me, it would have meant that I could expect greater opposition from them as I let our lives take such a course and later sought to change it. It would have been silly to think that they would have acted in a progressively-minded fashion when they had not previously.

It was before Thanksgiving 2007 when I communicated to each respective family member that I did not plan to extend my commitment to mom and Conchita beyond three years and asked them to consider a similar three-year commitment. I felt that that would give me time to accomplish some things that I wanted to and that I would be open to the possibility of a similar commitment to them in the future. I felt that such a commitment by other family members would be considerable but not unrealistic: a way for all of us to share in a responsibility that we should not mind until we could find the most suitable arrangement for mom and for Conchita. However, no one expressed the ability to make such a commitment at the time. Around March 2008, Conchita's energy level increased. I am not sure about the reasons but feel that anxiety about her living circumstances could have been a factor. However, she also seemed excited during that time about a potential suitor, and her enthusiasm seemed to correspond with an improvement in her memory and reasoning ability. She became very enthusiastic about the piano and was determined to become a good pianist. She really was full of positive energy I thought, which I welcomed in the sense that she was applying herself more to interests such as the piano and seemed happier. However, aspects of her behavior were excessive and inappropriate.

Conchita was up early, cleaning house, and doing things in the kitchen, and her behavior was relatively more disorganized, such as leaving breakfast on the table in order to do something before forgetting to do it or failing to come for dinner on time for a similar reason. This was not very acceptable in our household because mom prepared dinner at a certain time, Conchita's meal might become cold, she was expected to help out with the dishes afterwards, and the kitchen was beside my room and my place of study, meaning that prolonging dinner could delay some of my responsibilities. Additionally, Conchita's concerns were not of the sort that should have taken precedence over coming to dinner in a timely fashion. To make matters worse, she would be in the kitchen at 4:30 A.M. making enough noise to disturb my sleep so that I would need to arise, speak to her about staying in her room and preferably in her bed so that she would not awaken anyone at such an early hour, escort her to her room, and see her back in bed because she might not respond to my instructions otherwise. Even then, she was apt to repeat the behavior at least one more time before the night was over. I appreciated her positive energy but felt, at the same time, that she was matching wits with me at a subconscious level and that she could have resisted engaging me in such behavior more often if she had wanted to.

I had never considered placing Conchita in a group home. Mom recognized during this time that Conchita's behavior was disruptive to the household as she herself was experiencing effects from it. At her age then (she lived to be 94 years old), she was very sensitive to her environment. If something made her anxious, it could affect her sleep, and she might have more leg pain than usual, an affliction that was caused by a herniated disc and varicose veins. Much to my surprise, she informed me one day that one of her friends in a church group had suggested that she should consider placing Conchita in a group home. This was not only a friend that I knew and trusted, but one that had much experience in the field of mental health; and I had also been approached by a church member knowledgeable about group homes in a similar way. Subsequently, mom and I gave this idea serious consideration, had interviews with IRMHC staff members in Tuscaloosa who direct and supervise these programs, and visited two homes in the area. I learned from Conchita that her male friend at the day program often visited these homes and sensed some excitement from her, perhaps in anticipation of an added dimension to their relationship, which seemed a possibility; but she was also very nervous about this change, which we put into effect in April 2008. My commitment to Conchita was that this would be a time-limited event and that she would not have to stay if at any time her safety became an issue.

Conchita continued to be overactive at the group home. She did not sleep at all initially and was causing some havoc or disruption during the night as a result, and days were no better after sleepless nights, meaning that they had a restless, anxious, and tired person who is distractible to contend with. The choice was either let them take her to their psychiatrist and let him prescribe medication to help her sleep or take her back home. Actually, this was not a difficult decision because her behavior had become too much for mom to contend with and I had her health to think of, and she also had been disturbing my homework and sleep to the extent that it could have reflected on my work. They had her history, and we were accessible for any further questions. To our relief, in a short time, she was sleeping and following the routine better. In time, she mastered it.

There were some obvious benefits for Conchita to be derived from living in a group home. After her accident, she lived with her family members—either her parents or her sister Ana Maria—who were entrusted with assuming responsibility for her. One of the behavior changes we noticed was that she would say whatever was on her mind without any screening for the context or situation. Consequently, she often committed social blunders, which prompted remarks from us such as, "Conchita, how could you say such a thing?" about which she might find humor or smile but otherwise ignore. At least part of the problem seemed to be that with the protective oversight of her family, she did not feel that she needed to be responsible for her behavior, and she also was able to avoid that responsibility. During the first several weeks at the group home, she was so anxious that she could hardly speak clearly, like she was walking on pins and needles, and I think one reason was she realized that she had to guard her tongue lest she say the wrong thing. At any rate, this was a skill that she began to practice right away, in my opinion, and that she soon learned. Nothing like survival to motivate the will!

Conchita's accident, I previously mentioned, had caused her frustration in pursuing her schoolwork and in finding the right suitor, which had led her to become more family oriented over time. This orientation, which may have gradually become more rigid, did not seem appropriate to me. She was focused on family life and family personalities as well as some of her favorite friends at first, much like a person speaking about their friends while thinking about or planning on a class reunion: Conchita was oriented in the past. She engaged family members similarly, speaking admirably about them but often using her memories about them as a reference point in the conversation and hardly ever being forward looking, if at all. She acted like someone caught up in time rather than someone who has to live life on demand and thus tends to plan and tends to be forward looking. This changed right away at the group home. For one, she did not have access to her family, which meant that she could not dwell on past memories. Also, she had a definite schedule of things to do and had to meet the time demands of the situation, an imposed structure to her day that she was not accustomed to, which demanded greater responsibility. Essentially, the group home situation required her to respond to the demands of everyday living, which required an independent, forward-looking approach and some degree of planning. This skill, which she had neglected to develop and practice and which could have atrophied from lack of use, she soon began learning again.

Conchita's group home was very well managed, and I learned a lot as a result of that experience, often very directly or subtly from the wisdom of people who operated this one. I think one of the first things that I learned or that was reinforced was that I needed to let Conchita be more independent—to let her make more of the choices in her life. I picked her up on Sunday morning, we attended church and had lunch out together, she and mom did something that afternoon (I occasionally joined them), and I got her back at 4:00 P.M. I soon learned that it was best to abide by that deadline regardless—that it was a good practice for Conchita as well—and not to dawdle on returning her because that was her home or place of living and she would be perfectly fine. I soon got to know the staff and was made to feel very comfortable by them in regard to such assertive action. On Mondays, mom picked her up for music class and they had lunch, usually at home before her class, and they were apt to do something together afterwards. On Tuesday afternoons after work, I picked her up and took her to the YMCA, where she participated in a water aerobics class with an instructor that we both knew from church while I was in the Wellness Center working out. Otherwise, she was oriented to the group home and the program that they had to offer her.

Conchita accepted the idea that she had to live in the group home for a time, and she got along fine there, but she did not fall in love with it. I am relatively certain that she decided not to like it too much because she wanted to move on to other things, particularly living with her family, and she did not want me, mom, and the rest of the family to forget that and grow complacent at all with her stay there. Despite this attitude, I credit her with showing some pluck about staying there. On one occasion, she left the home without permission and was found at a nearby Publix, about which the day living skills instructor—a very young girl no older than college age who always seemed to have missed much sleep yet impressed me by her vigilance, knowledge of the residents, and managerial skills—called me about picking her up and returning her for a counseling conference. Conchita had given University of Alabama police my name, they had talked to police at Peter Bryce Hospital, where I am employed, and Bryce police also contacted me. This was a crucial situation because residents cannot just walk off from the group home without notifying staff and receiving prior approval after demonstrating the responsibility to manage that privilege, which Conchita did not have. To make matters worse, Conchita was preoccupied about the dangerous nature of the area, such as stating that she had almost been hit by a bus while crossing the street. Essentially, the counseling focused on the need to follow the relevant rules for safety reasons if she were to remain at the group home. I let her know that she would need to return home if she did not think that she would be able to follow those rules, but she agreed to follow them from that time forward, and she never had that problem again.

There was another occasion when I received word and responded about an incident related to Conchita's behavior at the group home. On this occasion, Conchita found some of her things missing, acquired the idea that one of the new residents had taken them, and went into the girl's room and took some of the girl's things. This led to a big argument during which another girl sided with the girl whose things Conchita had taken. The word that I got from Conchita was that two girls were ganging up on her and she was afraid that they were going to beat her up. The home manager and I counseled Conchita about bringing events like that to the attention of staff and letting staff manage them rather than taking matters into her own hands. We also had her return what she had taken of the other girl's belongings, which was not a perfect solution in that Conchita had used some of her toiletries and cosmetics and had no proof that the other girl, who had recently moved in, had taken her things. This was another moment of reckoning when I had to tell Conchita some of the residents there are from different backgrounds than hers and I could not guarantee her safety if she took actions like she had done because I could not predict what they might do. Therefore, I told her that I was prepared to take her back home if she did not feel that she could rely on staff to manage any further problems with a resident there by bringing them to staff's attention. Once again, she decided on her own to stay and had no more problems of the kind. Incidentally, it turned out that Conchita, who misplaces things, had misplaced the articles that she had missed. Also, the day instructor quickly became familiar with the new resident girl and put my mind at ease about her.

Conchita's chapter in Tuscaloosa came to a close on Christmas Eve 2008 during a visit to Montgomery, when she developed complications leading to the diagnosis of myasthenia gravis, an autoimmune disease in which lymphocytes, which are normally part of the body's immune system, attack acetylcholine (ACH) at the neuromuscular junctions or attach themselves to the muscle receptors for ACH, sometimes damaging them, thereby interfering with the transmission of ACH, which is how our nerves communicate with our muscles. The result of this action by lymphocytes is that the afflicted person tires very easily, apparently from the inefficient interchange of messages from nerves to muscles during any activity. Some of the symptoms that may help to detect it besides frequently feeling tired include visual difficulty, speech and swallowing problems, and a droopy eyelid. A thymoma or abnormal growth of the thymus gland, which may appear as a mass in the chest area, is a common manifestation. The muscles required in breathing, a repetitive function, may be involved and can lead to increasingly shallower breathing so that the person's tissues do not get enough oxygen, which is a life-threatening condition.

Conchita was returned to the hospital emergency room early on Christmas Day after complaining of a feeling like she could not breathe. In the hospital, she collapsed while being assisted to the restroom by a nurse, began having seizures—I think due to insufficient oxygen to her brain tissue—and had to be intubated for a couple of months until she became strong enough to breathe on her own again. She was cared for in Montgomery before my brother, an oncologist, had her transferred to the hospital where he works in Birmingham, where their able staff oversaw her recovery. She is doing as well as she can for a person who has myasthenia, meaning that she has to take medication, may need to limit her span of activity before a rest period due to tiring, and may grow more tired over the course of the day. I am not around her as often these days, but during our chats on the phone and periodic family reunions, her myasthenia is not a telling feature of her behavior.

I approached mom about moving into a type of nursing home facility on the University of Alabama campus around October 2008, Clara Verner Towers. I had received good reports about it from people whom I trusted, after which mom and I visited the facility. Mom was not opposed to it and had been giving it some thought before Conchita was diagnosed with myasthenia gravis. We completed the paperwork so that she could have moved in as early as January if she had decided to. This was not an easy decision but I felt that it was the right decision for me. Mom had not come around to changing her attitude about me, meaning that she was not going to be happy seeing me thrive, the essence of this being that instead of giving me psychological support, she was going to oppose me psychologically. This is a very subtle event when you are speaking of a mother and son who have so much familiarity from a lifelong relationship that it is like the status quo. I did not feel this would be a healthy relationship in such proximity to one another, with our everyday lives so connected, and I felt the alternative would be a very good one. This considered her proximity to Conchita, the Catholic church near the university where she often met friends, and the social opportunities that Clara Verner would provide her.

Mom began spending time in Birmingham during March and April 2009 while Conchita was undergoing rehabilitation there and moved to a very safe facility with program activities and some assistance in living, where she and Conchita shared an apartment. It was perhaps more quaint and comfortable but not unlike what she would have found at Clara Verner, which was a bargain. I felt that she and Conchita would have good support in the Birmingham community and that they might find its diversity to their liking. However, mom felt that they would be more comfortable in Baton Rouge with Ana Maria and her family, where they relocated in September 2009. In retrospect, I think this was a wise decision due to the level of care that she required, which Ana Maria and her family so aptly provided.

Our mom passed away on August 23, 2015. I think the cause could be described as old age. Her heart had experienced a leaky valve when she was in Tuscaloosa with me, and there was nothing to be done for it. I had talked to Ana Maria the prior day, when mom was so exhausted that Ana Maria had to bathe her, and John had to carry her to a recliner from the dinner table. She died in her sleep subsequently while Ana Maria was away from the home about an activity concerning one of her daughters. We were all grateful that mom died quickly without suffering. The world is now without one of the great children's storytellers and interesting autobiographers. The little lady with nine children: she lived to be 94-years-old and retained a sharp mind until the end. I shall miss her dearly. I am grateful that we were able to share each other's company during our family vacations in Destin during most every year before her death. We had a lovely get together in Montgomery for her funeral and were able to visit with old friends. Mom was an advocate of this book from the start. I am sorry that I will not be able to tell my story to her. I do believe that the truth won out in the end and that she recognized it, accepted it, and did not begrudge it. Tough love is not my idea of fun or pleasure, but it is necessary. If you think otherwise, then I refer you to Section 3 of this book.

CHAPTER 9:

GROWING UP IN CUBA

My father was a Cuban. He was raised in a rural area near or in the vicinity of Cardenas, Cuba, a historic city that is representative of Cuban culture at its finest, which I have gathered from my mother's commentary. His father worked aboard a cargo ship that transported sugar, a merchant marine vessel or one similar to it. He would come to the house early, where he would sleep. He was not around very much for family life, for which reason mom said that dad did not develop close relations with him. Apparently of necessity, he left the task of raising dad, his two brothers, and his two sisters, largely to their mother. Mom said that dad's mother was not part of the Cardenas society but an active woman in her own right who taught her five children well: Innocencio, the oldest, referred to as Tenso, Ester, Wilfredo (dad), Humberto, and Luisa.

My impressions from dad's commentary were that he was close to and very fond of his mother and that the children, in general, were dutiful and made the task of rearing them easy. Dad also indicated they were supportive of one another. He took a job working at a sugar manufacturing company in Cardenas that his older brother had before him, which was owned by a well-to-do family with whom mom was acquainted. He apparently used this job to fund his way as a young man to the United States, where he enrolled in school at Saint Bernard College in Cullman, Alabama, a path he became aware of through other young Cubans who had taken it. Not long afterwards, dad learned that another young Cuban was graduating from his studies in Montgomery, Alabama, would be moving on, and the small cottage that he rented from Edward O. and Mabel E. Harper, a married couple, would be available. Consequently, he moved to Montgomery, where he attended and graduated from Sidney Lanier High School under the thoughtful direction of Ed Harper, a partner in a well-established public accounting firm in Montgomery, and his wife Mabel Harper, an able clerical staff member for a mortgage insurance company with a Montgomery office.

Dad attended the University of Alabama after high school, where he was a member of the Sigma Chi fraternity, did Army service duty in Spain and Africa during World War II, and graduated with a Bachelor of Science degree in public accounting in 1947. He was in the midst of establishing an accounting practice in Montgomery with the help of Mr. Harper and another established accountant when he married my mother, a young Cuban girl of thirty years. This marriage was not quite as simple as that, for my father had married and divorced and had a young girl by his first marriage, my sister Rosemary, who was born two years before me. Rosemary's mother was killed in a motor vehicle accident following the divorce while Rosemary was still an infant or toddler. Rosemary informed me that dad had custody of her by that time.

My mother told me of their first date. She said that she had known Wilfred (dad) since she was twelve and he was eighteen. She would walk with her older cousin Lucita in the park, where dad would happen on them and greet them, or perhaps she would happen on dad and Lucita and greet them. Mom explained that it was traditional to hold a celebration on Easter Saturday after a week of inactivity because Jesus has already been buried and has risen. She said that on this occasion, there was to be a dance at the club in Varadero, a town known for its beautiful beaches some thirty miles from Cardenas, where many of the Cardenas residents liked to spend summers or established residence and commuted to work in Cardenas. The dance was not to be extravagant due to the Lenten season. Mom's mother's sister was staying at a beach house in Varadero with her two children, Ernesto and Ana Luisa, mom's first cousins, who invited mom to come from Cardenas to Varadero for the party.

Mom related that she had been hesitant to attend this Easter celebration because she had no partner but decided to join her cousins, noting that her parents were going to be by the party later and could drive her back to Cardenas if she desired. She said that dad also had been reluctant to attend the party but a close friend, who mom also was friends with, urged him to attend. And so it happened that they met at the entrance to the club: mom, then thirty, thinking that she may be an Old Maid, noting that all her friends had married, practically. She stated that her aunts and other family members would remark, "Mary, what happened to you?" and she would think that she had not found anyone.

Mom recalled that their friend in common introduced them: "Mary, you know Wilfred?" and they began talking. Mom said that one of her first remarks to dad was, "Wilfred, I heard that you married" or "Wilfred, haven't you been married?" She asked him this because she did not want to enter into a relationship with a married man. Dad responded, "Yes, Mary. But I have been divorced for eleven months," which she found acceptable, thinking, "Well, at least the relationship is over." She remarked that during the party, dad was fascinated by the new dance, the Mambo, during which couples dance like figurines, paralleling each other's moves. She also remarked that her cousin Ana Luisa was an accomplished dancer, whereas she mostly watched. She said that dad probably danced some due to his love of dancing. Mom described him as a superior dancer of the Jitterbug.

Dad and mom married that summer, on July 21, 1951, and I was born the following spring in Montgomery, on May 4, 1952, the first of eight children born by 1962 with my older sister Rosemary making nine. Within two years, according to my mom's wishes to be closer to home, dad took an accounting position with a company in Nicaro, Cuba, a northeastern coastal town rich in nickel located on a cove or bay of the Atlantic. He worked for the Nicaro Nickel Company at first but later took a job with the Hershey Company. One of my first memories of Cuba as a young boy of four or five years of age in the semi-rural area where we lived was of dashing across several yards from my best friend Tato's house filled with excitement and joy about keeping my promise to my mother that I would arrive home by a certain time. I had a love relationship with her and had a very joyful feeling whenever she was around. Otherwise, I have a few more distinctly visual memories of my early childhood in Nicaro before we settled in Varadero.

I recall once going into the recesses of our back yard with dad and Eddie, a young man who frequented our home, to a pool of water like a pond, which may have been formed by ocean water slamming against the cliff, because the area seemed elevated above the sea level. It seemed hidden from view by various green water plants until you came upon it. The pond was bordered by black rock that you could walk upon to navigate around it and view the area. Breaking the quiet of the morning on that occasion was the peculiar sight of a blowfish, which was filled with air and blowing as it made its way across the top of the water. Eddie, who was a helper to dad around the place, was also was quite good at entertaining me and my younger brother George, who was born on May 9, 1953.

I do not recall any negative experiences in Nicaro. If there were some, they are too vague to recollect. And I don't remember any family dissention or conflict. I mostly have fond memories. One in particular was when dad decided to make a chicken coop out of a large portion of the back yard—the clearing of the ground, chicken housing, and fencing—an unusual event that captured my curiosity. I imagine that dad and mom were a happy young couple with a growing family and a bright future and that dad was dedicated to his work. When I was perhaps five years old, we moved by train to Varadero, Cuba, a small peninsula known for its beautiful beaches. Dad had obtained a managerial position in a bank in Cardenas, the Bank of Cardenas, I think. We lived with mom's parents, Dr. Frank Smith, a general or family physician who had established his practice in Cardenas, and Concha Castro, his wife. Mom told me that my grandfather had once traveled to Boston as an exchange student with his brother Maximillian, where they studied English for two years. She had another anecdote about how my grandfather came to live in our house in Varadero.

Mom said that when she was about eight years old, Varadero was being developed. Her maternal grandfather, Ernesto Castro, built one of the first beach homes, where she was living with her parents. Her father, Francisco, or Frank, as he was called, was a nervous person (he always seemed a resolute spirit to me, but then, that is probably the impression most people have about my mother). The sounds of the waves bothered him so much that he could not sleep. Consequently, after a discussion with his wife, Concha, who consented, he began staying in a small country home that was owned by his father-in-law, Ernesto, in the town of Cantel, which was between Cardenas and Varadero. Mom described it as a small, comfortable wooden home with a small yard, much like the other homes in the area. She said that every afternoon, when my grandfather finished his work in Cardenas, he would drive to Cantel, where my grandmother, who was driven there from Varadero by the chauffer, would be waiting on him. After several years, he found a rental house in Varadero that was a couple of blocks from the beach and found that he could rest comfortably there without the sound of the waves. Consequently, after renting for a couple of years, he hired an architect and built a home in that area.

Mom described her father as a prudent man with his money and conservative in his ways also, I would think. She said that he was criticized for sticking to a seventeen thousand dollar agreement for the construction of the home because he was very well off and could have spent more. She said that he taught her to make purchases of good merchandise at a reasonable price rather than to be extravagant. She cited an aunt who was not very well off but who was extravagant in that if mom bought a watch, she had to buy her children one that was better, and so, her father showed her how not to make the aunt jealous. They say that behind every great man, there is a great woman. I have to wonder if my grandfather was mentored by my grandmother about economics. One of my distinct memories about my grandmother while we were living in her home in Varadero was of my grandmother promising me a quarter when I did a deed without complaint or did something to earn it, such as agreeing to take a shot of medication. She would take me back to her closet, where she kept a small, capped, clear cylindrical container that was about three inches high and just the size of a quarter, which was filled practically to the rim. Then, as if distributing part of her life savings, she would impart with one of the quarters, which filled me with thoughts of its purchasing power, such as a trip to the movies, and great appreciation for my grandmother's generosity, thinking that she had made a sacrifice for me. She was a great teacher of the value of money, and I was her pupil.

My grandparents' home was a beautiful place. It was located at the northeast corner of a large lot. To the north was one of the two primary streets that one could use to traverse Varadero. There was a garage entrance through a large, white wooden gate from this main street. To the east was a narrower street that was paved for a short distance, if I recall that bit correctly, after which it was a dirt road, of which I am certain. The front door of the house was accessed from this street through a small, white, wooden gate. The lot was surrounded by a cement fence that was about three feet high except to the north, where it raised to some five feet in order to provide privacy from passing cars. The fence itself was about a foot wide and, about one foot from the top, it flared out parallel to the ground for several inches on either side before angling to make a point at the top, much like an arrow tip that flares out from the wood and then comes to a point. It ran thus for some ten yards or so before coming to a cement post that was about half a foot higher and flat, so that a young kid could straddle and walk it doing a not-too-hard balancing act before coming to a secure landing. The back yard, which was quite large, was bordered to the east beginning some ten yards beyond the house and to the south by an eight-foot-high cluster of what appeared to be a small pine tree, where hummingbirds were occasionally seen, and there was also a coconut tree in the southeast area. The back yard was large enough that we could play baseball, with home plate being at the back of the house and the small pine trees representing the borders of the outfield. There was this great climbing tree in the west part of the yard not far from the house, from where one could jump to the soft white sand that my grandfather placed underneath it.

The house itself was a two-story, flat-roofed structure with a cement exterior that was painted a light green color, except for the windows, the shutters for the hurricane season, and the porch columns, which were painted white. The porch ran from the north of the house, where it met the far northeastern exterior of my grandparents' room, around to the east and for a short distance beyond the front door. It was raised several feet from the ground and had several comfortable chairs, benches, and swings arranged in an orderly way so as not to attract great notice and from where one could look down towards the yard and in all directions to the north and east at the hustle and bustle on the street. One took several steps to reach the porch or veranda and the front door, from where one entered a spacious living room that had a swirled ocean green and white marbled floor. As one crossed the room, there was a planter running the length of the back wall, where one accessed steps at the left end. They began a staircase that made two ninety-degree turns to access an open area that led to the bedrooms and a balcony above the porch.

The living room was fairly open and contained what appeared to be plain and simple bamboo and wicker furniture with sponge-like cushions for the seat and back that were covered with a veneer or polyester, such as one might find in a doctor's waiting room. As one faced the planter, the master bedroom, where my grandparents stayed, was to the right, at the front of the house. To the left of the stairs was a door that led to a hall from which someone parking in the enclosed garage, which was at the northwest corner of the house beside my grandparents' bedroom, could enter the house. As one entered the house there beside the steps to the upstairs on the left, there was a wall extending about eight feet on the right, which made a natural division between the living room and the dining room, a narrower yet fairly large room that had a long dining room table running lengthwise toward the living room. The two rooms together were spacious enough for the large family gatherings that might extend to the porch and yard in the typical Cuban balmy weather. Similar bamboo furniture at the south wall of the dining room that was somewhat low in height contained the dining ware.

There was a door at the southwest corner of the dining room. As one crossed it, one could make a left and cross through another door to enter a small room that accessed the maid or servants' quarters, consisting of a bathroom directly ahead and small, enclosed bedrooms to the left and to the right. That southwest door of the dining room primarily gained access to the kitchen, which was somewhat narrow and lengthy. There was some space to the right before one encountered a counter that ran the rest of its length, separating the cooking area from the dining area. Kitchen cabinets ran the length of the counter at the north wall of the room and there was a row of grapefruits on top of the cabinets for the reason that my grandfather always started the morning with half a grapefruit, most likely with sugar sprinkled on top. The open area to the right as one entered accessed a door that was the pantry, which was behind the cooking area. My favorite dish was the long wieners that we had on Sunday nights, imported from the United States and cooked and served right from the can. At the end of this long and narrow room, one found a door that led to the west side of the yard. The lawn there was large enough that my grandfather built a building that comprised an office for my father to manage his real estate business in Varadero toward the front, followed by a foyer that led to a bedroom area toward the back that in summer housed my uncle Alfredo, his wife Raquelin, and their four children. He also extended the kitchen southward to enlarge the dining area for the children.

There was an open area like a broad hall at the top of the stairs, which accessed the bedrooms and the balcony. Starting at the north, there was a room reserved for the summertime stay of my uncle Louis, his wife Elma, and their two boys (Elma later gave birth to three more boys) that was similar to the master bedroom on the first floor. Next, there was a door that accessed the balcony, which was used for such purposes as sunbathing or hanging clothing to dry, and that door was followed by a door across from the stairs that led to the room where my uncle Alfredo and his family stayed before my grandfather built them their new quarters. The south wing is where we stayed. My parents had a master bedroom at the southeast end that usually nursed a child also, then there was a boys' room—I remember that my brother George and I shared a bunk bed—that was followed by a common bathroom and the girls' room at the southwest end.

Varadero was an exciting place for a child. Let me try to give you a panoramic view. My uncle Ernesto was a doctor. He followed in his father's footsteps, attending medical school in Havana and setting up his medical practice in Cardenas. My other two uncles, Alfredo and Louis, graduated in chemical engineering from Notre Dame. Alfredo worked at a Rayon plant in Matanzas province and Louis worked at a soap plant in Havana. During summers, Ernesto, his wife Maricusa, and their six children, stayed at a beach house not far away that belonged to Maricusa's family (the Larieux's). Their children were older than me except the youngest, were both charming and endearing, and were my role models whenever they were around. They often organized and directed enjoyable events—a baseball game, a bonfire and marshmallows on the beach or the back yard, a game of cowboys and Indians—and added excitement when they were around. Also, during summers, Alfredo's and Louis' families stayed with us and were joined by Louis and Alfredo on weekends, so that, during summers, there were many aunts, uncles, and cousins around that added excitement to our everyday living.

Two blocks directly to the north of our house was the beach road, the other major road that ran through the town of Varadero. As one entered the beach there, there was a newly built complex much like modern day condominium units, only I think they rented out apartments, and the complex boasted a very popular, attractive, and spacious pool area and area for enjoying a view of the beach. Perhaps a block or so to the east was the club where my parents met and about another block or so to the east was the Larieux beach house, which began a row of beach homes that extended down the beach. These were my tromping grounds along the beach. As I entered the beach there by the new complex, there was a large expanse of beautiful white beaches on either side. At the shore about ten feet to the left began a swath of smooth black rock about fifteen yards wide and ten yards deep, I would guess, where colorful tropical fish running the full length of the color spectrum made their home. The beach itself was a crystal clear blue water that was shallow for fifteen yards, followed by deeper water for another fifteen yards, and by a sand bar that was shallow enough to stand upon for about another fifteen yards, after which one found nothing but ocean that deepened and became a darker shade of marine green. At this edge of the sandbar the strength of the sea could be felt, but the place was otherwise a haven for swimmers. It was a great swimming hole that seemed entirely safe, absent an undertow or the perils of the ocean.

My favorite activity was to get a line with weights and a hook and, using minnows or sardines for bait, cast from shore into the ocean in order to catch the minnows that were near the shore, always hoping for a larger catch, such as an ocean perch. I also liked to swim with my goggles along the rock to view the colorful tropical fish and liked to swim out to the sandbar to seek starfish basking in the sun. Down the beach, a short distance toward the club and my aunt's beach home, was a long public pier. Beyond it, the swimming hole became shallower so that the sand bar extended all the way to the deeper ocean. An enjoyable sight was the large schools of sardines that would come towards the shore there in front of the club, to be caught by fishermen who waded out and cast their large nets, and I recall the excitement on one occasion when the serenity of our swimming hole was disturbed by larger fish, perhaps Bonita, that darted out from underneath the sardine shadow to swim frightfully throughout the area, apparently experiencing temporary disorientation to their surroundings and feeling boxed in.

One took the mostly dirt road that ran in front of our house directly south for about three or four small blocks to access the South Sea, which was actually a large harbor for ships. The area on the way was not heavily populated. I remember that on the right side of the road, there was a home directly behind ours, followed by an open area from where one could view the street to the west, followed by some new commercial construction and another open area where we liked to ride horses along the South Sea. Heading south once again on that mostly dirt road, there was a large lot directly across the street, followed by a home and then a large field where horses that were leased for fifty cents an hour sometimes grazed, and thereafter until the South Sea my memory is indistinct. This was a black sea that could become quite rough when the wind picked up but was often calm.

The harbor was large enough that the ships, which seemed to dock across the way, and that area itself seemed foggy and unclear. I do not recall learning what the other side was about or being particularly curious about it. On our side of this harbor were mostly piers that had been neglected and damaged by the wear and tear of the sea, I presume, ranging from some that one could partly navigate with great care to others that were no longer anything but the poles that once supported the piers. I could not tell you whether this was once a wharf for ocean vessels or what other purpose it served. The beach was very narrow here, only five feet or so, and the sand was not altogether white, such as a light brown. One might find peculiar sights along this beach, such as heavy metal rope that was mostly buried in the sand. I liked to go out on the piers and catch some of the various shelled creatures that one could find there, such as snails, and light a match to force them out of their shell.

Hiking to the right near the shore towards the street to the west, the ground was loamy and became hilly all of a sudden. Along the way by the shore, one could spot seahorses bobbing in the water and probably needlefish also. The sea at this end was bordered by a rocky cliff against which it constantly splashed, spewing water on top of the cliff, which was a smooth black rock for about a twenty by fifteen square feet area. This was the top of the hill of which I spoke as well as the end of the street to the west of us. One could sometimes find their days catch on the black rock, which apparently was a not very publicized fishing hole. My uncle Alfredo took several of us there one afternoon. As we were sitting on the rock of the cliff looking down some twenty feet or so into what became clear green water from that view, a fish with a large snout that was narrow like a barracuda but extending some ten feet or more in length suddenly appeared. Just as suddenly, a white-haired and white-bearded man with a swarthy tan in faded khaki clothes and boat shoes appeared with a long line of rope like one uses to throw an anchor from a large ship and a large metal hook at its end, upon which he worked a large piece of bait and then hurled his fishing line into the sea. In the flash of an eye, this large fish swallowed the bait, bit through the thick rope, and disappeared into the sea. It was a breathtaking moment for a child. I was captivated by this event. I have countless such anecdotes about Varadero, which was a veritable kids' paradise, of which I felt that I should provide a glimpse. Before moving on, one experience that I should also share is my Catholic or Christian indoctrination.

We attended a Catholic school in Varadero that was taught and managed by an order of nuns that, I think, in English would be translated as The Nuns of the Brown Habit. They had the traditional robe and headdress like the nuns in *The Sound of Music*, only their vestige was brown rather than the usual black. What I remember most about this school was a very attractive first grade teacher and a tall, slender, elderly nun with an aquiline nose who wore rimless spectacles, was very efficient, and commanded respect much like a mother superior yet had a gentle manner. She was my mentor in the second and third grades, and I distinctly recall gaining in proficiency in mathematics under her direction: that soaring feeling of accomplishment.

I made my first Confession and my first Holy Communion at the church that served the school, meaning that I learned to ask Almighty God for his absolution from my sins as a means to prepare myself for communion and basic prayers such as the Our Father and the Hail Mary. I remember also the respect and admiration that I had for one of my classmates who was not very well-to-do. He was very devout and had sincerely made a decision to become a priest. He already seemed to be fitting the role. Cub scouts was an offshoot of the school and included a metal ring with metal beads for praying the rosary. At one school-wide gathering in the large playground, highly esteemed and colorful boy scouts, who behaved like mature teen-agers, put on a dazzling show with demonstrations of wood placement to start a campfire, starting it with sticks, and making an assortment of knots with rope that had specific uses.

My mother made a very significant contribution to my indoctrination into the Catholic faith. She was very good about showing me devotional prayers, such as saying the rosary. She was a gifted storyteller of children's stories and captivated my interest with her stories of personage in the Bible such as Saint Tarcisius, the young boy who risked his life by taking the sacrament to the Christians in prison after Jesus was crucified, who became a martyr when he was stoned to death for his actions. Mom was the object of our adulation as we frequently asked her to tell us such stories, very concrete examples of Christian faith and Christian virtues that for me became reference points and models for Christian living.

This sort of Christian deference permeated our family and way of life, such as religion or Catholicism and respect for Our Lord, Mary, and our Catholic traditions. They were at the forefront of everyday living: part of the fabric of our lives. By the time that I left Cuba in the fall of 1960, an eight-year-old in the third grade, I had sufficient instruction and practice in Christian living to begin to nurture a spiritual life. I was learning to seek out the spirit of truth, reconciliation, and peace, which is the calling of all Christians: to make themselves a dwelling place for the Holy Spirit of God. This is a spirit that provides direction in living, whose recipients are able to recognize the paths that God would have them follow. As such, the gifts of the spirit carry blessings and responsibilities. It is the force by which Christians are called to transform the world into a better place. It has only been in reaching a more mature adulthood that I have come to more fully understand and appreciate this inheritance, which has always been a beacon for me, if ever dim at low points in my life, when I did not see my way to God clearly or the ways of the world prevailed.

Were there elements of schizophrenia at this point in my life? They were not very visible, but I think so. Let me start with my mother. Mom was raised within a closely-knit family who saw to her needs very well. Our life in Varadero was but an extension of the Cardenas tradition. Mom tells me that her mother Concha's parents, Ernesto and Bernadina Castro, lived on the corner of a block in Cardenas when she was a child. As one walked the block to the west, the next home was occupied by mom's parents, mom, and her siblings; then came the home of their son Raul Castro, an engineer and architect, his wife, and their seven children; and then the home of their son Ernesto Castro, a lawyer, his wife, and their four children. Thus, until my grandfather moved to Varadero when mom was relatively young, perhaps eight years old or so, mom lived next to her maternal grandparents, eleven cousins, two uncles, and two aunts.

These homes in Cardenas, as best I can recall from a visit or two, had no exterior yards. Their front façade faced a large sidewalk. The front rooms typically contained the kitchen, a spacious living room that perhaps doubled as a parlor room, a dining room, and possibly a master bedroom. I remember that my grandfather had an office where he saw patients in a front room. The bedrooms in the house where my mother lived were to the west and followed one another in a row towards the back of the house. They were accessed by a hallway or covered pavilion that gave view to the courtyard, which was at the center of the house. The courtyard floor was cement or tile. It was bordered by a concrete fence on the east that was high enough to provide privacy and split into two fairly evenly divided courtyards by a similar fence that was perpendicular to the fence on the east and ran for three quarters of the patio's width. The back courtyard had a small grassy area on the east side and a garden. The courtyards were settings for outside socials and various games that the adults and children played, such as a game like handball but using a volleyball played by the adults that mom told me about.

There was perhaps a den at the back of the house, my mother also described a garret or loft room, and I believe one also accessed the garage there.

Thus, like our family in Varadero, mom grew up amidst numerous cousins, some who were close friends and a number with whom she has retained relations throughout her life. The characteristics that seemed to typify mom's family life and ours were that families were devoutly Catholic and the parents were loving and considerate of the children, who were in turn very respectful of their parents, and there was a vibrant social life for adults and children. Life was not without its usual challenges for children, including applying oneself in school, challenges to one's faith, and various situations that develop among peers and family members. However, overall, my impression of mom's childhood is that it was very well supervised and directed and I imagine that she was very comfortable.

Mom told me that after graduation from high school, probably after some discussion, suggestion, and encouragement by her father, she decided to attend a college for women in Pennsylvania in order to study interior design. This may have been in keeping with her brothers' decision to study engineering in the States. In describing this undertaking, mom's statements suggested to me that she did not become Americanized. She indicated that she spent most of her time with several other Cuban girls who attended the school and after two years, feeling lonely and homesick, she decided not to complete her degree and returned to her parents' home in Varadero. Was this a significant event in mom's life? I think that it is quite possible that this is one of those defining moments in our lives that we either rise to or we fail to develop the character that provides us a richer spiritual life, including leadership qualities, such as mettle, and the endowment of being progressive in our thinking. In other words, it appears that mom may have settled at this important time in her life for remaining comfortable instead of struggling to prepare herself better for whatever life would bring her, a shortcoming that comes with some psychological conflicts, meaning also that it acts to infringe upon one's spiritual life. Mom had a similar challenge after she married dad, which provided her the opportunity to make amends for her previous actions.

My father was a common man. His family was not very well off. The children had to struggle and work as kids to get ahead. Dad had ambition to do so and saved enough money to come to the States. He completed college at the University of Alabama and was establishing a practice in public accountancy under the guidance and direction of two prominent accountants when he met and married my mother. He was also in process of becoming established in the Montgomery community, where he had made close friends. Mom told me that she made some close friends among the people that dad knew in Montgomery, such as the Rainers, but she also indicated that she was not very comfortable at some of the parties that she and dad attended, where he knew and socialized with a number of the females and she felt left out. For whatever reasons, she said that when she spoke to her parents, they wanted them closer to home, and she was able to persuade dad to take the offer that he had for a job in Nicaro.

Was this a difficult decision for dad? It may have been, despite the fact that he had the blessing of mom and her parents, which proved to be fruitful. He had applied himself to gain the position that he had in Montgomery and had embarked on a career that had a lot of promise. Most likely, he would have continued that course were it not for mom's desire to return to her native Cuba, and perhaps he should have. He likely could have appeased mom with allowances for visits home and vice versa, and mom likely would have understood. He might have waited in order to acquire more in depth experience in the field of accountancy at the time. However, instead of asserting himself with a confident and independent air, he submitted to mom's will, which may have been a shortcoming on his part. He certainly lost some very good and able direction at an important point in his career. Mom, for her part, if she had made a mistake during her college days, she had not decided to reconcile herself with that past. Rather, instead of supporting dad in what was a noble endeavor, it appears that she once again sought the comfort of her native Cuban life.

Let's consider dad's decision further. My understanding is that public accountants are at the best training ground for the profession of accounting. They often have the opportunity for wide and varied experience in the field, such as taxes, accounting, auditing, and management advisory services, making use of recognized procedures, methods, and standards. They tend to use the latest tools in accounting and become aware of a variety of systems from the clients that they audit and serve. The opportunity to apprentice with established accountants who are at the top of this field is invaluable in regard to learning these practices as one advances within the field. There is usually a progression that is determined by knowledge, experience, and know-how, such as junior accountant, senior accountant, manager, and partner.

A senior accountant, in general, may be expected to become certified before progressing to the rank of manager, which may require the additional skills of being able to supervise other accountants as well as being able to communicate well with the management of clients who one audits and their office staff, who provide assistance during the audit. At this level, a proficient accountant effectively becomes a part of the management team, sufficiently skilled as to the company's accounting systems, business enterprises, and industry requirements to recognize the opportunity for management advisory services. Public accountants may gain wide experience in a particular industry, such as banking, telephone companies, hospitals, insurance, and various manufacturing concerns, which usually dictates the corporate area or company that they choose if they decide to leave the field of public accounting because that is where their experience lies and where they are most likely to be successful.

In my estimation, dad had everything to gain by remaining in Montgomery to receive training in public accounting. I am relatively certain that he had not acquired the skills to become a capable member of the management team at a corporate level without having to obtain additional supervision, training, and acquired proficiency in the particular enterprise of his choosing. I am not aware that he acquired special knowledge in an industry or that he provided accounting or auditing services for entities that may have been representative of companies such as the Nicaro Nickel Company or the Hershey Company. Presumably, these are manufacturing concerns that entail accounting methods such as process or job cost accounting, which, although not unusual practices, experience in these areas could prove to be invaluable.

I am not sure how dad came to choose the Nicaro Nickel Company, but I can say that he did not demonstrate to me any particular expertise in this area of accounting in his later practice in Montgomery, of which I was well aware, nor did he provide any services to clients of this type other than a residential home builder. I am also not aware of the degree and scope of his initial accounting experience in Montgomery before taking the job in Cuba, but I can say that the expertise that he demonstrated subsequently in the practice that he established in Montgomery was not of the caliber of a certified public accountant, and it did not reflect particular corporate accounting experience. This suggested to me that he abandoned public accountancy prematurely. As a minimum, he should have completed the requirements to become a certified public accountant, which would have demonstrated the entry requirements for success in the field. Also, it seems obvious that he would have benefitted from at least several more years of supervision and training. He might have also targeted an industry area that suited him in planning for his departure from public accountancy.

Consequently, I cannot help but think that mom persuaded dad to make these changes without adequate consideration and for the wrong reasons. I doubt that she sought the advice of Ed Harper, together with dad or otherwise, because I feel certain that he would have advised dad to become certified first. He might have also provided other invaluable advice to dad. Additionally, he might have made mom (and dad) more fully aware of the opportunity for dad in the Montgomery community. To have the opportunity to join an elite group of public accountants and to become a part of Montgomery society is a rich heritage. Ed Harper and Mabel Harper might have helped mom to look past her and dad's insecurities in regards to what appears to have been a hasty decision and guided them to assert themselves within the accounting profession and Montgomery society. Dad had other good friends that would surely have helped them to do the same. Instead, it appears that mom chose the security of her Cuban home once again and without due consideration. Quite possibly, my grandparents presented the promise of opportunity for dad, considering later developments, which would have been hard for anyone to turn down. However, due consideration should have helped them muster the courage to stay for a reasonable while longer.

Mom's and dad's decision closed the door to earning a rightful place in a richer life, broadly speaking, such as economically, intellectually, and spiritually. They appear to have compromised a higher value and the richness it brings to the quality of one's life for a more complacent lot in life, guised under the veil of doing for mom on dad's part, and the urging of her parents to be closer to home on mom's part. They were a young couple, very much in love, having the opportunity to make their own path, to gain the respect and admiration of their family, and to struggle nobly to better their position, with a good base of support and preparation; and, instead, they chose what seems to have been a more complacent path, from the looks of things. Dad's decision to become an accountant for a corporation at that point in his career and under those circumstances does not appear to have been thoughtful or properly motivated. His subsequent achievement in the accounting profession seems a testament to these inferences. To put it simply, by making this decision, mom and dad appear to have compromised their spiritual lives. They were devout Catholics in a sense.

They sought to practice Christian values in many respects. But that decision did not place them on the path toward growing closer to and becoming vibrant members of the Christian community.

When our decisions obstruct our spiritual lives, they affect those around us. I have previously described my indoctrination into the Catholic and Christian faith. I had many good role models in Cuba, and my parents themselves, from my recollection, were considerate and affectionate. I was in love with my mother, as many children are, and although dad was not around as much, I do not remember a cross moment with him. Even so, my conscious and subconscious behavior was beginning to reflect burgeoning Christian values, which my parents had access to daily. Although they meant well for me, they would not have been able to accept this.

Parents, in particular, are most likely well aware of the mental life of their children, not only consciously, but also subconsciously. In close relations, they are likely to be in constant communication as the children are growing up. The issue then becomes that parents come to recognize and have to accept that their child is pursuing a rich spiritual life that they cannot also enjoy. The only way for such parents to change this state of affairs in a progressive sense is to recognize what they have done to obstruct their spiritual lives and be reconciled with it. This is always the best course, and it may be very difficult or slow at first, but nevertheless always a choice. This course is likely unusual for people who have been set on another course, the result being that they are likely to harbor feelings such as anger, resentment, and jealousy. Parents in these circumstances would most likely try to change the course of a child by presenting situations that encourage the child to falter, such as offering the child something the child wants but in a way that compromises the child's values—which has from a psychological point of view been referred to as a double bind—or by mentally opposing the child in a way that forces mistakes by the child that compromises the child's spiritual life.

I do not remember any double binds during my years in Cuba. Considering my youth, the degree of support that I had, and my parents' success in living, it may be that mom and dad were mostly mum about how they felt about my spiritual growth. I remember but two events that I felt were perhaps of the sort about which I have spoken. I recall and gathered the impression from mom that she and my aunt Elma, her brother Louis' wife, did not get along very well. I am not sure about all the reasons why. However, I do remember from anecdotal information and general statements made by mom that she and Louis were very close growing up. Elma appears to have been less familiar in manner than mom, more of a businesswoman, and perhaps such a partner to her husband that she wanted him to be more of an individual in his own right and less reliant upon or "individuated" with his family members. In a sense, one might say that she was trying to come between the relationship that mom and my uncle Louis shared, though perhaps for a good reason. This sort of attitude, or Tia Elma's character, apparently led to conflict between her and mom.

Two of mom's brothers, Louis and Alfredo, and their families joined us at my grandparents' home in Varadero during the summertime. Louis' family had a maid living in the house who looked after their two sons, Luisito and Raulito. Their maid was like a part of their family and respected as such. We all had cordial relations with one another. Rarely did one observe open bickering. I was full of life and curiosity and very much my mother's child. She directed my life fairly much. There happened an occasion when my curiosity got the best of me. Somehow, I climbed from the outside of the house to peep into the maids' quarters where the maid that took care of my cousins Luisito and Raulito stayed and, I should add, hardly noticing or realizing what I was doing. The next thing that I knew, she was angrily chasing me across the yard with a pan that she had by the handle as if to strike and chased me away. This created a big scandal in the house, particularly among the servants. I remember sitting among those who cared for my family at a loss for words and feeling disgraced, but I also sensed that they felt at a loss about what to do or say under the circumstances. This event did not put me in good standing with my uncle Louis or my aunt Elma, I imagine, meaning that I may have lost some support. It may also have put me in less of a good stead among the servants. And, it could have been a source of conflict between my mother and Aunt Elma.

The other occasion that I recall occurred on Christmas Day, and it must have been in 1959, my last Christmas in Cuba. All the children were purposely kept very naïve about Santa Claus and about a number of other things. I did not learn that Santa Claus was not real until Christmas 1963, when I was ten years old and in the fourth grade. When there was a present under the tree with your name on it, Santa had brought it to you for being a good boy and that was that; it was meant for you and not someone else. I am not sure what Louis and his family were doing in Varadero that Christmas season. When Christmas Day arrived, we were opening our presents with excitement, and while we were doing so, my mother comes over to me, takes the rifle that Santa Claus brought me, and tells me that my cousin Luisito, who is one year younger than me, did not have any presents under the tree. Consequently, she wanted me to let him have my gun and she said that she would get me one later.

I reacted with indignation immediately and screamed to high heaven that that was my gun, that Santa Claus had brought that for me and not Luisito! Rest assured, my behavior was not acceptable to God Almighty, as considerate and understanding as he is. It created distance between me and the grace presence of the Holy Spirit, temporarily, but also in the sense of my lack of a mature faith, until I should grow up some. This is even though I could not have changed my perspective at the time, considering my mentality. It was every bit of me, resident in me, and brought out of me. In addition to some compromise on my spiritual life, this behavior also likely strained relations with my cousin and his parents, and it may have created the impression among the servants that I was something of a spoiled brat. I did not really fit that bill, but I did not want to part with the rifle that Santa brought me.

CHAPTER 10:

THE UNITED STATES OF AMERICA

Saint Thomas on the Hill in Birmingham, Alabama

My sister Rosemary, my brother George, and I caught a plane out of Cuba for Miami during the fall of 1960, around October, I would guess, the reason being that the Cuban dictator Batista had left the country for Santo Domingo, as I have been told, after being ousted by Fidel Castro and his army of rebels. They became a regular sight on the streets, and it became clear by their actions and their words, that communist and socialist rule would govern the country. They apparently from the first began to exercise such power as to make it clear to all who had acquired a desirable standard of living that they could not expect to continue with the status quo. Rather, they would be subject to the will and control of this new government and the process would not be democratic but autocratic. Overnight, all the professionals and merchants who had enjoyed such a standard of living were trying to get out of the country. My parents saw an opportunity to get the oldest three children out right away—I think the fact that Rosemary and I were natural U. S. citizens helped—and so my sister and I, along with my younger brother George, were the first to go. Mabel Harper met us in Miami, Florida, and from there we flew to Montgomery, Alabama. My memory about this event is a blur except for waving to my family from the plane as we left the airport in Cuba. I had no idea about what was transpiring and was ecstatic about going to the United

States of America, about which I had great expectations: an imagination of a truly wonderful place.

Ed Harper had died as a relatively young man. Mabel was now a widow. She had cared for Rosemary when dad divorced and when dad's first wife died. Having had no children of her own, Rosemary held a special place in her heart, and I am sure that she was excited about caring for Rosemary again. However, she did not understand young boys. George and I were very active little boys, who, to Mabel, it may have seemed that we were constantly in motion, and she did not know how to treat or manage us. Within three days, she made arrangements for the Sisters of Laredo, of the Laredo Catholic School in Montgomery, where Rosemary, George, and I were enrolled, to transport George and me to Saint Thomas on the Hill in Birmingham. This was both a boarding or foster home facility for children who had been displaced from their parents for one reason or another and an elementary school attended by these resident children as well as children from the community. It was managed by Catholic nuns who wore the traditional black vestige but wore a headdress that was white and that flared upwards and outward on either side, like that in the sitcom, *The Flying Nun*, unlike the traditional headdress of the Sisters of Laredo. I was eight years old, attending the third grade, and I recall that our teacher wore plainclothes: she was not a nun.

This sudden change was very traumatic for George and me. We faced the rear window and cried all the way from Montgomery to Birmingham. My mind was focused on the many miles that were separating George and me from Ms. Harper and Rosemary, the only family in the States at the time. The drive into the Dairy Queen and the chocolate ice cream cone that the sisters treated us to on arrival to Birmingham helped to soothe our hearts, which were aching at the time. Things went very well after that. First, the two Sisters of Laredo took us by the home of a Cuban family, it happened that the married couple were good friends of mom and dad, and they did wonders at appeasing George and me with plans of writing to mom and dad and visiting us. Next, on arrival at Saint Thomas on the Hill on Sunday afternoon, the big event was roller skating in the gym, which was like topping on the cake. My mood had changed quickly from despairing to enjoyment. George felt the same way. The only blemish to the enjoyable afternoon was an ethnic slur by one of the kids that raised my dander. It did not completely spoil my afternoon. However, it was the start of the negative connotation that the word "Cuban," used in an obviously derogatory way, held for me.

Saint Thomas on the Hill was partly about survival. Although I had been a good student in Cuba, the third grade in the United States was a struggle. I had no sense of rapport with the teacher or any of the students and felt rather lost. George and I did not make many friends right away and usually stayed huddled by ourselves during recess. There were some humorous moments, as I look back on the experience. On the day of our arrival, after we were introduced to our new quarters—a large, long room, which was a dormitory with many beds—the sister in charge told us to undress and line up for a bath. So there we were in this long line of naked boys who were going to get their bath. I also remember the stale, undesirable taste of a Tab, thinking that I had been served a Coke, and all the other kids finding humor in the heaping amounts of sugar that George and I put on our grapefruits.

We learned English overnight, literally. Athletics was always my road to friendships, and even though not quite as sporting as say baseball, George and I quickly became skilled at horseshoes, which led to challenging matches, new acquaintances, and some fun. We also were occasional altar servers for the daily benediction service, which helped our socialization. We were fairly homesick at times, but we managed to get by. There were other fun times and some trying moments. There were some older kids there, sixth graders. I am not sure whether I acted rightly, but on a couple of occasions while on the playground after school, when there was no one around to supervise events, I recall one of the older boys acting cross or just being mean, approaching me in a menacing way, and my reaction of hurling rocks to keep him at bay. I recall that we made friends later, when he impressed me as a nice boy, and I had some sense that I had done wrong.

The development of schizophrenia is insidious; at least, I think that it was for me. I recall that on one occasion during recess, George, who usually depended on me, got into some sort of conflict with a boy that was older and bigger than both of us. I do not recall the nature of the conflict, only that he seemed to be threatening George, and it did not seem that he would stop. In the heat of the moment, the solution was for us to team up on him, and we were able to best him in that way. What I find unusual about that is that George seemed to often put me in that position, and it got the better of me one day, which I will refer to later. I think that perhaps at this relatively young age, despite the fact that George was very dependent on me, there was an ulterior motive for this sort of behavior, another design than him simply experiencing some peril, and that design meant trouble for me.

I have another such subtle example at Saint Thomas on the Hill. By January 1961, dad had managed to get all my other brothers and sisters out of Cuba—Conchita, Ana Maria, Arthur, and Mickey—and placed them with good friends of his in Montgomery, Alabama. Mom was pregnant with my brother Raymond and did not come to the States until after his birth in March. Dad visited George and me that January and told us of the plan for us to remain in school there until the end of the school year, when we would join the rest of the family and mom in Montgomery. That time was approaching when, as was sometimes the occasion at Saint Thomas on the Hill, well wishers with philanthropist notions who visited gave each one of the resident children two silver dollars as we left the dining room. My first thoughts were that dad would be able to use that money, which may have been true but was also a kid's imagination. I told George of this and told him to be sure to save the money for that purpose. When I learned later that he had given away the money to a couple of older boys that he knew and formed the impression that he was trying to win their favor, I was very disappointed and could hardly believe what I was hearing. This may not sound like a big thing, but it made a deep impression on me at the time. This is because I was George's older brother, he always clung to me, and I always saw to his safety. I expected him to follow me about such matters as the request about the money, considering our relations, but I learned from that experience that he did not follow me. He heard the voice of a different drummer, which did not sound all right to me.

College Street and beneficial traditions at Cloverdale and Lanier

Dad picked a great place for us to live in Montgomery. He rented a house on College Street! It was a relatively wide street but not too busy with traffic that met two major streets—Fairview Avenue to the south, at the gates of Huntingdon College, and just about twenty yards from our home, and Carter Hill Road, four blocks to the north. Huntingdon College had a really nice indoor pool, exciting basketball games, and a beautiful, scenic campus as well as interesting buildings, such as a building that had science exhibits in a showcase like you might expect to find in a museum. Fairview Avenue had a nice sidewalk that was bicycle and roller skate friendly. Just one block to the west, one could find Pops, a candy store nicknamed after its owner, which was situated behind the dugout of the home to Dixie Youth Little League baseball. As one walked or rode further west on that block, there was a football field, a community center, and Cloverdale School, an elementary and junior high public school that claimed all that property. On the next corner was the Capri Theater, which had a matinee every Saturday for children. Across the street from the Capri was the Cloverdale Drug Store, which made some of the most delicious hamburgers and French fries in town, a real treat that I usually could not afford.

Little league baseball had a great nucleus of young boys at the time, great leaders among them, and a great coaching tradition also, including coaches that had played professional baseball. I spent many a day and night either watching their baseball practice from the bleachers or glued to the fence during their pep-filled baseball games. There was a sensation like magic in the air for me during those games. Those kids were my idols, heroes, and role models who made an impression on me that remains unblemished to this day.

Cloverdale Community Center was a hub of activity, especially during summers. One could play Ping-Pong, horseshoes, basketball, or jump on the trampoline. Older elementary and junior high school girls liked to play records on the Rockola jukebox and dance to the rock 'n' roll music of the times. There was often a pickup game of basketball or touch football to be found, and baseball with some luck. The community center staff members were always organizing fun activities for us during the summer, such as a horseshoes or a Ping-Pong tournament, a scavenger hunt, or a bus ride to Huntingdon College for a swim. We attended the Sisters of Loretta Catholic School that first year in Montgomery, starting with Rosemary in the sixth grade, me in the fourth, and George in the third. Conchita was held back one year and would have been in the first grade, I think, but I do not recall where she was enrolled. Some of my younger brothers and sisters attended kindergarten at the Cloverdale Church of Christ and later attended elementary school at Our Lady Queen of Mercy, another Catholic school in Montgomery. Frank, my youngest brother, was born in April 1962.

I made a number of friends at Loretta School, some that were later friends at Cloverdale School and in high school. There was a mixture of military and town kids there, and I did not feel uncomfortable. I was best friends that year with a boy named Kevin Bench, whose father was a colonel in the Air Force. We did what best friends do, such as make plays together on the basketball court, challenge other kids to a basketball match, and enjoy one another's company. He had me out to Maxwell Air Force Base one weekend and showed me a swell time, and I had him over to spend the night at our home one weekend also. For whatever reasons, convenience likely being a factor, my parents placed George and me in Cloverdale School during the following year. Rosemary continued at Loretta or Our Lady Queen of Mercy and later attended Catholic High. Mabel Harper, who often did volunteer work for the Catholic nuns, could usually be counted on for a ride.

I received a rude introduction to the fifth grade at Cloverdale School on the first day of class, during the first recess. A classmate who was about my height but much stouter and muscular—I was slim or skinny, like my mother—came up to me during recess, when there were a number of other kids from the fifth grade classes around (there were two fifth grade classes), reached his hand out to introduce himself, and when I took it, he tripped me over his leg and said something like, "Who cares about a lousy Cuban, anyway?" with a sarcastic sense of humor that was meant to draw laughter from the other kids. I was immediately on my feet and tried to return the favor but did not manage to. He then stated, "Hey, look. I apologize. I was just kidding around. I don't want you to have any hard feelings," reached out his hand again, and tried to do the same thing. I was feeling pretty lousy by the end of recess. As I was walking into the school, another classmate who was very blonde, handsome, and fairly stout himself, treated me especially well and told me not to worry about "that guy," support that I truly appreciated. The next day during recess, there was a copycat incident by a fellow from the other fifth grade class who was about my size, and I let him know right away that I was not going to put up with any monkey business from him.

These opening comments do not at all describe the character of Cloverdale School or my experience there. It was a wonderful place with a great tradition. To give you an example of some of the students, the daughter of the would-be U. S. Postmaster General was in my sixth grade class. Behind her sat a guy who always knew the meaning of the "big words" when the teacher sampled the class, the son of one of the attorneys who were involved in the landmark Wyatt vs. Stickney case in Judge Frank M. Johnson's federal district court, which established important standards in Alabama hospitals for the treatment of mentally ill and mentally retarded patients. Another student was the daughter of the pastor of the First United Methodist Church, a beautiful girl with long jet-black hair. These are just to name a few.

Many of these kids were bright and affluent enough to attend the Montgomery Academy during a time when it may have been traditional to rotate them into Cloverdale, perhaps because their parents had also attended Cloverdale and wanted them to take classes from some of the exceptional teachers that had taught them. I was fortunate to have classes with and get to know many of these kids. They came from excellent family backgrounds and provided important leadership qualities and strong Christian values to our peer group. This trend continued in junior high school, when we were joined by the kids from Bear School, which was the nucleus of McGehee Estates and the surrounding areas, kids from some of the most prominent families in town. Subsequently, at Sidney Lanier High School, kids from Cloverdale were joined by those from Floyd, Bellingrath, and Baldwin schools, the former two having a range from middle class to upper-middle class family backgrounds and the latter more of a working class background but good kids, just the same, who integrated well into the culture at Sidney Lanier.

I never had any difficulty making friends, which I credit to my athletic ability. I was an all-star on the Farm League baseball team that I joined after the fourth grade, which was not of the same caliber as our Little League teams but a good league just the same, and I was one of the top scorers in the YMCA basketball league where kids from Cloverdale played while I was in the fifth and sixth grades. In the seventh grade, I was the quarterback of our Pee Wee football team. Athletic ability helps to win friends among other athletes on your team. When there is a rich athletic tradition in well managed leagues that hold high standards, these tend to be people of character, often the school leaders. This ability for sports helped me to make friends with such people and kids that were not in athletics through association, the result being that I had a truly good peer group in junior high school and high school. I played football, basketball, and ran track at Cloverdale. I thought that I would be too small to play football my sophomore year at Sidney Lanier. They won the state championship in 1966 and 1967 and also won it in 1968, which was my sophomore year. I was in awe of playing football there, and more so considering that I was about 4 feet, 11inches tall and weighed about 110 pounds at the end of the ninth grade. In other words, I was sort of a runt.

The summer after my ninth grade school year, dad got me a job working at Alabama Concrete Silo Company, which was owned by one of his clients and a good friend of dad's. The job involved stacking ninety pounds of cement silo blocks after the wet cement dried and the metal forms could be removed. By the end of the summer, I had become muscular, weighed in at around 130 pounds, and had shot up to 5 feet, 3 inches in height. I made the Lanier B Team, which was an honor and prestigious—to be a football player at Sidney Lanier. They had this tradition where the boys that played football joined the Coaches Club and coached the Termite and Pee Wee football teams. The cheerleaders, who taught young girls cheerleading skills for these same leagues, and other girls, were members of Tri-Hi-Y. The YMCA provided the management for most of these activities. One night, we had this outing where the girls ask the guys to go out, and we all piled into several cars and had a lot of fun. I had a date with a junior by the name of Gypsy who totally charmed me. We also socialized at a place we called the coffee house at the YMCA, a room about thirty feet wide and sixty feet long where we held dances every Friday night that included music from some very good local bands of the time, when soul music was popular. These were well supervised activities with good student leadership that amounted mostly to good clean fun.

CHAPTER 11:

MY PARENTS: FORCES OR EVENTS THAT INFLUENCED THEIR BEHAVIOR AND MINE

I mportant decisions by mom and dad
My mother's history impresses me as an example of how our actions and choices in life shape our personalities: the people we become. She was well-to-do, attended reputable Catholic schools for girls, was ensconced in a broad social network, and had a strong Catholic faith. Her family valued education and high ideals. In short, her background suggested that she had a very good training ground for embarking on a college education. The exception is that she sought that education in the United States of America, another culture that was quite different from hers. However, she should not have been a total stranger to the American culture, considering that her father and uncle had been exchange students in Boston for two years and that two of her brothers were either attending or had plans to attend Notre Dame in order to pursue degrees in engineering. I would have expected mom to go to Pennsylvania in the spirit of not only seeking her degree and socialization with the group of about six Cuban girls that she became a member of, but also in the spirit of experiencing the American culture firsthand, meaning plans to also engage and make friends with the American girls that she would meet at the Pennsylvania college.

Mom told me that some of the Cuban women who attended her college when she did were a part of her social group in Cuba, though none were intimate friends. She told of regularly going on outings for entertainment with them during breaks from their college studies. She also indicated that with the passage of time, the group's numbers grew smaller and the group became less nurturing for her because she had not made good friends within the group and did not seem to have very much in common with the remaining girls. Thus, feeling somewhat lonely and isolated, she decided to withdraw from college and return to Cuba after two years.

I have never questioned my mother about why she was not able to make American friends. I would find it hard to believe that at such a fine women's college as she attended, there were not girls that would have welcomed mom if she had sought them out, of which she seemed capable. Although that may have represented a challenge, mom's failure to rise to that challenge suggested to me that at least part of the problem lay within her. It may be that she led a fairly sheltered life at home. It may also be that her culture had not sufficiently promoted leadership among its Catholic women in a worldly sense. It seems obvious that her Catholicism had not reached a mature level whereby she recognized her place in the world as a Christian woman and possessed the confidence to venture forth to engage other women, particularly women from other cultures.

It seems possible that mom had been faced with similar challenges in her life and had not acted in a lofty manner, such as being both congenial and assertive, or exhibited an independent, dignified demeanor. Rather, if faced with similar challenges, it seems that she might have held a lower standard that prevented her from developing the character and skills to more easily negotiate the task of reaching out to her American peers in college. For example, although she said that she was a good student, she may not have been inspired to put in the hard work and dedication that is required to provide leadership to peers, setting a high standard and upholding Christian and Catholic ideals. Instead, she may chosen the more complacent attitude of being part of a clique that maintained their favorable status quo, seeking out the support and comfort of the group instead of a more spirited and independent approach to living. It may have meant breaking with the norms of her traditional group to engage another culture and set a more independent path for herself—a path requiring change that she may not have wanted or been prepared to take. Such changes might have required her to tolerate some discomfort as she relinquished the more complacent attitude of her traditional group while striving to learn a path requiring greater self confidence and self reliance. For whatever reasons, it appears that this was an important challenge for mom and that she did not rise to it—to think that she could have invited American friends for a visit to Cuba, including Varadero and historic Cardenas! I imagine that many an American girl would have jumped at such an opportunity, including a chance to learn the Spanish language.

Mom chose to return to her parents' home without a college degree that would have opened doors for her professionally and given her the earning power to act and become more independent. She did not achieve the intellectual prowess that comes with that degree, which provides the opportunity for leadership and camaraderie with other well educated people and business leaders. She also did not make American college friends, which would have broadened her horizons to another culture. In short, she did not enrich her education in an eminent way that would have made her more of an asset to her Cuban culture, her family, and any would-be husband. She chose greater dependency on her parents of necessity by her choice. She became more reliant on her Cuban culture, choosing comfort within a broad Cuban subculture that she knew well, but necessarily limiting her horizons there also, because she most likely would not have been able to relate in a free and unencumbered way with the more accomplished people within that culture. Because she had not obtained a college degree, she would not have been in league with them; she lacked the endowment that comes with such an accomplishment. Thus, she most likely would have lacked both the confidence and skills to relate at their level of sophistication. It also would not have been unusual for the evoked memories to have filled her with chagrin upon encountering such people, an emotional hurdle that she may have been faced with during efforts to relate to them effectively.

How accurate are these inferences about mom? Could this mistake have been as costly as I have described? I will revert to my previous comments that our choices shape our personalities: the people we become. I do not have the information at my disposal to say how much mom's previous choices affected that outcome. But, I have good information that she continued along those lines and that this path promoted in mom the development of dependent personality characteristics and dependency conflicts, attributes that are synonymous with the encumbrance or obstruction of her spiritual life. She limited her horizons intellectually and culturally, which had a corresponding effect on her spiritual life: the two go hand in hand.

Mom remained single for the next ten years. She apparently continued to have a vibrant social life and a not-very-demanding lifestyle when she met and soon married dad, who had transcended his humble beginnings to be a match for her by obtaining a college degree in accounting, which was complemented by a bright future. He was a fledgling accountant, not yet certified, but directed by two proven leaders in the field, Ed Harper and Robert Troy Sr., who was president of the Alabama Society of Certified Public Accountants during his career. Such a bountiful providence! Dad was integrating into Montgomery society and brought mom to Montgomery to share in his good fortune. Did mom not see the opportunity that lay ahead for her and dad? Could she not see where this was taking dad and how she might complement him?

My mother tended to be prudent and thoughtful in her decision-making. Dad was also. I have known them to think things over until they reached a good decision and to act prudently about their affairs. I find it amazing that they made a mistake of the magnitude that they did at this point in their lives. They uprooted themselves from the Montgomery community before dad became certified in his field and seemingly also before he acquired sufficient experience to ensure that he would be an asset to management in the corporate accounting venture that he undertook in Cuba. In short, it does not appear that dad was adequately prepared for that venture. His decision to move to Cuba appears to have been made hastily or without due consideration.

Mom went to Montgomery as a newlywed bride with dad. She likely felt insecure after her Pennsylvania experience, considering that she withdrew from college without coming to know the American coeds at her school, apparently not showing pluck when it was called for, when it would have served her well. Additionally, she had to immediately contend with dad's outgoing nature, an inference that became evident in comments she made about this particular time in her life: "Wilfred would abandon me at social events while he socialized with his lady friends. I would be left alone and feeling awkward."

The challenge for mom at that time appeared to be gaining familiarity and competence within a Montgomery subculture that included relatively well educated people, members of a professional class, and refined people, who represented the sort of culture that would help dad to be successful in his own right as a public accountant within the established Montgomery society. Mom's background should have been a training ground for such an endeavor. However, her chosen path had become rather antithetical to the challenge before her, considering her failure to achieve the laurels of a college degree and acculturation in an American women's college followed by her complacency in pursuing a more traditional female role within Cuban society. She needed to gather her resources, consider her new horizons, and face the challenge of engaging this American subculture in order to acquire and practice the social skills, intellect, and business acumen that would complement dad well in his role of a public accountant and member of Montgomery society.

Earlier, I described how resourceful mom was in establishing a social network in Tuscaloosa at the grand old age of eighty-five. Mom did this with my backing as a source of support and with the purpose of providing social activities for Conchita. In our neighborhood, these were often mutually supportive and enjoyable experiences with other elderly residents who likely found Conchita to be entertaining and amusing. There was apt to be good social banter of a leisurely sort about mutual acquaintances, individual interests, or the day's events—entertaining chitchat. With church groups, sometimes there might have been a speaker on a relatively more intellectual topic or group leaders that directed a relatively more intellectually challenging conversation or one on a novel topic that might have subsequently been discussed by the group. Many of these people were elderly, and the church groups were a way for them to stay in contact with the church community, which added to their sense of belonging. Mom's role under those circumstances was one that she could fairly much pick and choose while having me as a base of support and Conchita's needs to think about, and it was one that she was very comfortable and familiar with. She is very adept in such a role.

Mom's role expectations as a Cuban lady in Montgomery society and newlywed bride to an aspiring public accountant appear to have been much more challenging. This novel role most likely required the exercise of social charm and composure or another effective social posture to match dad's outgoing nature and active socialization—to complement him well. The conversation was likely to be more elevated and refined, considering that these were college-educated and professional people. And, it would likely have required a degree of shrewdness or alertness to business affairs, considering that public accountants are necessarily vigilant to business opportunities amidst socialization, which is an important venue for acquiring new clients. Mom, on her part, is skilled at social banter. She is a good listener, a most interesting storyteller with a wealth of anecdotal information, and a student of people. I think that she was capable of acquiring the social skills to fill her new role expectations. Of course, dad would have been ready to assist her in that capacity as well as Ed and Mabel Harper if she had sought them out. Furthermore, I feel certain that the Montgomery society that she encountered was prepared to guide her and facilitate her new role—that its members would have helped her to become successful in that endeavor if she had given them a chance.

I feel that mom's influence on dad must have been a deciding factor in their decision to leave Montgomery for Cuba. She has given some indication that she was not entirely comfortable in Montgomery at the time, including some rivalry between her and Mabel Harper for Rosemary, my sister by dad's first wife; and she has directly stated that her parents wanted her and dad closer to home. She and dad may very well have spoken about the opportunities in real estate that dad would have in Varadero, which he later realized, and there may have even been talk about a job at the bank in Cardenas that he later obtained. In other words, I have gathered from mom that her father spoke to dad about opportunities that he would have in Cuba, which is probably so, although to what extent he did so on his own or at mom's urging I could not say. As to the reasons that mom was decided on returning to Cuba, I could not say for sure; I could only make a calculated guess.

The obvious is that this inclination by mom, this decision, had similarities to her shortcomings in college and could have been part of a pattern that began before then. Considering her past actions, such as her failure to acculturate within American women at her college and a rather complacent withdrawal to her locality, she may have felt daunted by the task before her, which required the very skills that she had neglected to develop. Thus, it seems possible that her decision could have been partly motivated by insecurity or fear. It is also possible that dad, on recognizing this, acquiesced. If mom had this degree of cognizance and was filled with some trepidation, she also seemed to lack maturity at this stage in her life, because her decision was not well considered. Given the immaturity that it showed, she may not have fully realized what was at stake for dad. Instead, she may have been primarily drawn to the comforts of home and that line of thinking may have prevailed over adequate consideration of the alternatives available to her and dad.

Mom may not have been sufficiently analytic to consider how this decision would affect dad's career and how such things as experience would weigh on his chances for success. The hastiness of this decision also suggested to me that dad, who should have known what was at stake for him, did not share his ideas with mom, either because he did not like to discuss business matters with her, or because he did not want to disappoint her, or for some other reason. I cannot help but think that if they had discussed these matters openly, greater reason would have prevailed. Their decision seems to have been whimsical. It likely blemished mom's spiritual life further, in my opinion, and it likely blemished dad's as well. They needed to see their horizons clearly and respond virtuously, which would have enriched their lives. Instead, it appears that they sought narrower horizons, such as security and complacency, without due consideration.

This criticism of mom may need to be balanced with practical considerations. For example, mom and dad may have judged that the road to success in public accounting for dad would be slow and arduous, testing their wits, their intellect, and their mettle. They would not enjoy affluence at first but would have to earn it through hard and diligent work, requiring a transformation of sorts, especially for dad. In essence, they would be striving to gain those very things that mom had enjoyed in Cuba all of her life, but in a more accomplished way, embodying more fully the ideals of this class. Regardless of their choice, prudence should have dictated that they exercise the patience to allow dad the time to gain greater mastery over accounting under able leadership and to strive to meet the requirements of the certified public accounting certificate. This would have been a noble struggle that could have helped them to decide on the best course of action for them; this sufficient training time would have likely helped to guide their future actions.

This decision by my mother, along with her decision to leave college, came to represent a maladaptive personality pattern, based on the understanding of mom that I have acquired. Her choices led to greater dependence upon her parents, her family, and her Cuban subculture rather than an independent air, an assertive and confident attitude, and a willingness to struggle with dad as part of a noble endeavor within a progressive social group, which would have likely furthered dad's professional career and helped them to mature as a couple. The consequences of her choices necessarily led to less self reliance and confidence. They promoted dependent personality characteristics and dependency conflicts that include passivity, timidity, and excessive reliance upon others, including an inability to be assertive and independent in decision-making. In my mother, as I contrasted in her behavior when she and Conchita joined me in Tuscaloosa versus when she went to Montgomery with dad as a new bride, the manifestation of these traits depends on the situation or context and her supportive network.

This personality pattern may have been supported sufficiently by mom's Cuban subculture after her withdrawal from college in Pennsylvania, such as her family, her friends, or both, that mom may not have felt dispirited and keenly experienced emotions such as guilt and shame that would have led to a greater awareness of how she had erred and motivated her to change her pattern of behavior so as not to act similarly again. If so, this appears to be the wrong kind of support. One's social structure should admonish a person when that person does wrong, which is the loving thing to do so that the individual learns from mistakes and does not repeat them. That is God's way, also. Apparently, this personality pattern went uncorrected and continued, as evident in mom's enticement of dad to abandon his public accounting practice. These choices, in my opinion, led to the formation of maladaptive dependent personality characteristics. These conflicts within mom became the lynchpin of my schizophrenia, as I will explain. These decisions did not immediately cost her and may not have proved as costly as they were if the Cuban culture had not been shaken up by the overthrow of the Batista government in a coup by Fidel Castro and his guerrillas.

My father never told me much about himself, about his background, his upbringing, or his interests. He never provided me a good chronology of his life that I could use as a reference when thinking or talking about him. He apparently did not like to talk about those events very much. He provided brief anecdotes on family occasions when the conversation was directed to him or on other occasions when I was with him and his memory was stirred. Most of the knowledge that I acquired about him probably came from mom, but she did not seem very descriptive or thorough at those times, if she could have been. His parents were elderly and frail when I was but a young child, and they needed to be cared for, apparently to the extent that we children were not taken to visit and provided the opportunity to know them, and they passed away during that same period of time.

Dad's vision or aspirations on coming to the United States as a youth may have been stirred by relations with well-to-do Cubans and information about Cuban boys who had followed that path. His ambitious venture into accounting appeared to suffer a setback when he left public accounting in Montgomery for a corporate accounting job in Cuba because he apparently had not obtained sufficient training and experience in public accounting to be prepared for that occupational change. I think that the practice that dad established when we returned to Montgomery after the takeover of the Cuban government by Fidel Castro in 1960 attests to his insufficient preparation. Dad provided a bookkeeping service to small businesses from which he generated financial statements to help them stay abreast of their profits. He used that information to prepare their income, sales, and payroll tax returns and financial statements for their financing needs. He also provided an income tax service to individual clients. Although he properly obtained his continuing education hours yearly, he did not appear to be a student in the field. He was not the sort of person who could pick up a textbook, absorb its contents, and apply its methods. He was better at hands-on learning. For example, he would return from an accounting convention with talk of a new technique that he had been shown, which other accountants were using, and seek feedback until he felt comfortable that it would help his practice, that it was something that he could do, and that his secretary-bookkeeper would be willing to tackle it. He enjoyed retrieving data entry information from his clients every month for his secretary-bookkeeper to process and mixing socialization with business advice as he sought to meet their needs.

Dad was very busy and had tremendous family responsibilities on returning to Montgomery and establishing a practice in public accounting, in which regard the support of some former close friends in Montgomery was invaluable. Even so, he might have taken a studious approach to the profession that leads to increasing skill and expertise. He was fairly satisfied with performing the practice of public accountancy that I described above and collaborating with fellow public accountants at conventions to learn a new technique or skill that could help him upgrade his service. He did not consider becoming certified at that point in his career. He seemed comfortable associating within the public accounting profession, where the content of conversation and fiber of people was more likely to include common and down-to-earth individuals in addition to the more advanced professionals or business leaders. He was less comfortable with and was not drawn to people who were relatively more intellectual or heady. His expertise did not progress to larger clients with more complex accounting systems, and he did not strive to increase his education and skills to become certified and thereby seek some of the lucrative services that are common to CPA's, such as auditing and accounting services as part of rendering an opinion. All this suggested that he did not have adequate education, training, and expertise when he got out of public accounting for a job in corporate accounting. My impression, which I describe below, is that he was undergoing a transition under able mentoring to achieve the abilities required for recognition of entry into the field of public accountancy; that is, passing the requirements of certification.

Dad, most likely, was a struggling young accountant at the inception of his public accounting career in Montgomery. He likely needed to further develop a studious disposition while acquiring additional knowledge of the standards, methods, and tools of the profession in order to reach the level of competence and know-how of a certified public accountant. Once that was accomplished, he would have likely required further study of auditing and accounting standards and methods within a specific industry or regarding specific clients in order to acquire greater mastery in the field of accounting that would have assured his success. That is a tall order that only comes from hard and studious work, but mentoring from very able professionals might have made the difference if dad had been willing. Mom was raised amidst professionals and might have provided him the balance to chart a steady course if she had been able to look beyond her insecurities and needs to visualize the opportunity for dad's professional development and their intellectual growth and cultural advancement. Instead, when she sought to persuade dad to return to Cuba, especially if her comments contained the promise of beneficial opportunities, given the struggle that lay ahead, she may have tipped the scales in favor of that course. That alternative may have seemed less daunting to dad, considering the apparent transformation that he would have had to undergo to become a successful accountant.

What kind of student was dad? Dedicated students that learn good study habits tend to keep them and are usually not satisfied unless they are able to achieve a fairly high standard that instills confidence in their ability and eventually, if gradually, earns them a measure of success. Their skills tend to improve over time. Dad's limited proficiency in accounting, his lack of good study habits, and his failure to make gradual progress in the field are indicators that he was not a good student. This may not be surprising. As I note in describing dad's family dynamics, he was raised in a working-class setting where academics may not have been stressed and where intellectual development may have taken a back seat to meeting life's daily needs. To support this inference about dad in particular, I previously noted that he was not someone who could pick up a textbook and readily absorb its contents and that he was more comfortable among members of the public accounting profession who used down-to-earth, common language rather than the more intellectual types. His task of becoming a certified public accountant was not unlike the task of becoming a good student: he needed to learn to apply himself diligently at academics in order to acquire the knowledge to help him gradually become more proficient in the field of accounting while setting high standards that would help to ensure his success. Once again, dad had able mentoring on his side, which my mother might have complemented well. With such support, to achieve such professional dedication, dad would have had to curb his penchant for socialization. He was an outgoing person who managed well the closure of business affairs to have the time to enjoy himself. But he was also a hard and dedicated worker who should not have had a problem studying diligently.

We stayed in Nicaro for approximately three years. Mom told me that dad became aware of and reported inappropriate business practices by employees at the Nicaro Nickel Company in positions that commanded greater authority than his, which led him to leave the company due to anticipated problems. He had made friends with Americans at the Hershey Company and transferred to an accounting position with them. However, it does not appear that he held on to either of these jobs for very long before he and mom moved to Varadero and into the home of mom's parents. Dad's position at those companies in Nicaro were most likely in the nature of an accounting assistant with specific responsibilities or functions that were supervised by or that generated accounting information that was submitted to a chief accountant or a comptroller. Most likely, he would have required training and supervision to learn them well and advance within those companies. He probably had not acquired the business and accounting skills to be able to readily absorb all the knowledge and information available about his area quickly and relate it to upper management in such a way as for them to increase reliance on his competence and ability. He likely needed mentoring and direction like that he was being provided in public accounting to increase his vision and help him to achieve greater competence. Without such mentoring and direction, he likely would have had to struggle to maintain his position. He did not give indication subsequently of specialized knowledge acquired during those corporate endeavors or, as noted previously, of mastery in public accountancy sufficient to consider certification.

My father was a practical man, a hard worker, a good provider, and a good family man. In Varadero, I think his and mom's plans on returning to Cuba came to fruition. Dad landed a job at a bank in Cardenas; I think that it was the Bank of Cardenas. Most likely, it was over a department, unit, or function within the bank, possibly as an assistant or involving shared responsibilities while he acquired the training and experience required to manage that area. I do not think that it was primarily an accounting function because mom referred to his position as that of a manager. Although his business degree and business experience likely helped him to obtain the job, I have the idea that the relative affluence and ties of mom's family within the Cardenas social, business, and banking community could have made a difference. Dad also became involved in real estate ventures in Varadero from an attractive office that mom's father built him, where mom's family owned developed and undeveloped beachfront property. His office was beside my grandfather's home, near the beach, with a good view of the area. Dad seemed to have a natural flair for this occupation. He was outgoing, entertaining, and knew how to be warm and make people comfortable. He was also Americanized, meaning that he was a natural agent to do business with American businessmen and tourists who were attracted to Varadero as a vacation spot and for investment in real estate. His banking connection was likely a good complement that could have presented additional opportunities for integration of services. At this point, previous business shortcomings did not seem glaring. He appeared to be attracting clients and enjoying some success in the capacity of being a real estate agent when we had to abruptly leave Cuba.

Mom flourished also. She resumed the tradition that she knew so well: raising a large family, devotion to Catholicism, and enjoying a rich family and social life. Surely she was satisfied and proud of dad for the strides that he had made in business since their move to Varadero. Pictures of our family at the beach and in other settings reflected dad, mom, and us, their children, with expressions indicative of peace, harmony, and contentment. One would have never guessed that mom had dependent personality characteristics within this culture unless one knew mom very well, and they would have only become evident in situations that cast her outside the traditional role that she was so comfortable in. Dad and mom were every bit the picture of a young, thriving, and happy couple. What this rosy picture did not reveal were the personality conflicts within mom resulting from poorly considered choices that did not uphold her Catholic teachings and limited her spiritual or mental life. Those conflicts, for example, may have resulted in feelings of discomfort in settings where Christian ideals prevail, which can be very revealing as to a person's underlying motivation, or in feelings such as anger and jealousy towards a child who was seeking a broader spiritual life.

What about my father's attitude and motivation in these regards? Dad was raised within a working class setting where the family had to scrap and struggle to survive. From what I know of dad, his sister Ester, and his brother Tenso, the children were taught to be honest and hard working. The parental intellectual level appeared to be that common to working class families, meaning a colloquial dialogue practiced within their subculture. It was not rich and abounding in its concepts and ideas but, rather, likely practical as required to meet the exigencies of everyday living. It seems unusual and quite remarkable that dad's family apparently supported his idea to further his education by traveling to America when a lad of about fifteen or sixteen years of age. That path placed him, a young man raised within a working class family that was limited in educational and intellectual achievement, on a path toward a college degree and a professional career. For him, as it may be for other people who have a similar challenge, this path required a transformation from practical learning, perhaps often by word of mouth, observation like an apprentice, and the reading of practical material, such as instruction booklets and trade journals, to becoming more comfortable with "books," which is a requirement to attain a higher education. He was seeking to leave his working class roots for entry into the more advanced professional class. As I have illustrated, dad did not successfully make this transition. The practical accounting practice that he established on returning to Montgomery, Alabama, lack of advancement into the certified public accountancy realm, and means of learning attest to this.

Dad pursued accounting in Cuba originally, but, being inadequately prepared, he apparently did not progress within that business and professional culture to join it as an accomplished professional. He could have been responsible for specific financial information as well as accounting functions and processes using established accounting standards and practices and been able to supervise less educated personnel under the guidance of a cost or chief accountant while working for the Nicaro Nickel Company and the Hershey Company, who would have been the managerial decision makers. Dad's success at those positions is hard to gauge, considering his brief stay in Nicaro. His subsequent job at a bank in Cardenas may have carried relatively greater responsibility and prestige, but, if an advancement over his former positions, it was likely fortunate, not earned or achieved by means of greater skill or competence at his profession, but likely through opportunity created or made available to him by making use of social influence strategies to some extent. Furthermore, it apparently did not require a specific degree of accounting know-how, because it was a managerial position; rather, it likely required learning departmental or bank functions, practical know-how that would have been within dad's grasp.

Dad joined the merchant class on becoming a real estate agent in Varadero and appeared to be having success at that venture. This might have been a very lucrative endeavor that would have increased his standard of living. Once again, although he appeared well-suited for it, it had not been attained by his accomplishments but bestowed by his wife's family, which is not necessarily a fault, particularly because dad might have managed that opportunity very well for all those concerned. However, his failure to continue his business and professional education in order to become comfortable relating to business leaders likely meant that he would not have had the broader scope of knowledge and intellect to court industry, real estate developers, and similar clients on his own. He had not fully shed his working class style to become an accomplished professional, which was illustrated well in his public accounting role later. He did not transcend his practical learning to become a studious person who continued to advance professionally as a result of dedicated study; he did not acquire the richer mental life that is represented by advancing from being a member of the working class to being a member of the professional class. Ostensibly, he may have been a member of the professional class, but in a real sense, based on the standards for a successful entry, he was not. He had not earned the rights of passage. Considering his choices and decisions, this necessarily meant that he had limited his spiritual life. He had made choices which compromised Christian ideals, including the opportunity to acquire a richer and more abundant life that God meant for him to have.

Class distinctions

What then would have been dad's reaction to my unencumbered spiritual growth toward a rich spiritual life? Let me elaborate on class distinctions before answering this question. Almighty God does not know prejudice. In his book, anyone can have access to the rich, abundant life that he would have us live if that person seeks him with a sincere heart and is willing to practice and uphold Christian principles. This is so regardless of one's class. It is the basic recipe for Christian growth. No one can escape this calling. We must be followers of Christ and subject to the will of his holy spirit. This is so whether we are rich or poor, well educated or illiterate, regardless of our national allegiance or racial or ethnic background. This is the equalizer among us, which at the same time keeps us humble and grants us access to a rich spiritual life that is shared by all of the Christian community. This is the gift of the Holy Spirit that Jesus left us: his legacy. Having said this, I think that it is important to recognize distinctions between the working middle-class that dad was born into and the more affluent professional class that I was born into and was being groomed for.

Traditionally, the working class has required less education than the professional class to meet its work-related agenda, such as a high school education in comparison to a college education. Presently, the greater demands for the working class to become more literate and technically skilled places a greater burden on the business and professional class to be knowledgeable of workforce requirements in their chosen industry or in general: to achieve greater mastery of the tools and techniques that are required by the skilled laborers in their chosen field or within the workforce at large. This is likely necessary in order to make them better managers and administrators. However, the point is that, as a general rule, a member of the professional class has developed better language skills than a member of the working class as a direct result of the standards for that class. Professional class members place greater emphasis on education, literacy, and intellect. As a result, they may have greater reading prowess, acquire a richer and broader store of concepts and ideas, and enjoy more advanced communication, both in terms of their thoughtfulness and their effectiveness in relating to other people. Such thoughtful and effective communication is likely to help the members of their household, their children, to negotiate their experiences without undue distress or emotional problems so that they can become well adjusted and thrive.

These class distinctions appear to follow Abraham Maslow's hierarchy of needs (17). That is, the professional class, enjoying greater affluence, can afford a higher standard of living. Its members are less concerned with meeting basic needs. They enjoy finer things in life, including greater opportunity for self and cultural enrichment. They may be more aware of the need to plan for their children's social and intellectual development, and they may be more likely to spend quality time with their children in order to ensure that they are happy and well adjusted. Effectively, their standards lead them to be more thoughtful and considerate as a class, in general. This is the equivalent of saying that they have a broader and richer mental or spiritual life. Although almighty God loves every one of us unconditionally without any form of malicious prejudice, the quality of our mental or spiritual life is necessarily determined by our educational and intellectual achievement and our corresponding language skills: the richness of our concepts and ideas, our reasoning skills, and our ability to communicate our ideas. Language skills are the medium for effective communication with one another. They are essential to negotiate our experiences in life successfully and to have a positive impact on the world around us.

Is the transition from the working class to the professional class difficult? As a general rule, I think that it may be somewhat difficult if it means transcending the typical norms and practices of that class, especially if these are the norms within a given family and the parents raise their children with the expectations that they will follow that tradition. The transition is likely to be less difficult if the norms within a working class family encourage educational and intellectual achievement, including proficient language skills. These people may be poised to advance due to their early training and preparation and their familiarity with working-class skills. Where did dad fit into this picture? I think that dad had the ambition to improve his lot in life and came to the States for that reason. I am not aware that he had very much in way of preparation for the transition from a working-class background to professional achievement, such as mentoring from a parent or someone else. He appears to have been more in the category of someone who had to struggle to make the transition, a task that he did not accomplish. Mom and dad's complacent choices did not place either of them on a path toward greater educational or intellectual development and, thus, compromised the development of their language skills. Alternatively, I was being raised in the tradition of an affluent, professional-class family. I was also being raised in a rich Christian tradition, not only by mom, but by a number of other positive influences: mentors and role models. I was happy and well adjusted. These paths were providing me with the opportunity for unencumbered spiritual and intellectual growth, including rich language skills.

I am sure that at some point, mom began to recognize the Christian spirit within me and to have reservations about my continued spiritual growth, eventually seeking to undermine it. I am sure that Dad was of a similar mind. The reasons are simple and evident, as the reader may have gathered. They both had had opportunities to pursue higher ideals that would have promoted their spiritual and intellectual growth and chose more complacent paths. While nestled within the bosom of a Cuban subculture of their choosing, where they could structure their social life to support their ways, they likely seemed the perfect couple: happy, warm, sociable, entertaining, and success-ful. However, it seems likely that in time, shortcomings in dad's educational attainment and professional development would have affected his advance-ment in the banking industry as well as his clientele or the quality of his busi-ness transactions within the real estate industry. Although such developments and the effects that they would have had on dad and mom's lives are hard to predict, we have firsthand knowledge of the effects that such shortcomings by dad as well as mom's academic and social-cultural underachievement had on their lives in Montgomery after they left Cuba for the United States in 1960-1961. They did very well, considering what their odds were and their children's accomplishments, but they did not thrive like they might have if they had avoided or made up for the shortcomings or underachievement mentioned. We were a solid middle-class family that provided the children opportunity for advancement, but dad and mom were not prepared to step into an upper middle class culture in Montgomery, which would have par-alleled their relations in Cuba. If they had made different choices earlier in life, they should have been so prepared.

Mom and dad, I feel certain, recognized my nascent spiritual life and Christian yearnings. This represented a dialogue that mom and dad were not promoting or did not embrace, and one that they could not share in directly without making some changes in their lives that would lead them back on a path to spiritual growth. It would, as a minimum, have made them uncom-fortable and it may have also made them jealous. Youthful Christians, striv-ing for ideals such as honesty and sincerity in relationships—for the spirit of truth—tend to bring to light wrongful motives and challenge people who are exhibiting those attributes to give them up. This perspective presented a chal-lenge to the way of life mom and dad had established for themselves—the paths they had chosen—which they apparently were giving no thought to changing at that time. Not that they were insurmountable, but considering one's past mistakes and taking action to correct them are both difficult en-deavors when a person has become accustomed to another way. Considering the difficult circumstances that mom and dad faced on leaving Cuba, they may have been more likely to rely on their habitual patterns. Most assuredly, they were not going to accept this form of criticism from a young child of theirs, however intended or unintended it may have been. Thus, the expected reaction may be what I have spoken of previously: they began fighting my spirit or mental life. I think that it happened as early as the conflict in Cuba with the maid of my uncle and aunt and my tantrum at age seven at Christmastime over a rifle meant for me that my mother gave to my cousin.

Mom (and also dad) made a decision to limit my undeterred mental or spiritual growth and its fruits: intellectual and social advancement. I feel that they did this by opposing me mentally at a subconscious level in ways that I have previously described. For example, in becoming unwelcome mental guests, they became privy to my thoughts and sought to undermine me by disclosing my weaknesses or vulnerabilities to people in my environment. They also promoted conflict between me and other people by subconsciously encouraging dialogue from them or me that the other would find fault with. Similarly, they tried to undermine or intimidate me by seeking to make it difficult for me to integrate reasoning processes and use good reasoning at important times, detracting from the quality of my ideas and my presentation of them. At a conscious level, they made comments or presented events to me that exploited my weaknesses and created binds that were difficult for me to negotiate without making a mistake and faltering along spiritual lines. Effectively, they sought to make me lose access to that mental state that provides a keen sense of direction and that facilitates enlightened thought. An early and limited example may have been illustrated by my feelings that there was something sinister about my brother George's frequent conflict with older boys during our youth, which placed me in the position of taking up for him as his older brother.

I do not know to what extent mom or dad may had exhibited this behavior, opposing another mind, in a relationship previously, particularly in a fairly permanent way, which I would regard as significantly maladaptive, in a worldly sense representing maladaptive personality traits and quite likely a personality disorder, at least in certain contexts. In a spiritual sense, this behavior represents a violation of fundamental spiritual laws, such as encroaching on another person's spiritual life for ignoble reasons. This maladaptive behavior, I feel certain, develops gradually. Like the illustrations of mom's behavior in college and as a newlywed in Montgomery, it can begin in contexts or settings that challenge us: situations that we have to negotiate well to avoid "hang-ups" or psychological conflicts. We are likely to break or ignore spiritual laws or warnings along the way, becoming more rigid, at least in certain respects, and sufficiently maladaptive that we violate another person's sanctity thus. The parallel behavioral characteristics that develop within us to reach such a state may be characterized as insecurity, fear, underachievement, low self esteem, jealousy, anger, resentment, greed, haughtiness, prejudice, hate, sloth behavior, and the like. This pattern is likely to violate some of the established commandments, such as "Thou shall not covet thy neighbor's goods."

Mom's motivation is not very clear amidst the immaturity that I have shown within my family over the course of my life and the many mistakes that I have made. However, there were a couple of family dynamics that I view as notable. One is that I became aware that mom did not want me and dad to get along, apparently because we might have then formed a bond that could have provided me the cognitive integrity to keep other minds at bay. This became increasingly obvious to me over the course of the many differences dad and I had in which mom often seemed to be caught in the middle. In a similar vein, I think she singled me out for attention during my upbringing, rather placing me on a pedestal before my siblings and dad. This behavior from her, I feel, was hard for them to take without promoting some jealousy, particularly from dad, who probably sensed some rivalry for mom due to the attention that she gave me. I believe that mom knew me very well, through and through. I recall recognizing her guiding hand in my mentoring of my brothers when they were young, but I do not feel that she directed dad and me in the same way to form good relations. This is like the reaction formation that I spoke about in Tuscaloosa: the lack of harmony with her and Conchita that I felt while we were seeking to build a life together here in Tuscaloosa as we socialized with neighbors and church members. I decided to place mom in Clara Verner Towers, a mutual decision that I spoke to the family about, because I recognized that she would not accept well my efforts to succeed. I knew that I could not count on her for that.

Dad, on his part, became very adept at evoking my anger, which tended to disturb my cognitive integrity or spiritual life. I think dad began to do this purposely for that very reason. This idea has been reinforced by negative transference that I have felt toward other similar persons in my life. That is a psychological term that refers to incidents when I have encountered other people that have evoked a similar negative reaction from me. These people likely had a role that resembled dad's and used similar tactics in their interactions with me, which had the effect of eliciting angry feelings from me due to the similar dynamics. Negative transference is most likely to occur during patterns of relating when the context, situation, and personality dynamics are similar to those that originally gave rise to the conflict or arguments. Although negative transference would generally be regarded as my problem, I have become more adept at recognizing this behavior that certain people elicit from me and rarely respond with any more emotion than becoming a bit emphatic. This is because I have had so many learning trials of this kind as to become skilled at recognizing the negative transference that is present and asserting myself rather than showing negative emotion in these situations. Just the same, these experiences have sensitized me to the personality features that dad employed to arouse angry feelings from me. Incidentally, the mental opposition and negative events in relations with my parents that I have described were not evident in Cuba as a general rule. This was likely so because I was yet very young, had many positive role models to affirm and direct me, in addition to my parents, and they had bountiful support and assistance to make them comfortable.

Some additional family information

I have previously described some of my role models and social influences. I will supplement those comments now with a brief sketch of some, including additional characterization of my father's family, which I have not provided previously. I will also make some brief additional comments about my father and mother's parenting styles in Cuba, in contrast to their parenting in the United States.

My socialization and education in Cuba were preparing me for a college degree and a professional career. I was also becoming indoctrinated in Catholic principles to become a member of the Christian community. The expectations of my grooming likely included development of proficient language skills and a vibrant spiritual life. There were a number of people who were an important part of my socialization in Varadero, who helped to shape my character and personality. First of all were my maternal grandparents, in whose home we lived. They were serious, reserved people who observed everyone's comings and goings and whose general demeanor commanded respect. My grandparents were fairly much in the background. They saw to much of the planning with assistance from the head servant, a young man who had been with them since his teens, so that everyone in the household was comfortable and things ran smoothly. They enjoyed the conversation around the dinner table with the "grown ups": their children and children's spouses.

My grandfather, Frank Smith, was a general practitioner who made house calls if necessary. His chauffer drove him to Cardenas and back daily. His oldest son, Ernesto Smith, was in practice with him. My grandfather made small impressions on me that formed the larger image. He prescribed a cup of pureed calf liver for me when I lost my appetite, and he burned off the wart on my forearm that I picked to a bloody mess. He drank bottled water and liked to have half a grapefruit every morning. I remember him calling me to his side at breakfast early one morning and asking me to taste from a golden, bead-like concoction that was simply delicious: my first taste of caviar, fish roe. He also firmly planted the toe of his shoe in my rear when I mischievously knocked over and broke the enamel eagle that decorated the dining room. One of my few memories of weeping occurred when I learned of his death from cancer of the liver as a 10-year-old in Montgomery.

My cousin, Francis Smith, who is several years older, informed me that our grandfather was not only a physician but also a businessman. He invested in the stock market in the United States, owned real estate in Havana, and owned a grocery store in Varadero that provided fresh milk and other products to the Varadero community. My grandmother, Concha Castro, I remember for her sweetness and kindness. Her share of her family's land in Varadero was managed by my grandfather. One fond memory of her was when she whispered for me to come to the pantry and treated me to the divine taste of a small shot of Sherry cooking wine with egg yolk. She came to live with us in Montgomery after my grandfather's death. She died much later from Alzheimer's disease at the Little Sisters of the Poor convent in Mobile.

We were a big and happy family, and there were many uncles, aunts, and cousins who influenced me. In particular, my cousins, the children of Ernesto and Maricusa Smith, were role models, probably because they were older, but also because they were so entertaining. They introduced me to such activities as baseball, bonfires, and cowboys and Indians. They were athletically minded, such as Pancho (Francis), who participated in rowing competition, which may have spurred my early participation in a swimming meet. They were always organizers of good, clean fun. I remember that my mother was having difficulty weaning me off the bottle of milk as a young boy when my cousin entered the dining room and proclaimed, "Freddy, you don't want to be a baby! Only babies drink milk from the bottle!" which cured me right then and there. We affectionately referred to them as "The Ticos" after the eldest son, Ernestico (Little Ernest). There was also the influence of the Sisters of the Brown Habit at the Catholic school that I attended from kindergarten until around November 1960 of the third grade.

I do not know very much at all about dad's parents, such as what sort of models for parenting they were, and how that reflected on his parenting style. He never spoke about his father to me that I recall. Both he and mom indicated that his mother assumed the primary responsibility for raising the children due to his father's inconsistent presence and corresponding limited contribution to family life. They depicted her as a woman of character, a positive role model who guided or influenced her children to espouse desirable values.

The oldest daughter, Ester, married a chemistry professor who was also a pharmacist, Dr. Pedro Vazquez, who had a reputation for being a studious man. Anecdotal information about him on coming to the United States during the exodus of Fidel Castro's takeover of Cuba was that he scored in the 90's on his pharmaceutical boards, which was unheard of. Ester was simple and kind, a good homemaker, and a gourmet cook. She preserved the peace Dr. Vazquez required for his studious work and was dutiful to him in every way, structuring her life and daily affairs to satisfy him, which was not apparently difficult anyway because they had similar simple, conservative values. Ester's youngest sibling, Maria Luisa, who was referred to as "Luisa," suffered from mental illness: schizophrenia based on the little that I recall about her, although mom, who said that Luisa's problems began during menopause, did not entirely confirm that impression. I have a vague and uncertain recollection of having met her once, about her requiring a caregiver due to her condition, and about her death as a relatively young adult. Mom informed me that before the Cuban revolution of 1960, Luisa was living in the home of her mother in Cardenas, where Pedro was teaching school. He and Ester had a home in the same neighborhood. They had Luisa over for lunch every day as well as looked after dad's mother. I remember the adventurous and benevolent spirit that prevailed within me when I had occasion to visit their home as a child, which I regard as good treatment.

I lived in Tio Vazquez and Tia Ester's home during the first semester of my freshman year of college while attending the University of Dubuque, where Pedro was the chair of the Chemistry Department. I recall that they enjoyed socialization with the families of other Cuban professors, looked forward to a good television program or two, and were regulars at church on Sundays. Ester portrayed the simple values that also guided my father, such as a strong work ethic, a belief in being altogether honest, devoutness in their support and devotion to one another, and a strong faith; namely, that if you walked a right path God would be with you, and they were God-fearing in that sense. Ester and Pedro both exuded positive energy along with their values and were very kind, nurturing, and affirming toward a nephew like myself.

Dad also had two brothers, Innocencio, the oldest, who was referred to as Tenso, and Humberto, the youngest, who followed Luisa. Tenso married a piano teacher, Mercedez, who bore their two children, Tensito and Luisito. Mom told me that Tenso had a superb mechanical mind. She said that he was an excellent electrician who made a living at this and other mechanically minded trades in Havana. Luisito informed me that his father also did clerical work for the Ministry of Finance and described him as a politician; that is, a man who took an interest in politics. Mom said that he got along well socially but was something of a wandering spirit: a nervous man who moved about. She felt that dad had similar characteristics, but dad was serious-minded and had acquired conservative values, which helped him to recognize boundaries clearly and prevented him from getting carried away on socially festive occasions. His ambitions were apparently more firmly rooted and clearly realized than Tio Tenso's, who may have lacked such direction. He was a more liberal man who did not have sufficient distinction of social boundaries for a family man to please his wife Mercedez, who decided not to stay with him. Mom felt that he needed dad's guiding hand. I did not see much of Tio Tenso in Cuba but acquired a favorable impression of him as well as fondness for my older cousins, Tensito and Luisito. I recall his familiar, engaging nature when he came to visit us in Montgomery.

My mother informed me that dad's younger brother, Humberto, married a Christian woman named Nora. Mom felt they were a happy couple even though they did not have a lot of money and did not have any children. She said that Humberto was not ambitious like dad or Tenso. He fairly much went along with what he had without seeking to change his lot in life. I do not have a recollection of becoming acquainted with him or Nora.

My recollections of my father in Cuba are of a cheerful, happy man with a good sense of humor who usually greeted me with a positive note. I do not recall ever being spanked and only occasionally scolded or admonished, such as when picking up a baby precariously from a crib. I remember my excitement when he purchased me my first bicycle, a colorful red bike with streamers at the handlebars that I quickly learned to ride. Dad, who worked in Cardenas and did a real estate business in Varadero, was often not around.

We had servants or maids assigned to supervise us. Most if not all of the household chores, cooking, and many of the errands were done by servants, which provided dad quality time with us when he could provide it. Given that he was usually satisfied with his business pursuits, we children usually encountered him at his best. Occasionally, he took me into his office or took me along when he engaged a business client, but not so much that I acquired a good glimpse of his real estate business.

My mother and I bonded well in Nicaro and Varadero. I was filled with wonderment as she told me endless stories about biblical people: of Mary, Joseph, and Jesus, martyrs and saints, miracles, and the like, which were concrete descriptions that became the foundations for my values and my faith. My imagination was similarly captivated by her children's stories: traditional stories about the Big Bad Wolf, the Three Little Pigs, Little Red Riding Hood, Cinderella, Snow White and the Seven Dwarfs, the Tortoise and the Hare, and biblical stories with a moral or virtuous theme. I adored every minute of our engagement. She showed me the panoramic view of Nicaro and Varadero that I came to know. I usually let her know what I was up to, and, I imagine, that she learned to trust that I was not going to fall in harm's way because she gave me a free rein.

My tromping grounds in Varadero were bounded by the beach to the north, the South Sea to the south, across the street to the east, and one street over to the west. To give you an idea of my free rein, I would walk to school with my sister Rosemary and my younger brother George, which was ten short blocks to the east. At lunchtime, a minibus would bring us home for a span of an hour or so, during which time I would be off to the beach for a swim or surf-fishing. There were countless things to do within these bounds as to captivate a child's interest: roller skating in the bank parking lot across the street, playing marbles with children that resided catty-corner from us, straddling the fence surrounding the house, drawing earth crabs from their holes, catching chameleons, flying a kite, catching snails in the South Sea, dogging the two Perez teenage boys on the street to the west as they shot blackbirds with their BB guns, swimming with goggles along the black rock formation of Varadero Beach to observe and try to catch the tropical fish that made their home there, and swimming out to the sand bar to grasp starfish basking in the sun. Like dad, mom was not encumbered by many of the regular household duties and seemed to have plentiful quality time for us children. I do not recall a cross word between me and my mother in all my time in Cuba or even before high school in the United States.

Mom and dad's parenting styles or parenting was much different in Cuba than in the United States as a result of the different demands presented by their circumstances. In Cuba, we were ensconced in a rich family and traditional way of life that promoted desirable values and behavior. The structure of our lives, including the assistance that my parents had with the daily routine and the typical congenial, positive atmosphere made parenting easier and allowed for opportune parental intervention to promote learning. Even though their parental roles were favorable in Cuba, mom and dad's complacent decisions about the course of their lives limited their ability to take a more active leadership role in directing their children's lives and to be visionaries for their children. The limits their choices placed on academics, intellect, and professional development, each in his or her own right, affected their language skills and spiritual growth, all of which had a bearing on their parenting skills. Their choices also affected their parenting attitude towards me by leading them to undermine my strivings for an abundant and fulfilling life—socially, intellectually, and spiritually—my strivings to become an accomplished Christian person.

Socialization in the United States of America entailed a different culture that provided much more room for error. I was no longer ensconced in a supportive and affirming environment but one that was sometimes rejecting. Similarly, I could no longer take comfort in a tradition that served my needs well or a structure that I knew well. It was all new and subject to learning, by trial and error rather than proven paths, providing a much wider margin for mistakes, problematic situations, and the like. I had lost the broad, guiding hand of thoughtful mentors and positive role models. Additionally, for the reasons that I have explained, I could not expect my parents, who were now more exclusively my guiding forces, to have my best interests at heart, at least not in some respects, while I was pursuing a rich and vibrant spiritual life that they could not share in without first making some basic changes in their lives.

David Anders, the Catholic theologian who reviewed my book, commented that he was not convinced from my opinion that dad settled for a less advanced career or that dad had compromised his Christian ideals, such as his Christian vocation to family and God. He also felt that my claim that "the quality of our mental or spiritual life is necessarily determined by our education" was greatly overstated, noting that many saints have been uneducated. He felt that the text confused spirituality and social advancement.

My response to David's first point is that God calls us to a rich heritage if we but put him first in our lives. He provided dad a rich training ground and tremendous opportunity to advance his lot in life and grow closer to him. Dad did not capitalize on that opportunity. He settled for a less lofty and more complacent goal. This affected his academic, intellectual, professional, and spiritual advancement as well as his place with the Christian community and with God. He did not subsequently take steps to rectify his mistake.

My response to David's second point is that a saint is in a special class that requires me to point out that I spoke in general terms about the relation of education and social advancement to spirituality. A saint is someone who has responded to God's call and become baptized into a life with Christ. His bounty is the inspiration and enlightenment of the holy spirit of God, a great teacher. God will lead him along right paths to become ever more perfect and knowledgeable. He will be capable of recognizing and rectifying his mistakes and will be capable of communicating very clearly, explicitly, and convincingly within his acquired body of knowledge. This is a course to ever-greater social advancement. It is also a unique form of education.

CHAPTER 12:

GROWING UP IN MONTGOMERY: EARLY PARENTAL INFLUENCES AND FAMILY LIFE

The United States of America represented a challenge for all my family. We were thrust from a world in which we were very comfortable, where our basic needs were well met, and where we had considerable guidance, direction, and opportunity to find our place in society, to a world in which we would have to struggle and succeed relatively more to find such direction and opportunity. It represented a major adjustment for all the family, especially my parents and the older children. My mother and father's roles as parents were more challenging, demanding, encompassing, and visible to all of us. My younger brother George and I had adjusted fairly well at Saint Thomas on the Hill in Birmingham. We had been fairly close in Cuba and stuck together as well as made friends with other boys at the Birmingham school. We had learned the English language but were struggling in school within a culture that we did not know intimately. I had always been a good student and had to settle for being average or less. George was not faring quite as well.

We were relieved and assured when dad and Rosemary visited us around January 1961 to tell us that the family would be reunited in Montgomery after we completed the school year. At the time, Rosemary was staying with Mabel Harper along with my sister Ana Maria and my brother Mickey, who was an infant. Arthur, who was but one year old, and Conchita, were residing with the Joe and Mary Louise Troy family, good friends whom dad and mom had made previously in the States. My mother was to deliver my brother Raymond in Cardenas, Cuba, in March of 1961 before coming to the States by way of Puerto Rico, an arrangement dad had previously made. My youngest brother Frank was born in April of the following year. Dad had been busy re-establishing himself in accounting with the help of Robert Troy, Jr., a certified public accountant whose father had mentored dad previously. Other friends that he had made, such as Fred and Mary (Troy) Schaum and Albert and Mary Roemer, were very supportive. These were also members of the Catholic community in Montgomery.

Mom and dad were good parents. They made a good team. They never bickered among themselves. Dad liked to have a good drink after work from time to time to relax him, but he never got carried away. Mom drank occasionally with dad. Dad was a good provider. He was busy from sunup to sundown establishing his accounting business. We were struggling financially at first and accepted help from friends occasionally, such as clothing. We never seemed to lack for anything in a substantial way. Dad was a bundle of positive energy. He found time for family in events such as church functions, invitations from former friends or from clients, and our annual vacation to Destin, all of which were enjoyable. He was not the type of parent who could talk to you or talk things out with you in order to explore your ideas or concerns and give you feedback, at least he was never that way with me. He and I did not relate very well. I do not remember that he ever sat me down and had a good talk with me other than as part of an argument except for when he encouraged me to enter the accounting field when I was a young man of 21 years. Considering his responsibilities, it would have been difficult for him to contemplate his parenting methods in order to change or improve upon them. He also may not have had very much time to get personally involved with me during that period of time.

Dad and mom were not the sort of parents who could talk things over with you at a meal in order to explore your activities and relationships so they could discern that everything was okay, at least they were not that way toward me that I can remember. Dad kept up with us though, either by asking us questions, learning from mom, or from our response to his wishes. His parenting was fairly simple. He would be happy with you if you had done as he expected you to do; otherwise, he tended to get on to you, to chide or scold you, and if you were not willing to cooperate, then that would lead to an argument and sometimes a spanking if he lost his temper. That was not so unusual considering his responsibilities for such a large family. He did not relate to me very well, which may have been partly due to our class differences; that is, although he was my father, my vast role models, schooling, and other influences in Cuba had led me to a scholarly, or upper-middle class, or affluent identification and the corresponding mental life at both a conscious and subconscious level. He, on the other hand, was more of a practical, down-to-earth, common man. He had not been able to transcend those origins to also become a member of the class that I was being groomed for in Cuba. We never grew close in Cuba—not as close as I was to my mother. I knew very little about what he was truly like before we came to Montgomery except that he always treated me well, he was my father, and I cared for him for those reasons.

Dad and I did not relate very well, but he did try to do things for me. For example, when I did not make the elite Dixie Youth Little League bunch that played baseball at the Cloverdale School field, he was one member of a group of parents who formed a new league, the Southeastern League, in order that a considerable number of other aspiring baseball players would have a chance to play. He became treasurer of the league and had a minor accounting role, I think, which may have been an enticement for him to become involved. I think that dad and I, as father and son, would have been an ideal union if we could have mustered it, like a child who develops socially, academically, and intellectually and brings up the family in doing so, but that does not happen without the unselfish support of the parents. I honestly do not think that my father was ready for such a role or relationship with me. If he had come to recognize its merits, my mother would not have stood for it, I feel certain. I think that our class difference made it hard for dad to relate to me and me to him. I have the idea that he may have been a bit daunted and envious of me, recognizing the difference, including some sense of competition for mom's attention. I did not have the capability at the time, all things considered, to understand him well enough to make an impact on our relationship without him or someone imparting knowledge to me of the way that he was.

Dad and I had some conflict from the start in Montgomery. He would regularly assign chores for me to do such as washing the dishes or raking the carpet of leaves that two large pecan trees would drop on the front yard. These tasks were not beyond my capabilities, yet they were not easy either for a nine-year-old boy. I would sometimes complain to mom, who would then plead my case with dad, who would become angered, and who would occasionally become upset with mom for assuming that role. Dad's common retort would be to chide me with comments such as, "You're not too good to do the dishes!" or "You're not too good to rake the yard!" Of course, he was right.

Mom, it seemed to me, was fairly much in the background. She was socially capable but had not, in my estimation (as I discussed earlier), developed assertive leadership skills, just as dad had not achieved the transformation in the accounting field that would likely have made him a better parent. At an individual level, a little talk from her might have done me a world of good. I adored her and would not have wanted to do anything to violate her trust in me. She might have sat me down and spelled it out for me by saying something to me such as, "Look, Freddy. Your dad is working day and night to build an accounting practice. He is tired and weary at the end of the day. I have to see to the needs of all the children, including a baby and a toddler with very little help. You are the oldest son and we are counting on your help. Please don't let us down. I can let you know what is expected of you in the way of chores. You will still have time to do a lot of the things that you enjoy." I may not have liked it very much, but I feel that I would have complied and learned a valuable lesson. It would have made me closer to dad, more than likely, and I would have set a good example for my brothers and sisters.

It is hard for me to judge my mother's motivation at this point in my life. I described previously her and dad's psychological development to their established lives in Cuba, what that would eventually mean for their offspring, and what it would mean for me. I could only recall a couple of instances during that time when I felt my mother's hand may have been at play in undesirable behavior by me. In this particular situation in Montgomery, she had me. I was making a big mistake by not being a dutiful son. I could plead or bargain with the best of them. I pleaded my case with mom, and she beseeched dad on my behalf. This was a pattern until I finally had a falling out of sorts with mom during high school. I remember that day. I came home with just one more excuse, she looked at me for the first time as if to say, "Son, that's not acceptable," and I looked back and said (not in words), "Mom, something doesn't seem right to me, but I do understand that things are not the same between us."

Looking back on it, I feel that by this time mom had had her way; she had compromised my spiritual life. I think that statement by her also meant that she felt that she had gotten the upper hand and could now support dad more directly. I did not judge or criticize my parents at that point in my life. The first time that I looked at their behavior in a critical way was during a visit to my younger brother George's grave one evening when I was about 32 years old. I remember how difficult it was to scrutinize their behavior. To do so even a little, I would encounter a punishing superego, in Freudian terms. I had already had a couple of bouts with schizophrenia, and my mother, as I eventually came to understand, was one of my primary antagonists: an unwelcome guest that was privy to all my thoughts, all the time. She was aware of my every move at a subconscious level. I have also come to understand that the rest of my family—my father, brothers, and sisters—similarly opposed me in varying degrees, some not very often and only in certain circumstances. They were my superego, and to try to scrutinize any of their behavior in a critical way, at the onset, was anguishing for me. I was filled with guilt, as if I had sinned and fallen from grace. I would have to recover from that state and consider their behavior again when I regained myself.

Did mom exploit my attitude toward chores and toward dad when we were starting out as a family on College Street in the summer of 1961 when I was nine years old? Today, I cannot say for certain. Mom's behavior has puzzled me throughout my life. I found her to be shrewd, keenly alert, thorough, and quick to grasp information within a social realm that she was familiar and at a customary level of intellect. At other times, in apparently similar situations, I found her to be inept and slow-witted, seemingly unable to grasp the gist of things. In addition, to my incredulity, I learned that mom, regardless of the situation—whether having a medical problem that I was assisting her with, considering an important decision such as whether to allow a needy neighbor to stay with us temporarily, how dire the situation and how demanding it was of us, and her dependence on me due to her old age—was also alert to any mistake that I might make that might compromise me psychologically or spiritually, if you will, which she might then exploit. Once again, I feel that she acted that way not only because she would have had me fall from grace to bring me down a few notches from the spiritual or mental life that I enjoyed, but because she was also able to compromise my cognitive integrity at those times: to access my mind for her own thought. I will continue by saying that if mom had had the parenting skills to coach me when we were starting out in Montgomery, or if she had been motivated to do so, I may have avoided a serious mistake and we may have fared better as a family for it. She did not rally me like that, and neither did dad. I also did not observe that they motivated and promoted us to improve as a family in that way. They would promote a family spirit on social occasions, but their differences and mine were there beneath the surface and liable to emerge. This was a disharmony that my siblings were aware of, and which I feel that the public sensed and gradually came to know during their encounters with us.

I eventually came to the conclusion that the variability in mom's behavior was representative of maladaptive personality characteristics that I have spoken of previously. That is, if the situational dynamics were right, say a group of people that shared her values, such as being smart about living but not totally scrupulous, among whom mom could build support at a conscious or subconscious level, so that she would become entirely comfortable among them, mom could be confident and capable socially, take on roles that did not seem customary for her, and so on. In that similar situation, I could expect trouble, such as conversation that included content to make me uneasy, events that tested my principles, and other challenges to my general well being. Alternatively, among a more scrupulous group, mom was more likely to be dutiful, scrupulous herself, and more in the background: timid and meek. She often created that impression while she was raising us—that of a meek, timid, unassertive little Cuban lady who was very sweet (she was 5 feet, 2 inches tall and weighed around 107 pounds). She kept up with all of us as did dad. That is, she asked questions to learn our activities and would ask us if anything was wrong if we looked the part. She was not inconsiderate of us, nor was dad. There was just this other side to her that I came to recognize as her unconscious motivation and her reasons for it. She would act the best she could as often as she could, but if pressed to it, she would show her other side. It was either that or change her behavior for the better. She was not going to do that in the family or social culture that she built for herself.

I have faced a number of antagonists in various settings who have become permanent mental adversaries for periods of time. It is well near impossible for people who experience schizophrenia as I have known it to escape this legacy because their families are adept at keeping potentially supportive people at bay and collaborating with other mental adversaries to perpetuate the mental opposition of the person who is experiencing schizophrenia. I have had mentors who have been successful in helping me succeed at my endeavors, increasingly so as I have gained knowledge of what schizophrenia is all about. This knowledge or experience has helped me to be better prepared for and respond to situations wherein I face people who would take advantage of me if given the chance. This seems to speak ill of a lot of people, but it is a facet of human frailty and failing that we all need to work to overcome—these negative thoughts and emotions that we can harbor toward another person—due to their limiting nature in terms of our spiritual life and what that means for both the victim and the perpetrator. They are as subtle as insecurities that we experience, feelings of needing to best the other person so as to come out on top, jealous feelings because someone demonstrates a skill we do not possess, and so on. In the subconscious or spiritual world, if we hold on to these ideas and emotions, we are adversely affecting those toward whom we harbor them. We are not aware of these effects that we have on other people very much and can only change them by immediately recognizing that ours are the wrong ideas and emotions and resolving how we might respond better or by arriving at that conclusion later so that we do not repeat the behavior.

My family is not any different. I have to be thankful for the good my family has done for me despite any shortcomings. We would have to be considered a closely-knit family. At a conscious level, we have always supported one another in time of need without hesitation. We have put differences aside at such times. I could have had a family that failed to give me such support or that abandoned me in times of need, but that has never been the case. They have been outwardly supportive in my endeavors as a general rule. The issue is that they sought to place me in the design they had for me and not God's design, and I would not acquiesce to their design for me, not at the cost of my heavenly inheritance. That is not to say that their subconscious opposition has not been daunting and difficult, overwhelming me with mental illness at times. I have had an epic struggle with them. This is also true of other people who would exploit my vulnerability arising from a lack of permanent bonding with someone who can shield me from a mental opponent.

My mother and father, as I have noted, made a good team. They were both capable of being sociable and warm. Dad was a source of positive energy as he built a practice in Montgomery. They had support from a number of friends and clients. Dad was an outgoing, extroverted personality. He loved to engage and entertain his clients. They enjoyed his company, liked or loved him dearly, and continued to retain him year after year. Mom complemented him well on those social occasions. They both knew how to entertain and make others comfortable. Mom may somewhat have been the little Cuban lady in the background at times, seemingly rather shy and reticent, but she was alert socially and got along well. She was as well liked as dad in her own way. She knew how to portray him to clients and friends in a comical way, and how to tease him. They were still having a romance, very much in love, and she was his song and dance. When he was courting and socializing with clients, taking a drink and being very extroverted, she may have seemed reticent, but she was right there with him. As I have noted previously, she was a socially active person. She loved good food and good entertainment. She liked to get out and do things.

Dad and mom were intimate. They were in close communication daily. Probably not one thing transpired that the other did not know about. They communicated about their children also. People involved in such a relationship know one another's thoughts. They communicate intimately at a conscious and subconscious level. They recognize one another's feelings. For these reasons, I feel that it would have been impossible for dad not to have recognized mom's motivation toward me, such as any misgivings that she had about my development on a spiritual plane, insecurities that this may have created for her, her growing possessiveness towards me, her efforts to undermine me or change my course to one of her making, and the like. Recall also that in terms of their intellectual growth and spiritual development, they had both made compromises and followed an agreed upon course, so that they were of one mind in terms of motivation and action. Considering that, I feel that dad was not only aware of mom's feelings about me but likely had similar sentiments.

Dad was very sensitive emotionally, very aware of class differences and the like, and more likely to display basic emotions, such as anger, spite, and jealousy. He really knew what to say to get under your skin, which reflected his underlying sentiment. I remember his cat calls during the days when I would shirk my responsibilities at home to have a good time with more affluent friends: "You're just a pretty boy!" and "You're living in an economy that you can't afford!" If dad did not have similar feelings as mom, and I feel that he did, mom saw to it that he did and that I did not form good relations with him. She gave me a lot of attention as her first child. At some point, I feel that mom used this for her ends. I am referring to when we established residence in Montgomery. She often placed me on a pedestal during family gatherings before my dad and my siblings; she singled me out for discussion in an elevated way to the extent that other family members at some point would have likely felt left out or have become somewhat envious, especially someone as socially sensitive as dad and particularly in regard to his and mom's relations. If that were not enough, her pleads to dad on my behalf made him feel that she was favoring me and playing a dual role rather than being a dutiful wife, which also hurt our father and son relationship.

Mom and dad's motivation was not known to me at the time, but it became obvious to me later that they fought me on a psychological or spiritual plane. The same can be said about my brothers and sisters. We were a closely-knit family. We interacted every day. All were privy to many of the events of the others, including their friends, activities, interests, social interaction, and the like. During those circumstances, over time, subtle behaviors and nuances come to light, and this was so in our household. Dad and I frequently argued or bickered about my failure to shoulder more of the responsibilities at home. These scenes were visible to all family members, who were influenced to form their opinions and to eventually take sides, whether they expressed their opinions or not. There is usually a complementary internal dialogue that follows such argument or actions, usually led by the parent or family leader—their internal voice—which can take many forms, such as a statement by mom like, "Don't worry about your brother. He is just going through an immature stage. He'll come around to being responsible about his chores in time, I feel certain. You don't have to be mean to him" or "Your father is right. Please don't listen to your brother." Of course, I was in the wrong about that, which could be made clear to children, either directly, or indirectly by means of internal dialogue, or by both means. What then were my brothers and sisters to think?

My vindication here lay in the soul and conscience of every brother and sister and parent. Granted that what I was doing was wrong. However, each one of us has a further sense of right and wrong than the obvious or the visible, which is determined by our subconscious or spiritual life. It is hard to follow that inner conscience when faced with contrary visible evidence and the inner voice of a parent that is swaying you in a similar direction. But we can often feel it when we say something that is wrong, or think it. We can have a deep sense that there is more to a situation than meets the eye, and we can stake steps to uncover such events in order to bring them to light for our awareness. That can arouse our ire or anger when we witness an event that can lead us to side with a brother or a sister against a parent. It takes a lot of courage but it does happen in such a way. This was not an easy go for me. I always found it difficult to agree with dad on things—things that were reasonable, such as the requests that I have spoken about. He was practical and had much energy for fixing this or that about the house, yet I never felt that energy imparted to me. I never felt at home around him when I was assisting him. I always felt a sense of disharmony that was distressful psychologically, even when I was trying to be a dutiful son, which makes me think that there was something else at work. This, as I have come to understand it, could only have been psychological opposition from dad, or mom, or both, and, possibly, from some of my brothers and sisters. Once again, I always felt as if I was working against the grain when helping dad and similarly found it difficult to agree with the things that he asked of me. I believe that internal as well as external dialogue can be very helpful in these instances, such as, "Help your dad out, Fred. It is not going to take you very long. And he will truly appreciate it." That can change a person's demeanor to become agreeable. I was deeply religious. I find it hard to believe that I would not have responded to appeal and support of that sort from my mom.

My dad and I argued and bickered throughout my school years. We were not always at odds. We got along when there was not some contentious issue to settle, when I was complying with his requests, and at a number of other times, but this difference that we had came between us. He did not approve of my behavior, and that was not going to change. It did not until I matured, after I completed college, married, and got a job. Whether he and mom meant to adversely affect my spiritual life, my failure to be a dutiful son affected it. At the core of my being, whether I showed it or not, I was deeply religious and faithful. My relationship with God was the most important thing in my life. However, throughout my upbringing in Montgomery and into my adult years, I could not be at peace with myself in a variety of family and group situations, and this was because I was not reconciled to these differences that I had with my father. They stood in the way of my peace and harmony, and they affected my social adjustment. It was like an albatross around my neck or a thorn in my side. I remember once that one of dad's farmer clients invited our family to his stead for a lovely afternoon with his family that included horseback riding, rustling with calves, and good food—lots of fun. I recall the sense of humility when our family of nine children

piled into the small Opal station wagon that was our means of transporta-
tion. And, I recall at the end of the day, when our families were gathered for
dinner, how I felt disgraced at this family event. I could not share in the blessings of the day.

David Anders makes reference to the claims that I make about my parents opposing me on a spiritual plane and asks me to provide support for
this assertion.

The entire body of ideas contained in this book is designed to support
this assertion by me. Broadly speaking, God calls all of humanity to grow
closer to him, out of his love for us, because this is the path to happiness.
He provides us the opportunity to do so, fairly, according to our merits, giving us choices. Good choices gain us a greater share of a spirit life with him
and the Christian community, meaning insight and enlightenment to light
our path and direct our way. We enjoy a better mental state for reasoning
and comprehension, which influences our academic, intellectual, and social
development. Poor choices obstruct us from obtaining this measure of God's
grace, which has such a profound influence in our lives. Essentially, God
wants us to apply ourselves so that we can access more of his grace, achieve
greater perfection, and be more successful in every way. When we fail to rise
to occasions or opportunities that he provides us, there are repercussions.
Our psychological selves are obstructed and limited by those poor choices
unless we take corrective actions, which means we will eventually face the
consequences of our choices, whether in the short or long run. Some examples of these consequences might be decreased ability to relate to other people
successfully, including emotional and personality problems, a less vibrant social life, more limited parenting skills, and less success in our work.

These choices and our consequential development then act to support
the premise that our psychological makeup resulting from our choices influences the world about us and the people with whom we interact, whether in
a positive or negative way, according to our spiritual development. The more
advanced we are along spiritual lines, the greater the positive impact we have
on the world around us; the less spiritual we have become, the more likely
we are to have a detrimental effect on those around us. It does not always
work this way, but it is more difficult for the less enlightened to act in a lofty
way, though that struggle is at the essence of their opportunity to improve.

This aspect of our lives, referring to our influence on the world about
us, is governed by the spiritual or subconscious world in many respects,

which is a consciousness that we may not be much aware of or understand. It is a marvelous world that everyone will enjoy learning about—another dimension to living that will make our lives more meaningful, giving us greater direction and understanding. In chapter 3, "More About Subvocal Speech," I discuss ways that the subconscious complements the conscious world in everyday living and provide various examples of subconscious life and subconscious influences in group and individual situations. In chapter 2, "More About Mental Opposition," I discuss two apparent reasons for the mental opposition and provide some examples of how I think it has been manifested.

The support for my assertion that my parents opposed me on a spiritual plane is grounded in my explanation of how they made complacent or poor choices, which affected them to have a more limited spiritual life and more limited development in other important areas. I specifically described choices they made that did not appear to be well considered, opportunities they likely missed as a result, and how these poor choices likely affected their spiritual life and their corresponding progress in such areas as social advancement, academic skills, and professional development. When we have such shortcomings, we may have a more detrimental or less positive effect on the world and those around us. This is caused by the attendant emotional and personality conflicts, such as envy of people who seem to be more skillful than we are; resentment of people who appear to be more charming, charismatic, or sociable; and discouragement about our achieved status, which can lead us to affect other people negatively. Consequently, if a child does not accept parental efforts to limit his development along spiritual lines due to their shortcomings and, instead, pursues Christian ideals that will lead to a vibrant and abundant spiritual life in which the parents cannot share, the parents may become indignant at this action by the child, and they may begin to oppose the child subconsciously, on a spiritual plane.

CHAPTER 13:

A FALLING OUT WITH MY BROTHER GEORGE

My life in Montgomery had parallels with my life in Varadero, at least initially. That is, I had my tromping grounds and was into everything and anything imaginable that boys like to do, which I made reference to previously. Mom knew pretty much what I was up to from asking me and George, my younger brother, who was usually at my side, particularly at first. Despite the fact that I was not doing right by dad, I had a strong spiritual foundation from my Catholic upbringing in Cuba and sought rightful paths. I had strong values and was drawn to people with similar values, as a general rule, and I sought to instill those values in my brothers and sisters. For example, I did not like cursing, did not tolerate prejudice, and valued honesty. I liked good, clean fun. Our sports games were always fair-minded. We played by the rules, chose sides evenly, and played in a spirited way. I was drawn to those athletes who were exceptional leaders on the field and likable off the field. They were good and decent people. Thus, my spiritual life had been compromised, but I continued to nurture it. I did run into challenges, including some that tested my mettle, and some that got the better of me.

It was not soon after we moved to College Street when George and I became acquainted with a neighbor who was several years older and much taller and bigger than we were. We were not in the same age group, but I think the newness and curiosity that we both shared led us to regularly spend time together. As can happen, there was some conflict that he had with

George—an argument that led to shoving and the like. I felt responsible for George and reacted like I had on a similar occasion in Birmingham. That is, we teamed up to bring him down and got him to back off. Some time passed before he came around after that, but he eventually began to come around again. Well, it happened that he became angered at George again and hit George, right in front of the house. I became indignant and reacted by socking him in the belly with all my force. To my relief, he doubled over, and I think that he began to cry, but the best thing was that he left. It was one of those occasions where I felt that I had taken on more than I could chew.

I previously mentioned that George seemed to always get me into these sorts of situations. Even though he was always at my side, and I did not forsake him, he and I did not seem to be of one mind, and I felt that that meant trouble for me. Later events in our lives led me to believe without doubt that George was working with my parents to undermine me during those times when I was placed in the position of acting in his defense—that he instigated trouble for me. It got the better of me one day. It was around the summer following my completion of the fifth grade at Cloverdale and George's completion of the fourth grade. Dad had purchased a residence on Felder Avenue that became our home and which we all liked, notwithstanding that Dad had to build two rooms and a bathroom in the attic as well as turn the garage into another bedroom to accommodate our large family. The home sold for something like $12,000 dollars in 1963 and required a monthly payment of $100. One of my classmates at school lived nearby. We often encountered him at the community center or ran into him on passing his home. We were friends and did things together. He was better developed physically than most of his peers, so that no one cared to challenge him.

This classmate tested my mettle a number of times. There was an instance during the fifth grade when the exterior of the school building had been freshly painted. He reached outside a window, swiped paint on his fingers, and smeared it on the interior wall, leaving two streaks of paint on it. The teacher, on entering the classroom, immediately remarked, "Who smeared that paint on the wall?!" and he replied, "Fred did it," to which I retorted, "No, Mrs. Rogers, it was him," referring to my classmate, who was then admonished by her. Afterwards, word got around that I was going to get my butt beat at recess, which did not surprise me, but when the time came, this classmate apologized. I think that he did not want to challenge me at that point in time because he did not have the upper hand. On another occasion, he got the better of me. It must have been the summer after the fifth grade, when it happened that George, him, and I were together and paid a visit to the Cloverdale Drug Store, where George, who apparently had some money, purchased an ice cream cone from the soda fountain. As we exited the store, there was some difference between George and this classmate. Perhaps he asked George for a bite of his ice cream cone and George said no, or perhaps he was just being mean. At any rate, he knocked the ice cream cone to the ground, and George started crying. I had no reply. I should have challenged him right there and then, but I did not.

This was one of those situations that I have relived in my mind a thousand times. I am not sure what got the better of me, whether he had whittled at my confidence successfully or some other reason, but I do know that I backed down by not challenging him and that I acted like a coward. After that, I screamed to high heaven. I was very angry and took it out on George. It was my reaction, not something that I thought about or that I was aware of as to what motivated it: only that I was angry at George and began putting him down, such as calling him stupid and not wanting him to be around me any more. It was behavior that I did not seem to have control over or know how to right. My parents obviously became aware of it but never questioned me about it that I recall. Years later, on considering this recurring issue in regard to my association with George and the development of his mental illness, I became convinced that he and my classmate were working together that day and got the better of me. I think that I reacted so because I felt disgraced. I had made a mistake on a spiritual realm that brought me down. George and I continued to associate, but we did things together less often, unless the situation called for it. We engaged in similar activities, such as basketball and baseball, but he began associating more with his friends and I associated with mine.

George and I helped dad build the upstairs of the house except the bathroom and the stairs, which were done by contractors. It was not a good time for me, although such an endeavor sounds like it could be interesting, worthwhile, and a good learning experience. Dad needed to put it up fairly quickly because he had business responsibilities and because the family needed to settle in. Once complete, the house was a lot roomier. I did not like the thought of being around the house. I sensed that it was not going to be good for me. I think that it was because I felt that mom and dad were not grooming or stimulating me in ways that helped me to thrive, whether it was something that had been contrived by them or that had developed from my failure to follow their wishes. I think the two reasons could have been complementary.

I felt a strong need to break into the peer group for my age at Cloverdale Junior High School. I did so in Pee Wee football during the seventh grade, when my ability to quarterback the team led me to be accepted and recognized by my peers. The rest seemed easy. I was a good athlete and became a member of an upper middle class group that nurtured me. On days when I felt distressed due to home life, such as when I had disagreements with dad, they would lift my spirit. They spoke my language. Let me draw a parallel. Working with groups of people who experience mental illness, personality disorders, and behavioral problems is a very challenging and emotional experience. It is most important to greet them with a positive air and confidence that comes from preparation and experience. At the end of the day, it is not unusual to feel drained and rather low. I go to the YMCA and work out regularly. There is never a day after a workout that I do not feel positive and upbeat, ready to plan another day and excel at my job, and excited about what I am doing. My peer group renewed my flagging spirit. I was more upbeat and more of a source of positive energy at home. Would it have been so bad to stay at home in order to please dad, who felt that I was overdoing it by playing football, so as to please him and my mother? If I had had the insight to follow the mold they designed for me, I think that Almighty God would have blessed me all the more, and they would not have been able to hold me back if they had intended to. I did do that in a sense when I joined dad in his office after becoming a certified public accountant. After five or six years of that, God began calling me to do psychological work.

My brothers and sisters knew of my friends and my peer group from my relations with them. Although they recognized the differences between dad and me, they all seemed to recognize me because of my social standing, to look up to me in varying degrees, and to admire me, or to at least act as if they did. My four younger brothers—Arthur, Mickey, Raymond, and Frank—who had but five years of difference between them, stuck pretty much together. They also were paired, the two youngest, Raymond and Frank, being separated by just one year in school, and the next two, Arthur and Mickey, by just one year also. They were always around when I was home—drawn to me fairly much like magnets—and I felt mom's guiding hand in the values and rules that I implored of them. This was fairly much a supervisory capacity that she delegated to me while they were relatively young, before they reached their teenage years. They were all studious and did well in school. Arthur and Frank are engineers, Mickey is a doctor, and Raymond is an accountant. I always encouraged them to study and apply themselves in school, and I was very proud of their accomplishments. They were boosters throughout my pursuits before college and beyond, always giving me their attention and affection, though they stuck together fairly much, fared very well, and were dutiful to their parents. They were young enough when we came to the States that they did not seem to have any adjustment problems, at least none that persisted and got in the way of their goals.

George had some very good friends that comprised a very good peer group like mine, but he was easily influenced by some that were perhaps less conforming. I was also. He got in some trouble in the eighth or ninth grade that hit the news and was very embarrassing to me. I know that that was the wrong sentiment to have, but that is the way I felt. Looking back on that time later, when I better understood George and my family dynamics, I felt that George may have acted that way—become involved in those activities—out of anger toward me, in order to get back at me. That may seem far-fetched, but he recognized that we had experienced a falling out of sorts, that I was pursuing an independent path, and that I was thriving in relations with my peer group. My parents recognized this also. Thus, as far-fetched as it may seem, I think he may have engaged in that behavior in order to get back at me, a pattern that I think continued until and after he became mentally ill. The embarrassment that I felt about his behavior created greater distance between us—I rather pushed him away—which may have made him feel more isolated and estranged and could have been breeding ground for his mental illness, although I do not think that it worked that way necessarily. He got in trouble again around the 10th or 11th grade and had to attend Lyman Ward Military Academy. He attended Sidney Lanier High School subsequently during my freshman year of college, but he began to have problems and had to drop out of school. It was then that he was hospitalized due to mental illness.

CHAPTER 14:

HIGH SCHOOL, COLLEGE, AND TWO BOUTS WITH SCHIZOPHRENIA

My senior year in high school at Jefferson Davis (JD) High School in Montgomery was memorable. My football coach used a defensive strategy that promoted my quickness at middle guard, which helped me to excel. We won all our games except for a tie with Lee of Huntsville and were ranked seventh in the state. It was a memorable football season for all of us, with many standouts. I made the first team all-state roster. I already enjoyed good relations with my peer group. Beyond that, my popularity soared. I began dating a girl that I had dated less seriously in junior high school and gave her a promise ring. We were promised to one another. Her father was a radiologist. He welcomed me as her suitor. She attended Stratford College in Virginia her first year while I went to the University of Dubuque in Iowa. We had plans to attend the University of Alabama the following year.

This girlfriend brought a new dimension to my life that I did not fully recognize at the time. It was a dimension that I received in a more transitory way from my peer group, but it was more constant from her. This was the origin of some degree of spiritual life between us. That is, we started an internal dialogue that began to help me at home and later in college: that bonding that can act as a protective shield from an unwelcome mental opponent. She got along very well with my family. My brothers and sisters simply adored her. She invited my sister Conchita and one of Conchita's girlfriends for a visit to Stratford College on a special visitation weekend, which thrilled

Conchita. They had good relations. During my freshman year at the University of Dubuque, we were frequently in telephone contact and saw one another several times during the course of the year. I developed good study habits and made practically all A's. When I reflect on that time, I recognize that our bonding was helping me in regard to my ability to grasp and retain schoolwork. I did not recognize then what our relationship was doing for me cognitively.

My decision to attend the University of Dubuque was not well considered. I think that I was experiencing the origins of what we describe in psychology as schizotypal thinking—a prodromal (early, preceding) symptom or precursor to schizophrenia. Schizotypal thoughts are unusual ideas that may not be sound or that lack good judgment; they are poorly considered, eccentric ideas that can lead to problems if they are carried out. This was the time when Vietnam antiwar sentiment was at its peak and students were questioning our institutions (e.g., established societal ways). High school and college kids began trying to make a strong cross-cultural statement by their clothing, hairstyle, and other habit patterns. The lyrics of the rock groups of the time complemented these trends with their statements and had large followings, some promoting or glamorizing a drug culture that had grown up alongside the anti-war movement. Marijuana sporadically found its way to selected members of my peer group after my senior year of high school. These patterns were not prominent within my peer group but were portrayed in varying degrees and influenced me. I decided not to follow the traditional course that many of my friends were following, perhaps listening to some of the eccentric or non-traditional members. That is, I decided not to immediately attend the University of Alabama and join a fraternity, for which I was fortunate enough to have been recruited by virtue of membership in my peer group and some of its members who spoke up for me. I decided to "go off to school," my first year, to see another part of the country and learn what "other people" are like. My uncle, the husband of my father's sister Ester, a learned pharmacist, taught chemistry at the University of Dubuque. They offered me their home if I should want to attend school there.

I still had a love for football. I had been recruited by a couple of small Division 1A college schools in Alabama, one of which was Livingston College. I had some films sent up from JD and was offered a small scholarship to play at the University of Dubuque. I started on the varsity my freshman year. I lived with my uncle and aunt during the first semester. After making some friends from playing football, I joined a small fraternity and moved into a dormitory for the second semester. I had been introduced to marijuana once during the summer after my senior year of high school while in Montgomery. It was at a party of my peer group, around which I was entirely comfortable. I had not been exposed to much of the lore of marijuana at the time. I remember the spacy, surrealistic feeling, getting the munchies, raiding the refrigerator, and acting silly. I did not give this experience much thought. It was not particularly good or bad, but I did not like my mental state the next morning, a sort of dullness and some degree of distress or dysphoria. It was not a refreshed mental state. I smoked marijuana at the University of Dubuque a few times. It was around, and some of the guys I knew smoked it from time to time, including my roommate, who was a member of the football team. He was a nice guy from a good family that lived in a small town just outside of Chicago. We became friends and had other friends and associates throughout the school. Mine were from football, classes, and the fraternity I joined. My roommate was one of my closest associates.

Marijuana rarely turned out to be a good experience for me. I think that I was very vulnerable whenever I used it. I felt more sensitive to influences from other people, including opposing forces from my subconscious. I seemed to lose the cognitive integrity to be assertive and felt inferior. I feel certain this was the result of subconscious opposition that downgraded me very effectively. It created a mental state that made me susceptible to mental illness. Similarly, my mind would always contemplate religion and God, the purpose of our existence, and other heady religious thought related to my Catholic faith. I was also filled with a sense of guilt due to my shortcomings, which I could not escape. I withdrew into myself. This was not a good experience. Sometimes, I would have a sense of paranoia in social settings due to my misgivings and some degree of distortion in perception related to the speech, tone, and expression of other people—the magnification or greater intensity of emotion from them that I would feel. I had heard about the lore of LSD. It was something I never intended to do. One evening, my roommate approached me and told me that he had done a "hit" of LSD. He acted like it was great and said, "You should try some." I told him that it was not for me. He began to plead. I told him, "No thanks." He started becoming upset and told me that he was going to have a bad trip if I did not do it with him just this once. I acquiesced. I did LSD a few times. It affected me much like marijuana, but to a heightened degree. It was a more intense experience. I sometimes felt entirely dispirited and depressed at the end of the experience.

I had an attractive offer from the University of Dubuque's football team quarterback to share a dormitory room during our sophomore year. My girlfriend wanted to transfer to the University of Alabama. I was not acting like a proper suitor, such as doing things with her that showed commitment to mutual plans for the coming year and career choices. I was searching for direction and unsure of what I wanted to do. I was noncommittal about our plans. At times I spoke to her about some of the heady ideas that I had about religion and existence. I also spoke of some of the challenges to society and established ways that liberal college students and other liberal groups of the times had raised. This dialogue continued into the summer, when it became necessary for us to make choices. When I could not decide, she decided for us. She broke our relationship and decided to attend school in Texas, where she could pursue her interests in teaching. I finally decided to attend the University of Alabama.

I lived in apartments at the University of Alabama with friends from my peer group in Montgomery, some of who were in a fraternity. They would invite me to their fraternity house so that I did not feel left out. I had my heart set on medical school, which was not a very realistic idea because I had a poor foundation in chemistry and algebra. After I made a "C" in my first chemistry course, I reasoned that I had not made the grade for medical school. You don't get in medical school with C's, or so I had been told. I anguished over this result, which was discouraging. I decided to change my interests to psychology, but I was not sure if that is what I really wanted to do. My occasional use of marijuana and LSD did not help. Periodically, I had an experience that made me susceptible to mental illness, such as withdrawing into myself, low self esteem, guilt feelings, and general distress or dysphoria. I think this was the effect of my punishing superego getting the better of me at those times: my subconscious opposition. These events were distracting influences that kept me from focusing more determinedly on academic goals. I needed a guidance counselor to direct my education because I was unsure of the direction that I wanted to take and feeling mounting stress or distress from the knowledge that I was living on borrowed money that I would have to pay back. However, I did not have the good sense to seek one out. No one had guided my education before.

My junior year, around November 1972, the mounting stress from these experiences overwhelmed me psychologically. I began to get messages from the television. How does this happen? When your subconscious mind begins to awaken from sufficient distress, lack of sleep, and the resultant twilight state, you begin hearing the voices of other minds. Thus, I could watch The Tonight Show and hear Johnny Carson say something to me at a subconscious level. Television personalities are capable of hearing you in your living room and responding to you. That is a miracle of the human mind, which can transcend space and time. It could be a recorded show, yet television personalities can perceive you watching their show and respond to your thoughts and ideas at a subconscious level. They can even display affective expressions on the television that are consonant with what they are saying to you at a subconscious level if your unconscious mind is awake enough to perceive their persona. Johnny Carson can do that today from the grave. He can be revealing about the person that he was like.

This idea may seem difficult for the reader to conceive. It is an elaboration of the subvocal speech ideas that I have introduced, such as the idea that we hear every idea that we think, that subconscious communication occurs mind to mind (we hear the voices of other minds), that we are capable of getting such messages from people who are not in the room, and that in fact, we communicate in that way with significant other people in our lives regularly, throughout the day, as we plan and organize each day, such as our children, which may help to explain why some parents intuitively sense when something has gone wrong with respect to a particular loved one. Thus, why would it be far-fetched that we could communicate with a loved one who is deceased, particularly during the period immediately after his or her death?

I think also that our relative state of spiritual enlightenment may be a determining factor in these regards, meaning that relatively more enlightened minds may be the most privy to such communication, such as a deceased parent and a living child who continue to communicate. Although this may help to explain the phenomena reported by the mentally ill—that they have references from the television—I agree that this is a most unusual ability. That is, that the mind of a person who has never seen you, by virtue of appearing on a television show, and a taped one at that, can recognize those people who are watching and respond to them at a subconscious level, mind to mind. I may not be able to provide more proof or corroboration for this virtual miracle of the human mind than, for example, to tell the reader that I have had immediate concerns relieved by subconscious messages from reporters or other radio or television personalities. They recognized my concerns by reading my mind and responded to them from the television set, at a subconscious level. My concerns were then relieved from pertinent information that satisfied me. I would add that before I understood schizophrenia and mental adversaries, I was more likely to be influenced by television messages that promoted paranoid experiences, such as messages that preyed on my fears of falling short of Jesus' expectations of a Christian. Just like people whom we encounter daily, at a subconscious level, television personalities can be adversarial or supportive.

These messages from the television, as I just mentioned, and other influences, such as my ideas or perceptions when I smoked marijuana, took on religious connotations for me. These influences were primarily adversarial, such as antagonists that exerted their influence at a subconscious level. They seemed to recognize my vulnerabilities and exploited them. These experiences were an aspect of what is termed paranoid-type schizophrenia. I felt compelled to lead the life of Christ more directly, as one might do by following the Bible. I was not acting rationally, seeking guidance, and planning accordingly. This culminated in a psychotic break. I dropped out of school and returned to my parents' home in Montgomery. Subsequently, I was hospitalized at Jackson Hospital in Montgomery due to a schizophrenic episode. At the time, 1972, one of the prevailing treatments for schizophrenia was electroconvulsive therapy (ECT). Dad told me something about it beforehand, I think, but I really was not sure what to expect. After two or three treatments, I called dad and told him that he "had to get me out." I felt that I might experience permanent harm because after each treatment, I was very forgetful, to the point of not being able to remember people I knew. Dad got me out.

I enrolled at Auburn University at Montgomery (AUM) during the winter quarter of 1973. I was having mildly mentally ill experiences in school, such as a heightened sense of negative emotions from other students during their class participation, as if their emotional tone was directed to me in a negative way. One of the courses I took was Zoology. It requires a lot of memory work, which I was not entirely up to after ECT and the mild mental illness that I was experiencing in class. I got an incomplete in Zoology and obtained C's in Economics I and Economics II. After a lecture from dad, I decided to pursue an accounting curriculum. I had been working part time in his office during tax season, preparing income tax returns. However, I was not quite up to school yet and withdrew from Introduction to Accounting I during the spring of 1973, but I enrolled again in the fall of 1973 and made an A.

The holiday season arrived. I had been experiencing some degree of depression after broken relations with my girlfriend, not making the grades for medical school, having a psychotic break, and dropping out from the University of Alabama. I was not my usually confident, pleasant self around friends. The attendant negative emotions made me susceptible to mental illness again. I began to receive more intense messages from the television. This was a harrowing experience. In the midst of another psychotic break, I ran my car into a tree. I was in the hospital for injuries to my knee, ankle, and heel.

I resumed my accounting curriculum in the winter of 1974 and made A's and B's. I began frequenting a residence that had become a hangout for local friends, where I was drinking more than usual. Occasionally, I struggled psychologically. When the next holiday season arrived at the end of the year 1974, I struggled more. On one particular occasion, I had a serious bout with mental illness, when I was overwhelmed with compelling paranoid ideas like those that had preceded my previous accident. I was filled with trepidation. It was my good fortune that I saw college friends, a couple, at a residence in Montgomery shared by several female friends. This couple invited me for supper and also invited a girl named Pam whom I was acquainted with from high school and college. She had attended Sidney Lanier High School. We hit it off pretty well and began to see one another. She was and is a very practical and bright girl whose common sense and organization were just the treatment that I needed. I made the Dean's list the last two quarters of school at AUM and graduated in September 1975. We married one week later. After a honeymoon in Destin, Florida, I began work for one of the leading accounting firms in Montgomery, a middle-sized firm where dad had received training early in his career—one of the successors to Ed Harper's old firm.

David Anders made this comment on reading the chapter: "Fred, the material about Johnny Carson is deeply, deeply troublesome and incredible. You present absolutely no evidence that this takes place, only that it takes place."

My response to David is that I have provided substantial evidence that we are essentially bilingual: that we communicate daily at a conscious and subconscious level. Subconscious communication does not require someone's physical presence. That someone might be a boss, co-worker, teacher, someone we have recently called and are about to engage, people with whom we have a joint, vested interest in some enterprise or task, and other relationships that we have. Subconscious communication occurs between these parties to facilitate their relations and coordinate their activities. It is a facet of everyday human existence, although it may become clearer and more helpful as we grow along spiritual lines to develop a vibrant or charismatic spiritual life, meaning subconscious dialogue. Thus, we can communicate mind to mind in this fashion with anyone across the world. There are ample signs that this occurs if we but consider them, some examples of which I have provided. This is a miracle of the human mind.

When I began to understand this phenomenon of our subconscious, on hearing messages from the television, I reflected and thought, "How can Johnny Carson communicate something to me right here in my living room?" I then realized that our mind is not only capable of communicating with a person who is across the globe, it can perceive people who view a motion picture or a live or taped television program that the television personality is in (e.g., as an actor, a newsperson) and respond to that person from wherever they are, including the grave, at a subconscious level. Usually, this is not trite, although it might involve tomfoolery if it occurs between a television personality and a mentally ill person who has bizarre ideas or whose opposition the television personality aligns with, which is unfortunate because the television personality can make the mentally ill person's experience worse. My impression is that, as a general rule, we may not often communicate with a television personality unless we have some common interest that is pertinent for such an exchange. Furthermore, it would be less intimate to the extent that neither has conscious awareness of such an event.

The idea that we can communicate with a deceased person is not hard to conceive, such as a parent with whom we have communicated at a subconscious level throughout our lives. I agree communication with television personalities is hard to conceive. Perhaps it would help to consider my comments that a mind or soul can literally grab another mind and become entrenched there, set up permanent residence, become privy to the unwilling host's every thought, and influence the host's environment, recognize complete strangers from such a perch, and create difficulty for the host-victim. Additionally, people in the victim's environment can, in turn, at a subconscious level, receive those messages and act on them to influence the victim. That is a remarkable capability of the human mind. I provide some support for its occurrence in this book. This phenomenon, which I have specifically encountered and know to be real, provides my explanation for the schizophrenic signs and symptoms described in chapter 1.

CHAPTER 15:

ACCOUNTING, MY MARRIAGE, AND ANOTHER BOUT WITH SCHIZOPHRENIA

I was grateful for this accounting opportunity. It was a tremendous challenge. An accountant for such a medium-sized firm had to relate well to seven partners, fifteen to twenty other accountants who had varying levels of authority and responsibility, and a bookkeeping staff amidst a friendly yet competitive atmosphere. To advance within such a firm, one had to also relate well to business owners or business managers and their employees while sizing up financial information and communicating it to the client and the partner in charge, ever alert to new business opportunities and managerial advice that could help the client to prosper. In my four years with this firm, I became certified and advanced from a junior accountant status to a senior accountant status. I was not ready to be a manager and departed at that point.

I experienced some resurgence of schizotypal thinking during one engagement, which I spoke to Pam about and overcame, and I had resurgence of schizotypal thinking during at least two other engagements, during which I struggled but managed to complete satisfactorily, likely due to able help, yet lacking the discipline and mental integrity that is incumbent during a public accounting job. I became more meticulous or exhibited perfectionism during one of these engagements: obsessive-compulsive behavior that has been referred to as the glue that holds the personality together to avert a psychotic break. I helped the firm to profit during my stay but did not make money for them when engaging that particular client. These schizotypal experiences that

I have mentioned, including the perfectionism noted, I feel certain, were mediated by subconscious forces.

I have a good example of an experience that I attribute to oppositional forces or unwelcome mental guests while working for this accounting firm. It occurred while I was the accountant on a job for a local builder under the supervision of a partner that I particularly liked. The job involved cost accounting. Under the partner's able mentoring, I was proceeding well. I had firm grasp of the accounting concepts involved. What happened next was puzzling. It seemed that I lost his good direction, became entangled, and had to figure some of the work again. Although I had not identified oppositional forces at the time, this event was so palpable to me that I sensed something unusual or beyond my control had happened, and I sensed that the partner realized it also. I did not do so badly on the job, but I did not excel like I should have. Today, I attribute that event to the anger of an unwelcome mental adversary coming between the alliance I was building with the partner. I remember another audit engagement with this firm, which was my last one before my employment with them came to an end. The partner in charge was a bright, young guy whose genius became obvious to me during the engagement of the rope or cord manufacturer, which also involved cost accounting. Under his able tutorage, my work was steady and true to the end without any hitches.

Many young accountants leave a firm of public accountants to successful careers in accounting. These firms are good training ground that provides newcomers to the profession an opportunity to become certified. Oftentimes, these young accountants join the management team of a client of their accounting firm as a chief accountant, controller, or other middle management position. The most viable opportunity for me at the time appeared to be to continue in public accounting as a sole proprietor or to form a partnership with dad. Dad and I did not relate well enough with one another at the time to form a partnership. It appeared that such a form of business was going to lead to misunderstanding and argument from the inception. Ultimately, we decided to share offices and expenses, which proved to be a good arrangement. We had no problems after reaching that decision. This was a mutually beneficial endeavor. I was able to help dad upgrade his income tax practice and computerize his bookkeeping services along with mine, and I was able to retain some of his clients for year-end accounting or tax services that were needed, such as those requiring financial statements with an opinion. I was also able to pick up other clients requiring an audit or accounting opinion. Furthermore, on dad's advice, I purchased a small tax practice that provided me as many tax clients as I could manage (and as many additional tax clients as dad wanted). Thus, fairly quickly, I was providing a full range of services and kept very busy.

Ours was fairly much a family atmosphere, although dad and I managed our mutual businesses independently. My older sister Rosemary, who had received training from dad in the past, became my able bookkeeper and tax assistant. She was shrewd about my relations with dad and advised me to merely share expenses with him after witnessing the contention that a partnership was creating. Dad had trained a young girl from age 18 who was like a family member due to her long association with and dedication to dad. After Rosemary and her family moved to Lubbock, Texas, around the end of 1983, Rosemary found someone to take her place. At that time, I retained my mother to pay my bills, do my personal bookkeeping, and do general office clerical work, which provided her the business sense to manage her household expenses after dad's death.

My son Matthew was born in March of 1979, the same year that I left Jackson, Thornton, & Company, the firm where I received my training, and became a sole proprietor. Pam, a graduate from New College at the University of Alabama in three years and a statistician for the Retirement Systems of Alabama (Dr. David Bronner's place), took off from work to nurse him for 20 months. He was an active, energetic child and a joy to raise. Pam and I were both raised in the traditions of the Catholic faith but were from quite different backgrounds. As a result of my psychological problems and needs, I had not been able to be sensitive to her emotional needs. During Matthew's early childhood, we began to have some conflict, some related to my desire to be more assertive in the marriage with regard to parenting methods, and some related to my business practices. I had become more of a perfectionist in my business again, the so-called glue that holds the personality together. This was a sign of stress that showed in less efficient management of my business, which required more of my time, excess worry, and disturbed sleep. I was not keeping opposing forces at bay quite as well. I became more preoccupied with religion, what we refer to as religiosity, and had another psychotic break. This was around the late fall of 1982. To the best of my recollection, this is when I began hearing voices in a sustained way.

Mom and dad took me to Meadhaven (now Crossbridge Behavioral Health) on a Sunday. I had become rather non-communicative with the growing realization of my behavior and the consequential dismay. I remember speaking to June Hassell, a very nice counselor who was part of a group of mental health professionals in practice with a psychiatrist at Baptist Medical Center South in Montgomery, of which Meadhaven was the hospital's psychiatric unit. She and my parents had to decide whether to hospitalize me or treat me as an outpatient. In what was a gutsy decision, she told me that she would be willing to try outpatient services if I would agree to take Mellaril, an older antipsychotic medication that was commonly used at that time for the treatment of schizophrenia, and if I would agree to participate in weekly individual therapy with her. My relief and gratefulness to this person (and my parents) at a time when I felt helpless was immeasurable. As it turned out, this marked the beginning of marital therapy, which provided me the additional validation that I needed to work things out and thereby achieve greater psychological well being. Incidentally, after a brief time, I asked my therapist if I could discontinue the Mellaril, because it seemed to be compromising the mental integrity that I needed to be at my best at work, which we did on a trial basis initially and permanently when I had no further problems.

Pam and I decided over the course of therapy to break relations. We divorced on January 13, 1984. She retained custody of Matthew, and I had visitation rights every other weekend. Matthew had participated in counseling from another member of the same group that Pam and I used for individual and marital counseling. Later, in kindergarten at the Montgomery Academy, his two quite exceptional teachers called Pam and me together and told us that Matthew was showing some rigidity, likely a sign of stress from our divorce. They advised that it was usually helpful for children under similar circumstances to spend time with their friends. Subsequently, Matthew and I enjoyed getting together with a number of his friends on weekends, doing such things as swimming, attending basketball games, playing in the park, visiting neighbors, playing putt-putt, and hiking nature trails. It was fun getting to know his friends and their parents. More importantly, his rigidity quickly passed.

June, my therapist, and I, had two sessions before we began marital therapy, and we continued for several or more sessions after we terminated marital therapy. I remember how distraught and distracted I felt before our first session due to the adversity that is a part of schizophrenia: the mental struggle and internal stimulation. However, June seemed to reach to the core of my being and to draw my undivided attention, so that I was able to focus on her every word and perceive everything that she said with great clarity. I think this was the beginning of my ability to live in two worlds simultaneously and tame the voices. I quickly learned that my daily achievement at work tamed my mental illness—the voices and mental opposition—insulating me from the effects of mental illness. The voices were not all that prominent after our first meeting, and I was able to keep them at bay so that they were not altogether bothersome. However, I also learned that schizophrenia is not an experience that goes away. No matter how successful I was during the day, and I often soared, there were unwelcome guests, opposing forces if you will, ready to greet me at night, undermining me while in bed when one has less mental control, keeping me awake until I became exhausted, and awakening me to a distressful mental state that follows a restless night. At those times, the subconscious mental experiences—voices, subconscious messages, and mental antagonism—became more prominent and more distracting. It took me longer to get organized.

I may not have fared as well if I had not been a sole proprietor who could determine his schedule. My response was to stay in shape, such as running 10 K races, the 6.2-mile outdoor races that became popular. I only ran in two but was in regular training and built up to running about seven miles daily, after which I was always exhilarated and obtained a new lease on the day. Additionally, if I needed to, I was prepared to do extra work in the evening so as not to get behind. With this formula, I was able to succeed in my practice. Additionally, I was beginning to master the simultaneous influence of the conscious and the subconscious.

CHAPTER 16:

SEVERAL PSYCHOLOGICAL BREAKTHROUGHS

There were notable events that I became aware of from an awakened subconscious. In that state, I was more aware or likely to perceive the emotional component of a conversation. Dad's secretary was like a family member. She had been with dad for many years, had fairly much the run of the office, and was fairly set in her way of doing things from long practice. She was not well educated and was somewhat sensitive to a professional like myself who sought to upgrade dad's services. One of the first things that I did was to set up a checks and balances system for income tax returns to ensure that any errors in preparing a return were caught. I am not sure whether it was demonstration of that technique or something else, but one day, when she and I were the only ones in the office, she said something to me like, "Freddy, I don't know who you think that you are coming in here and telling me all this stuff. Your father and I have been working here for years without any problems. What makes you think that you can come in here and take over things just like that?" I was quite surprised by these statements but became much more sensitive to her feelings after that and did not have any further problems with her. Dad supported most of the recommendations that I made to him, recognizing how they would benefit his practice, and she learned to adapt and probably liked the changes, which were beneficial.

My office was situated next to dad's secretary's office and his office, which were part of a suite. I could readily hear their chatter. By this time, I had trained myself to maintain objectivity and focus while also having greater cognizance of subconscious influences. Without any intention, I began to notice from where I sat in my office, the emotional component and subconscious dialogue between dad and his secretary, which was frequent and ongoing for considerable periods of time. What I began to notice about it was that they seemed to be keeping up with my business dealings throughout the day at a subconscious level—a sort of running commentary of what I was doing—with some of their opinions or feelings interjected. In other words, they would frequently chit chat, and this dialogue between them seemed to have a primary motivation of tracking my ideas at a subconscious level. To my recollection, I discerned this because I could hear some of their subconscious statements. A consistent theme was that when everything was going well with me and my practice, negotiations with my clients, and what not, the emotional component of their commentary was like one of concern or disappointment; but when I ran into problems, such as when I made a mistake or had a dilemma, the emotional component of their dialogue took an upbeat turn, as if they were relieved or exhilarated. It seems possible that dad did not feel so much this way as his secretary, but there was enough corroboration for me to discern that both she and dad experienced some jealous feelings, apparently due to my higher achievement and know-how. That is human nature to some extent, meaning that similar dynamics may often take place in similar situations, which creates a climate wherein a business is not likely to be as successful as when its members are able to work together cohesively.

I felt these aforementioned events were significant. They went a step further than me hearing the content of statements by adversaries to discern that an adversary was reading my mind or becoming privy to my thoughts; they identified the motivation of adversaries by noting positive or negative responses from adversaries based on the content of the thoughts they heard. Let me expound on significant events at the office a bit further.

It was the 1985 tax season. I had divorced two years earlier. I had a good income tax system in place and had polished my tax practice. In the midst of regularly interviewing income tax clients and completing their tax returns, there was one particular day when I was encountering a lot of mental opposition. I am not sure if I immediately noticed that it was coming primarily from dad's secretary, but at one point, amidst the struggle, perhaps because I was more tired that day and had less mental fortitude, though I felt alright, I noticed, unequivocally, that she was affecting my ability to perform operations on my calculator. Neurologically, she was affecting my hand to be less coordinated—stiffer, if you will. She was affecting my motor nerves. This was brief, and I was able to overcome it, but it opened my mind and made me much more aware of the effects of this omnipresent interpersonal experience and all that it may explain, perhaps not all the time in some disorders, but at least some of the time. Such events as waking up with back pain, as if I have been sleeping wrong and my back has been twisted, a possible course to scoliosis; spontaneous seizures; cerebral palsy; some severe cases of arthritis that I have noticed; and countless other medical conditions or physiological effects. Some of the basic, everyday functions affected that I have become aware of include urinary frequency and bowel movements.

I have sometimes been affected by a mental opponent to have to urinate at sporadic times, when it is an inconvenience to do so and when I do not have a very full bladder, to the extent that I am literally about to pee in my pants and have to constantly flinch not to do so or to avoid having a preliminary squirt. When I make it to the bathroom at these times, I may experience great resistance, such as a strain that holds back the stream and slows it down. Similarly, when having a bowel movement, I have noticed the facility or difficulty in having one, depending on the ambient culture. Furthermore, during a relatively long-range relationship with a mentor, including a potential romantic partner, I noticed her beneficial effect on my digestion and elimination, such as my ability to ingest large amounts of food and both digest it and eliminate it well, without becoming constipated, unless under circumstances when I was temporarily not subject to such mentoring or my would-be partner and I were not having harmonious relations, particularly if I was eliminating at a location where the ambient culture was unfavorable to me neurologically. Besides the elimination functions, one physiological effect that I notice keenly from mental opponents is their ability to induce drowsiness beyond that which I would normally experience and particularly at inopportune times.

This is a constant struggle, especially because I frequently sleep fewer hours, a pattern that has become the norm for me during the past six years and which I am able to accomplish by staying in good physical condition. I am relatively certain that my mental opponents are deriving mental energy at these times, which provides the motivation for then to affect me in that way. To counter this mental opposition, I have learned a number of tactics to stay awake, such as standing to do my work, taking a little break from office work by going out into the patients' living area, reading or working at another location, washing my face, and doing another task, if it is not itself a distraction. My best tactic is a catnap. I have mastered this strategy. I can take a 5 minute catnap almost immediately, almost anywhere, and at anytime. They are refreshing and invigorating and can pick me up for the balance of a morning or an afternoon, although, I must say, my opponents have become very determined in this regard. These physiological and neurological effects of which I have spoken here are a facet or our daily existence. We all face them when under interpersonal stress and seek to counter them in various ways, perhaps oftentimes with medicine, a primary example being the tension headache. They are a reflection of the relative sensitivity and compassion with which we regard one another and why we instinctively or intuitively recognize an environment as being friendly or unfriendly for us or our loved ones.

These experiences are surely more frequent and ongoing in mentally ill conditions where the victim is subject to the mental adversity that I have described. These comments are not meant to discount purely physiological explanations, such as the natural bodily response of the need to go to the bathroom as the bladder reaches fullness or the need to have a bowel movement as the digestive tract fills with waste. They are also not meant to disregard impaired bodily functions caused by injury and disease. But they can be imposed on these conditions due to interpersonal conflict or the ambient culture. Thus, I hope that increased awareness of this phenomenon will lead to positive steps to remedy these problems as we recognize them, such as the need to be sensitive to one another, to provide the most beneficial structure for various populations, to demand character from personnel, and other criteria.

John Toppins, a learned psychologist who reviewed my book, effectively asked me a number of questions like one might expect in defending a dissertation. My responses to his questions have led to helpful editing throughout the book that have enhanced understanding of and provided support for my ideas. On reading the comments about the neurological effects that I detected from mental opponents, he challenged me with a number of questions, such as, "How can someone influence another person's behavior to this extent? … Is it possible that there is another explanation?…" He noted that the reader may have experienced urinary and bowel problems that were related to stress or anxiety and may ask, "How is this different from what I experienced?" and also, "What is the evidence that it's one and not the other?"

Furthermore, he remarked, "The reader may be wondering if drowsiness isn't simply occurring because you weren't sleeping very much," and added, "The familiar question comes up, 'What is the evidence?'"

My first response to Dr. Toppins is that I think that I know myself well enough to recognize when someone is badgering me in such a way. In addition, I would say to Dr. Toppins that because these experiences have become a part of the fabric of my daily life, I sometimes do not pay them a lot of attention, but I can provide corroboration. Recently, at times when I have been very tired or fatigued and hardly able to stay awake, a mental opponent has fairly much had his way with me. That is, on catching myself about to nod off to sleep, I have been awakened to the anger of the adversary literally shaking my head robustly while I have been in such a susceptible state. I was not mistaken about this force that was extraneous to me.

Catholic priests have provided among the most illuminating psychological discourses that I have heard. I recall one such homily by Father John Fallon, a former pastor at Holy Spirit Catholic Church here in Tuscaloosa. Part of his homily went as follows: "If Jesus could speak to humankind today, he might tell us: 'You have developed such technology as to achieve great control of your environment, which has provided you with greater comfort and a longer life span. Your architecture has shown tremendous advancement. You can harness energy to provide power in order to meet your needs. Advancement in flight, electronics, and communication has transformed the world into a village of cultural exchange (this was before the proliferation of the Internet). You have advanced modes of travel, command of the air, the land, and the sea. You have placed a man on the moon, built a space center, sent aircraft to explore the planets and return information to you. Your knowledge has advanced to make you skilled at these endeavors, and you have developed great institutions for learning and governing. But, you still have not learned to live with one another.'"

Pam continued living in our home after the divorce. I moved in with mom and dad for several months and then moved into the second story of a nice home in the Old Cloverdale area, which was in a nice section of town. The second story had been converted into an efficiency apartment with two bedrooms. The owners, who lived in the spacious first story of the home, were a relatively young couple with two children younger than Matthew, who was five years old. There was a nice couple with four children across the street with whom we became acquainted. Our next-door neighbor was a nice person who worked in state government. She was very good at entertaining Matthew, often with a young girl who lived next to her, the daughter of a partner in an established Montgomery architectural firm. It was not too far from our family home, and I felt that it would be a suitable place to raise Matthew, as it turned out to be.

It must have been around the spring of 1985 when I invited Conchita to live with me. I felt that she was much too dependent on mom and that it might help her to become more independent. I realized it would not be easy—an added responsibility—but I was managing relatively well at the time and decided to give it a try. It did not work right from the start. When I lived at home after my divorce, Conchita occasionally exhibited what I recognize as passive aggressive behavior. She could often seem in the way, trying my patience, and so on. Recall my comments when I tried to teach her how to manage our home in Tuscaloosa—when I provided her training in household chores. In this apartment, Conchita seemed passive aggressive all the time. It seemed that everything I did, or planned to do about the house, she beat me to the draw. She was right there ahead of me in the way, whether I needed to use the bathroom, open the refrigerator, wash the dishes, or go down the hall from one bedroom to another. And, she was not facing me; she had her back towards me. I soon had irrefutable evidence, if I had not had it previously, that her subconscious mind was tracking me, hearing and visualizing my every move, and she was placing herself in position to obstruct it. I think that after several weeks, I decided that my idea to help Conchita become more independent was not working very well, after which she moved back in with mom and dad.

CHAPTER 17:

MY BROTHER'S SCHIZOPHRENIA (AND OTHER EXAMPLES)

I was at the University of Dubuque when George began to experience schizophrenia. I have previously mentioned early influences that could have had an impact on his later adjustment and development, such as our falling out and some trouble that he got into. There was also the placement at Lyman Ward Military Academy away from home and the subsequent change of high schools in Montgomery from Jefferson Davis to Sidney Lanier. During that period, a primary influence appeared to be friends who followed the culture that had migrated from the hippie movement in San Francisco and the West Coast to Montgomery as to music, dress, drug use, and other elements of that culture, including gathering places.

George had musical talent, acquired an electric guitar, and was "into that scene" so to speak. He had not seemed very stable after getting in trouble during the eighth grade and needed direction that he did not have. He had friends with good backgrounds, but he did not need the influence from the lyrics of the hard rock bands of the time or the mind-altering experience from marijuana or LSD. He was not a good student. He seemed to struggle in school academically, and I think that he sometimes got into trouble for behavior such as skipping class. Thus, school was not the steadying influence for him that it can be. That result, his involvement in the counter-culture or subculture that had arisen during that time, and his use of mind-altering drugs were forms of stress and precursors to mental illness. Another factor could have been dad's disapproval of his behavior, which led to conflict between them at home.

George experienced the type of schizophrenia that has been termed "disorganized type." I say this not from having firsthand knowledge of the diagnoses he was provided but from his behavior and my knowledge of this pattern of mental illness. Disorganized schizophrenia, as you might imagine, is characterized by disorganized speech and disorganized behavior. George would look at you, grin broadly, and might say something such as, "Freddee!!" really emphasizing your name, and he might repeat this sequence of behavior regularly. He sometimes assumed rather fixed stares for long periods of time without saying much of anything. He had a penchant for cigarettes and would regularly ask for one. If he did not get one from someone such as mom, who was weaker than him, he might become angry and say, "You better give me a God damn cigarette!" His mood could change abruptly, particularly if he got the cigarette, at which time he might say happily, "Maria!" with exclamation while patting mom on the back. Once he had the lit cigarette in hand, he might talk some and was liable to regularly drop the cigarette and pick it up again while speaking, making everyone uneasy.

I would take George places for entertainment—the mall, AUM, and other places—introduce him to people, and otherwise try to make him feel comfortable. He would regularly exhibit odd behavior, such as turning a cartwheel, the lateral move whereby a person makes a circle like a Ferris wheel by placing his hands on the ground while rotating so that his feet turn up to the air and come to the ground again at the end of the rotation. He was liable to do this several times during an outing with him. George was also apt to wander away, use drugs, or become aggressive to family members. Due to his disorganized behavior features, the unpredictable nature of his behavior, and the poor control over it that he would exhibit, including aggression or poor judgment that contained safety risks, he could not be managed at home and had to be hospitalized. He resided at Bryce and Searcy Hospitals within the Alabama Department of Mental Health most of the time until his premature death in 1983, when he ate a hot dog too fast and choked on it.

I would like to expound on disorganized-type schizophrenia. George, I mentioned, seemed to hear a different drummer. He did not seem to follow my lead as his older brother. He seemed to frequently get me in situations with older or stronger boys during which I had to take up for him, and this eventually got the better of me. I feel that he was following mom and dad instead of me, that they were trying to best me in those situations, and that they eventually did. I previously mentioned that when he got in trouble in the eighth grade, after we had had a falling out, I felt that he may have been angry at me and wanted to embarrass me by his behavior. He recognized that I had put him down and his behavior would reflect badly on me for that reason. I noted that I was not just referring to George, but also to mom and dad. I felt they were working in tandem with George to exploit my mistakes and thereby affect my spiritual life. This is not unlike the mental opponent who seeks to bring conflict to the victim-host by influencing his environment. I would extend these ideas to George's behavior when he got into trouble and had to attend school at Lyman Ward Military Academy. At that time, I was immersed in a very affirming group at my high school, and his motivation may well have been to undermine that affirmation and the positive mental state it generated.

George's behavior reflected on me as his older brother, particularly within our family and in a community that understood some of the dynamics that had occurred between us. I was in the midst of a romance in college when he became involved with the counter-culture of the times and became mentally ill. As incredulous as it may seem, I think that George's association with a more marginal peer group and related activities at that time may have been partly a reaction to our changed relations. That is, I think it is possible that he did not want to follow the path of conformity because he wanted to get the better of me. I may have been central to his motivation at the time. Furthermore, I think that it is also possible that mom and dad's natural inclinations to be traditional, conservative, and conforming people could have been superseded by their design for me amidst those circumstances: that they may have outwardly chastised George for his behavior but inwardly condoned it. I regret casting my parents in that light when I could be wrong, but such has been my observation of the unusual personality dynamics that are present in mentally ill disorders, personality disorders, and basic human interactions, particularly regarding disorganized-type schizophrenia, in this example.

I anguished about George for a long time, blaming myself for his mental decompensation: his mental illness. I tried to help him a number of times, but I never had any success. I have worked with other patients who have had a diagnosis of disorganized schizophrenia. One case was a man that I became acquainted with some years ago. He was in regular classes in school until a traumatic event in his life led him to become mentally ill. Almost from the onset, he appeared to experience a regressed form of schizophrenia, which had disorganized features. In meetings with one of his parents and a sibling who visited him regularly, it seemed obvious that they—the parent, sibling, and patient— were cohorts, not antagonists, aligned together and of one mind, so to speak. Furthermore, during the time I worked with him, my impression was also that his disorganized speech and behavior represented passive aggression: resistance to performing according to societal expectations. Although no two cases are alike, his presentation reminded me in some respects of my brother's schizophrenia, based on the limited information about him that I had on hand and that I acquired. I could not say more about his other family relationships because I was not privy to that information.

Another case that I became acquainted with indirectly and but briefly happened while I was working in our Psychological Assessment Services Unit between 1990 and 1992 while a young man visited with his mother in the common foyer to the receiving wards and our unit. I felt this young man had obvious disorganized features of schizophrenia based on speech that was not sensible most of the time and mildly disorganized behavior features, such as being demanding and loud. What impressed me was his relationship with his mother. They were obviously aligned together in a relationship where I would say that he depended on her, and it became obvious to me that she was his guiding source.

There have been at least several cases in the hospital of people whose histories indicated to me that they experienced episodic schizophrenia that required hospitalization for stabilization. What became notable to me is that these people appeared to regress due to hospital dependency needs; that is, their schizophrenia evolved to the disorganized type or they developed a delusional disorder. The events that led to the change in their psychological presentation and their hospital dependence were sometimes similar. One of these cases involved an individual who had some medical issues that would act as stress on his psychological functioning in the community, where he would typically face a tough time, whereas in the hospital, where his medical conditions were closely monitored, he tended to do better. He had never exhibited hospital dependent features and had related effectively during his course of treatment. However, he also had a significant other person who was a constant source of guidance and support: someone who he knew that he could count on. When he lost this source of support due to this significant other person's premature death, his schizophrenia gradually evolved to the disorganized type. My impression from working with him and having access to the dynamics involved was that he decided to regress as a way to depend on the hospital because, given the difficult times that he had faced in the community and the loss of his only significant source of support, he was not ready to try community living again. I also provided psychological services to another client diagnosed with schizophrenia who experienced similar circumstances and whose regression also appeared to evolve out of hospital dependency needs. In this case, rather than disorganized-type schizophrenia, he developed a delusional disorder that very effectively promoted his need to rely on the hospital.

These cases of disorganized schizophrenia and delusional disorder involved resistance on the part of these patients to represent themselves accurately, whether due to passive aggression, meaning an indirect expression of anger, or a need to present themselves as more sick than they were due to a dilemma they could not resolve. I have treated other patients who have experienced such regression. For those who exhibited disorganized features (and also the ones who developed a delusional disorder), their behavior typically appeared to spring from their subconscious motivation. Those displaying disorganized features exhibited behavior such as speech and expressions that were not consonant with efforts to engage them, disjointed speech, odd mannerisms and expressions, repetitive behavior, and aloofness. More than just being out of touch with reality, they did not seem to want to relate effectively, improve behaviorally, conform, or get better. There was no obvious bonding that occurred with me as their caregiver or any sense of rapport. If passive aggression was at issue, their problems were often ill timed, sometimes creating the impression that they were obviously being disruptive.

These are some of the antecedents, developments, and motivation for cases of disorganized schizophrenia. There may well be numerous other explanations for it. For example, another explanation could be a person who suffers from such a severe thought disturbance—such severe mental opposition, if you will—that his speech in not very organized; or someone who is so distracted by strong mental opposition that he exhibits odd behavior, such as inability to sit still, frequent pacing, occasional shouting, and, under extreme stress, smearing feces. Disorganized schizophrenic features can also spring from the patient's own lack of motivation to relate—an indirect form of anger or rebellion—which would be an illustration of passive aggression.

An apparently common reason for schizophrenia may be the type experienced by the parent, which the child who is mentored by the parent with that type of schizophrenia becomes vulnerable to. As I have mentioned, situations involving discordant relations within or between groups that have regular relations can progress to the extent of mental opposition, which would make the unwelcome host susceptible to schizophrenia. This places emphasis on good case histories so that influences within the family and the community and other relevant factors can be identified early in the course of the disorder. With this knowledge, we might better understand the pre-morbid events, the development of the disorder, and what is motivating or sustaining the behavior, which should lead to improved treatment for schizophrenia.

CHAPTER 18:

A CAREER IN PSYCHOLOGY

I made a decision to pursue a Master's degree in clinical psychology after my 1986 tax season. I had been working long hours as a certified public accountant and not making enough money. I think a primary reason was that I was too particular in my work and was not making good economic decisions for that reason, what I previously referred to as obsessive-compulsive personality features. There were continuing elements of this pattern during my employment in public accounting at the time, which can be a good pattern when things are going well, meaning that my work is not only thoughtful and thorough, but also completed in a sufficiently timely manner as to be profitable. However, the problem with this pattern is that with increasing stress, the person with these features can become more meticulous at the expense of being practical, which can result in failure to meet time constraints, a backlog of work, and less profitability. The task for these individuals is to be able to remain practical about their work, to recognize the proper order of priorities, and to learn how to negotiate them without undue anxiety. Pam's practical nature and the 20 weeks of marital counseling helped me to develop a more flexible personality. By this time, I have learned to do what needs to be done within the time frame allowed, considering the need to do a satisfactory job while recognizing the time constraints that I am under. I remain very thorough and thoughtful in my work otherwise and put in extra time to better assess and understand the patients that I work with because a good assessment can make such a difference in the course of treatment. Today, I consider my obsessive-compulsive qualities a strength.

I decided to expand my business by hiring someone who could fill the role of a junior accountant before I changed careers. When this did not turn out to be profitable, I decided to make the change to psychology. This was not because I felt that I would not succeed in accounting but because I had become increasingly drawn to the psychological aspects of interpersonal dynamics, and I felt a divine calling to pursue that degree. The employee that I hired and I had a satisfactory trial at this new scope within my business. When my plans were not quite so successful, I was able to provide him a good referral with the experience that he obtained. Subsequently, I learned that he was hired by a successful corporation in an area related to the work that he had done for me, which was also his major.

My pursuit of a master's degree in clinical psychology included a practicum at a substance use facility, where I subsequently worked for a year, which was an experience that has proved to be invaluable. While obtaining my degree, I was prepared for all my classes, made the grades to pursue a doctorate, and had recommendations from several teachers, but I was not accepted by the four programs where I interviewed. Typically, I was not able to get any sleep the night before and did not interview well. I do not feel this pursuit was right for me at the time because I had accumulated some debt and was paying monthly child support, which was going to drive me further into debt.

I became a regular counselor at the substance use treatment facility where I did my practicum after I graduated with the master of clinical psychology in December 1988. When I was not promoted at that facility, I applied for a job at Bryce Hospital and was ecstatic when Violet Perney, the director of psychology at the time, hired me. After all, my degree was in clinical psychology. I could not have found a better training ground than Bryce Hospital. I began work in April 1990. Matthew was eleven years old and more interested in peer group activities than before. We saw each other during vacations and holidays and kept telephone contact. He was or became more aligned with his mother and his peer group in Montgomery and did not seem to need me as much.

My first two years at Bryce Hospital were spent in Psychological Assessment Services (PAS), our testing unit. This was a great experience. At the time, we had about 12 doctoral level psychologists and 24 psychology associates like me, usually holding a master's degree, scattered about the various units throughout the hospital, in addition to PAS. We tested all new admissions and tested by referral from all the other units about the hospital, which cut across the full spectrum of the psychiatric disorders listed within the *Diagnostic and Statistical Manual of Mental Disorders—III, Revised*, the manual that all clinicians in the field of mental health were using at the time to determine an individual's psychiatric diagnosis. Our reports usually consisted of a review of the history, a clinical interview, intellectual testing, neuropsychological screening, and personality testing to provide opinions as to intellectual, neuropsychological, and personality functioning along with a list of problems, our diagnostic impressions, and treatment recommendations. We were expected to complete one report daily, which was quite challenging.

I have been fortunate throughout my life to have had able mentors, caring people with high ideals, usually good Christians also, who created the mental life for me to absorb, learn, and apply myself to my work without opposition. They made the difference in my successful accounting and psychology studies in college and my success in my psychological work. With Dr. Perney's able mentoring, I soon began writing good psychological reports. After two years, when I had the opportunity, I decided to work more closely with our patient population on a unit.

My new supervisor had a strong behavioral background, which was a good experience for me. Besides a general behavioral emphasis on the unit, I became more skilled at performing a behavioral analysis and writing behavior management plans for patients who needed a more specifically structured treatment. I also developed a plan with Dr. Perney's guidance and the hospital director's approval to recruit a "recovering addict" from the community in order to hold weekly Narcotics Anonymous meetings for candidates on our unit and about the hospital, a program that served substance use needs of our patient population for some 18 months.

My new responsibilities on this unit involved responding to the psychology needs of the patients on my workload as part of a multidisciplinary treatment team consisting of a psychiatrist, a social worker, a nurse, a recreation therapist, mental health worker representation, and myself. This was a challenge that I was inexperienced at meeting and that I did not master until later. One key was learning to manage the workload, which seemed a never-ending job. Another was negotiating well interpersonal relations with all staff working on the unit, which met each morning; with the variety of members of my treatment team, which all have to work well together; and with a large patient workload where it is important to manage relations well with each and every patient. This unit closed after two years as the hospital began to downsize, at which point I was reassigned to PAS, where I worked for about another four and a half years.

I soon took up where I left off at PAS by continuing to write good psychological reports. The daily case studies helped me refine my skills as a diagnostician. Around 1996, the director of PAS transferred to another unit. This left us without a director, a position that Dr. Perney filled temporarily. She originally practiced as a neuropsychologist in Missouri and has tremendous psychological aptitude. To illustrate my point, she would come over to the PAS unit several mornings during the week after she had become oriented to her general duties as the director of psychology for that day or week. She would then review the accumulated psychological reports of the five or so staff at PAS, go to each of our offices to discuss her findings and any necessary changes to the reports, and leave before lunch. Within the six weeks or so that she filled this capacity, before it was assigned to the neuropsychologist, I learned to write more efficient reports and important rules of consistency, which subsequently saved me time and trouble in doing psychological assessments and writing reports. Some afternoons, Dr. Perney would return to do a neuropsychological battery for a patient and write the report. She departed that same year to be the director of psychology at the forensic hospital here in Tuscaloosa, Taylor Hardin Secure Medical Facility (THSMF).

I think it was the following year that we moved to the new Admissions Unit, which, like the old Admissions Unit, contained the Department of Psychological Assessment Services. Our new director of psychology, the former chief psychologist on the Admissions Unit, Dr. John Toppins, helped me to negotiate through the process of change. At that time, we had reduced our testing emphasis to only provide testing by referral for specific referral questions. Dr. Toppins helped me to recognize the need to write less comprehensive reports, with less historical information, as was requested by our new director of PAS. He also designed and recommended a format to help us meet time constraints of writing initial psychological intakes in four hours, a service we assumed for the admissions unit psychology staff. Dr. Toppins has very good people skills. He tried every maneuver that he knew to satisfy psychology staff by placing each of us in a job position that we liked and was usually successful. This was a most considerate skill that made him very popular among the psychology staff. In March 1999, as part of our contin-ued downsizing or because we did not need as many staff at PAS due to the less demands for testing, I became a psychology staff on a unit once again. It was not long after that when PAS closed and the unit psychology staff began doing their own testing.

I had not mastered the role of being a treatment team member who was assigned to one or more wards of patients. During my first assignment in 1992, I worked with a good variety of patients who had a primary mental illness such as schizophrenia or bipolar disorder; lower functioning patients, such as those with a diagnosis of intellectual disability, some with a coexist-ing neurological condition, such as a seizure disorder or a history of head trauma; and a number who had a coexisting personality and/or substance use disorder. The unit I was on in 1999, though it had a good variety of men-tal disorders represented, had patients with greater medical or nursing care needs, such as more elderly patients with a diagnosis of dementia, Parkin-son's disease, or Huntingdon's chorea, with behavioral problems; head injury patients; severe cases of schizophrenia or bipolar disorder; and chronic pa-tients who were low functioning and behaviorally unstable, who tended to decompensate under mild to moderate stress. Few of these patients met the criteria for traditional individual therapy unless you include supportive forms of individual therapy, which was often what was indicated. One of my suc-cess stories was a token reinforcement program that I implemented for a pa-tient on my workload, which I had not attempted before. I was transferred to the Behavior Rehabilitation Unit (BRU) in February 2002, around the time that Dr. Toppins replaced Violet Perney, who retired as the director of psychology at THSMF. I remained at BRU until July 15, 2014, when we moved to our new hospital.

I worked with the full range of the patient population on BRU, a variety of treatment teams, staff from the various disciplines, and several unit direc-tors. Some of the patients on BRU resided on a closed ward due to severe behavioral problems with violent tendencies. The population of patients on BRU included patients with the schizophrenia or bipolar disorder diagnosis, some with a co-existing personality and/or a substance use disorder; mentally retarded patients with a head injury or a seizure disorder, some of whom warranted an additional diagnosis of dementia; and other conditions. Some were forensic patients: those with a criminal history who were deemed to be insane at the time of their offense. This population includes a good sample of patients that are candidates for individual or group therapy. I achieved greater mastery of psychological services over the 12 years on this unit. I have continued to perform good psychological assessments to help treatment teams respond to the psychological needs of our patients, have become an assertive treatment team member in communicating patient needs, and have acquired skills in providing the needed treatment services to help patients make progress toward discharge from the hospital. These services include individual therapy, violence risk assessments for forensic patients who are under consideration for discharge, a variety of educational services using a classroom format, and referrals for other needed services (e.g., work, school, substance use, and psychiatric rehabilitation).

One of the most important skills I have learned is to always have a good plan and to be as prepared as I can be. Preparation helps to organize our staff and patients and prevent problems that arise from poor management of resources. I was impressed by an observation of an instructor in an annual alcohol and drug studies class who felt that expertise is so critical when you consider that the success you enjoy in helping a client over the course of a therapy hour is entirely dependent on that. I have appreciated the contribution of cognitive-behavior therapy (CBT) to the treatment of the severe mental disorders for its benefits in treating patients with a diagnosis of schizophrenia, bipolar disorder, and major depression, including enhanced understanding, better management, and remediation of symptoms.

The psychiatric rehabilitation emphasis for the mentally ill has added a most important dimension to treatment, looking beyond hospitalization to helping clients prepare for a community role (8). My role as a day treatment or psychiatric rehabilitation instructor has also provided me the opportunity to communicate CBT and substance use strategies in a group format and has helped me to improve and refine my skills in presenting classroom information. One of my rewarding and challenging experiences on BRU was therapy with a small group of female patients with a diagnosis of Borderline Personality Disorder that I conducted with a psychology intern using dialectical behavior therapy (Linehan, 1983). One of the keys to my success, in addition to being prepared, advancing my skills and proficiency, and able mentoring, has been physical fitness. I have been a regular at the YMCA and recognize the benefits of good physical health. I am always positive after a good workout, which helps me to maintain a confident and a positive attitude.

CHAPTER 19:

MY SCHIZOPHRENIA, REVISITED

The basis for my schizophrenia syndrome, which I have described, was a difference in spiritual principles or values from those held by my parents. They appear to have made choices that thwarted their spiritual growth without corrective action, which can act as a limiting condition for their offspring, like a status quo. Under the guidance and direction of a broad reference group and related Catholic teachings, which mom herself provided, I sought to follow a spiritual path that was consistent with this religious foundation that I was acquiring. These differences in our spirit life appeared to lead us to have an epic struggle, as I have described, such as lack of bonding and mental opposition at a subconscious level. This has been a handicapping condition throughout my life. Eventually, mistakes such as lack of sufficient preparation for college led to events and conditions which created sufficient distress that I began to experience symptoms of mental illness.

I believe that I am a high achiever and that I am at least partly that way because mediocrity, lack of success, and failure affects me keenly, likely more than it does most people because I lack permanent mental support, such as someone in my corner telling me, "Don't worry. We're going to make up for that." In contrast, I am likely to experience mental opposition creating a feeling like, "You're not very smart" and publicizing that to those around me, which is a letdown.

I was not prepared for college. It took me a while to gain familiarity with the American culture. I was never a struggling student, in general, though I struggled with specific subject areas at times, but I did not develop very good study habits, and so, I did not excel as a student. Athletics were always high on my list of priorities because they enriched my social life. I remember as late as my junior year in high school, after sitting out from football that year, how important it was for me not only to make the team during spring practice for my senior year, but to be a starter. I was totally prepared for that experience and had an outstanding year. But I did not have the vision and did not prepare myself for a planned college experience, which worked much to my detriment.

I remember how much I enjoyed and excelled during my seventh grade English class at Cloverdale Junior High School when my English teacher, Mr. Goolsby, stirred an interest in English grammar by his very concrete diagrams of the parts of speech, which kept that interest alive from that time forward and made me into a better English student. Alternatively, in the same grade, I did not feel a sense of rapport with my algebra teacher, Ms. Peake, and never quite got the new math, which was humiliating to me. I had always loved math, but algebraic equations were a foreign subject. Even though I had quite an exceptional math teacher in high school, Dr. Joseph Piazza, I did not grasp the algebraic principles he was teaching during one 6-week period, when I made an F, which had never happened to me before. I have difficulty with the "hard" sciences because beyond understanding the material, I have to learn all the little bitty details, which my mental opponents are relatively more successful at preventing me from encoding in memory and learning. I have to get the principles and facts "down pat" during individual study, which I was not up to in high school due to insufficient dedication to schoolwork. I was not aware of any tutors at the time either, which is help that might have made a difference. This F in algebra during that 6-week period was embarrassing and humiliating. I loved geometry in Ms. Jones' class during my sophomore year at Sidney Lanier High School and made an A or B in that subject.

I think that what I really needed, what may have made a difference in my life, if anything might have prevented the problems that I ran into in college, was a guidance counselor as early as the ninth grade. Someone to point the way for me and tell me, "Fred, now is the time to think about your career goals. Let's consider your interests and abilities and determine what you are most suited for" and "Okay, I am not saying that you cannot go to medical school. But if you really want to do that, then you need to obtain a good foundation in the algebraic and chemistry principles that are being taught at this level and show proficiency in a beginning physics course." Or, "Fred, accounting is a very promising field, but to excel in tomorrow's accounting world, you will need at least a minor in information systems" and "Have you ever tried to visualize a business operation, such as their primary source of revenue, where their costs lie, and how they account for them?" "Do you know the difference between job costs and process costs?" "What about internal controls? Do you know their importance to a business and how to test them in an automated system?" "What would be pertinent about accounting for plant, equipment, and inventory on hand?" and "Are you aware that there are accounting, auditing, and industry standards that you have to follow?" I did not need study hall in high school; I needed a guidance counselor.

I feel that such guidance during that time in my life could have helped me identify my interests early on and given me much needed direction that would have helped me to be better prepared for college. I had not developed good study habits. Additionally, I remember that it was a struggle for me to study at home. The subject matter did not seem to sink in very well. I remember that the noise factor was sometimes a problem in our large household. Furthermore, I do not think that the ambient culture at home was conducive for me to develop good study habits and become a good student. It was part of the opposition that I had for the very reason that my parents did not want me to excel. Nevertheless, I was capable of developing good or better study habits.

Dr. Toppins, on reading these comments, remarked, "One theory about schizophrenia is that it represents an impaired ability to screen out sensory input, resulting in sensory overload from things that most people can ignore— low levels of noise, for example." My experience has been that a mental antagonist can sensitize me to the noise in the environment so much that low levels of noise are bothersome, or conversely, to prevent me from effectively screening it out, essentially supporting this view about schizophrenia. My classroom behavior depicts a related event. I get at the front of the class and listen intently because I have to override or overcome the mental adversary who seeks to prevent me from effectively hearing and absorbing the message; a casual or relaxed attitude does not work for me because my mental adversaries are more capable of affecting my sensory perception with such an attitude.

I made a 24 on the ACT, showing strengths in English and arithmetic. Furthermore, I developed good study habits during my first semester at the University of Dubuque in Iowa. I remember a cynical, dry-witted English teacher, perhaps a frustrated medical student, who was quite superb in his field. He taught me to appreciate poetry and to enjoy English literature, and he spurred me to work assiduously on my grammar. One proud moment occurred when I went to his office to get my grade and he told me that I had made a B in English. That was not just a B; that was him telling me that a C student in English had been transformed into a B student. Still, I had to be practical. Recall that I was also playing football, which required a good bit of my time. I used my paper in Western Civilization titled, "The Life of a Serf," as my English paper also, ensuring that I used good grammar. In retrospect, my English teacher was not the least bit naïve. I feel certain that he became aware of that, but he never mentioned it.

Many people who experience schizophrenia do so during the period when they are making the transition to independent living, and it can start during their college days. This may not be surprising considering the important tasks of the period, finding a partner and a career, in face of much novelty and change. Young people for the first time in their lives are able, in many instances or to a large degree, to set their own schedule. They are responsible in varied ways for independent living needs such as meals, laundry, and upkeep of their premises. They are also responsible for establishing their classroom schedule and study habits in face of unlimited recreational or leisure time. They are relatively unchaperoned or do not have to account to their parents for the first time in their lives. They are faced with such decisions as whether to remain active in a church as well as dating practices and standards, all amidst an environment of influence from peers who may be from different walks of life and who may espouse different standards than they are accustomed to. All this may often occur amidst a liberal culture in which such practices as marijuana use and open, same-sex partnerships may be evident. A lot can go wrong. For people like me who have had a lifelong battle on a spiritual plane with an adversarial parent(s) and other adversaries, it means that they must negotiate this period very well to keep these adversaries at bay.

I had liberal friends among my peer group. The fashion of the times had an influence on our dress and customs. We mixed it up, but there was occasion for longer hair, bell-bottom jeans, embroidered blouses made of a light cotton-lace material, leather crafts, and braided hair. You could find Boone's Farm wine and marijuana at some of our parties. One could fairly much take it or leave it, but these trappings of the hippie culture were there among us, in our midst. My peer group did not identify strongly with that movement, such as the liberal element that was placing at question our established way of doing things and our social institutions, including the Vietnam War. I was not a social activist, but I listened to these ideas and tried to keep an open mind. They influenced me to a degree for a period of time, but I do not think they made a lasting impression. That was not really me.

Marijuana was a significant stressor in my life. I did not have any formal religious education at the time, but I had always taken an interest in religion. Most of my education had come from the many Sunday homilies offered by learned priests, which I had contemplated and considered. Whenever I smoked marijuana, it seemed that I was often immediately drawn to consider very profound subjects in a self-critical way, such as whether I had been leading the life of a Christian. It was an experience that would get at the core of my being and make me feel that I did not measure up, which would "shake me up." The attendant feelings of guilt, disharmony, and bewilderment would make me feel out of place and lead me to withdraw socially; I did not feel a part of things. During stressful times, the emotional tone and statements of people in my vicinity would seem consonant with my experience, contributing to it, which could lead to paranoid feelings. At the University of Dubuque, where I used it infrequently, it did not get in the way of my studies, but I would have to say that the combination of the liberal views circulating and the marijuana experience were somewhat of a distraction. In retrospect, I think that whenever I smoked marijuana, I lost the cognitive integrity that insulates me from mental opponents, and they directed me to have the negative experiences that I did. I was flirting with mental illness. At the University of Alabama, it had become a recreational drug that was often around, and I used it more than I should have. I should have been smart enough to say no to it. It consumed time that could have been better applied elsewhere and led me to experience transitory mental illness.

I feel that my primary problem in college, despite these comments, was insufficient preparation. I was not prepared for the rigor of a college program, such as putting school first, absolutely, and my recreational and social life second. When I entered the University of Alabama for my sophomore year, I was interested in a pre-med program, but I had not done the preparatory work. It seemed too challenging at the time to remedy my academic weaknesses while taking the requisite courses. I might have done better with the help of a guidance counselor to assist me in career planning. I had improved my study habits at the University of Dubuque, but that was not enough without good preparatory work for medical school. When I did not perform at the expected level during my first pre-medical course, I figured my chances of getting accepted into medical school would be slim. At that point, I was not sure of what career to pursue, which was distressing, considering that I was borrowing money to pay for college. These were some of the stresses that precipitated my first psychotic episode.

My grades remained satisfactory, but I lacked important direction and guidance. Schizotypal ideas began setting in: those odd, unusual, and eccentric ideas that are often the prodromal or early signs that precede the schizophrenia experience. I took a course in religion that absorbed me. It was around that time that I began receiving messages from television personalities, which exploited my insecurities about religion to confuse me. I felt compelled to become more religiously active. I began trying to walk the biblical path of Jesus without being adequately schooled in the Bible and a common sense understanding of Jesus' fundamental messages. This had the semblance of a paranoid posture. I remember an instance of approaching another student or other students on campus in order to preach the gospel of Jesus Christ as a response to these schizotypal notions that had a paranoid flavor, which was improper motivation. When this pilgrimage of sorts led me to drop out of school and landed me in the psychiatric ward at Jackson Hospital in Montgomery, I became depressed. When I surfaced from my initial mentally ill experience and got my life back on track, the adversity represented by mental opposition did not go away and was present to affect my self esteem and my judgment, once again seeking to undermine me, with varying degrees of success.

I think one of the reasons I prevailed over schizophrenia is that I rebounded quickly. On both occasions during college that I suffered an acute schizophrenic episode, I enrolled in school the next quarter, and I usually found part-time work as well. I was back in Montgomery, living at home, and began attending church again, something I had neglected to do in college after the first semester of my freshman year. The demands of work and school, the drive to obtain an education and earn a living, and the rekindling of spirituality on Sundays helped me to maintain a desirable mental integrity and bolstered my self esteem, which were indispensable attributes during that period of time. Those activities also provided me a social structure that was mostly beneficial—the work, classroom, and church environment—which helped me to fit in. However, I had lost direction or perspective about school, the jobs that I had were not career-minded jobs but semi-skilled work, and I was not yet attending church regularly. Without greater direction and the self-confidence that comes with it, I was more susceptible to the effects from mental illness, which sometimes affected my mental state in those generally positive activities that I mentioned. I had friends that were supportive, but I was lacking career goals and the confidence that comes with such direction. Furthermore, my self image had been tarnished by mental illness, all of which affected the quality of my dialogue or socialization. Amidst those circumstances, the richness of my social relations declined; peer relations became less satisfying. At times, I felt that I was just "hanging out," which was not very rewarding or uplifting.

My decision to pursue an accounting degree after struggling with schizophrenia for over one year was an important goal that gave me direction. Additionally, from the time of my first accounting course, which was Principles of Accounting, I became acquainted with an accounting teacher, Dr. Mary Golden, who became my leader. Like the direction of a career, her mentoring and affirmation were a stabilizing influence in my life. There were other teachers who were very positive influences as well at AUM during my coursework towards the Bachelor of Science degree in business administration. I was not being very smart socially, however, because I was still "hanging out" with the guys, and I was starting to drink more. Effectively, my social life was having a detrimental effect on my mental life. I should have found a better way to bide my time while pursuing a college degree or at least been smart enough not to consume alcoholic beverages except for lightly on occasion. Although I had a relatively good year, I was about to succumb to schizophrenia yet one more time when I had the good fortune of being introduced to Pam Tillman by a couple who were both good friends.

Pam made a difference in my life at that time for several reasons. First and most importantly, she is an intelligent and practical person who reverberated with those ideas when I spouted my schizotypal thoughts, the odd and unusual ideas that precipitate and maintain schizophrenia, so that I had a healthy dose of practical reality every day. She also pulled me away from hanging out with peers and drinking to our more satisfying dialogue. And, because she was also Catholic, we attended church regularly, which began to increase my spiritual life. With her friendship, I finished my accounting curriculum well and embarked on a career in accounting.

I was elated and thankful for the opportunity to work and train at Jackson, Thornton, & Co. The skills required for success in that firm were considerable. They included mastery of accounting principles and accounting, auditing, and client industry standards; the corresponding tax law; tools of the trade both in the practice and with regard to the client; and people skills. This was an experience during which one gradually acquired competence through training and education. Practically speaking, at least a minor in information systems was required. This was quite a challenge for me and one that I was not prepared for psychologically. I was not prepared to relate to people quite that well, and I needed further academic preparation.

I advanced from a junior accountant to a senior accountant and became certified, but I was not ready to advance to becoming a manager. Competition was very keen. I was vulnerable interpersonally due to the very nature of my schizophrenia; namely, psychological opposition that seeks to undermine you in various ways and creates controversy for you rather than set the stage for congenial relations. These mental dynamics make management of people in such circumstances difficult. Additionally, although I was a good student, I was not sufficiently assertive interpersonally at that time to reap the full benefits of the training that I was being provided or the client experience. However, I accomplished a primary goal for all public accountants—to become certified—which provides numerous opportunities on leaving a public accounting firm. I was usually an efficient accountant for this firm, which was the norm. I struggled in some industries with which I was not very familiar, although one could usually do the detail assigned without much complication. I was not very well acquainted with computerized client data systems to take a more responsible assignment if that knowledge was required.

I was influenced by schizophrenia in way of mental opposition that makes it difficult to relate to other staff and clients confidently and harmoniously, like someone constantly seeking to introduce doubt and create controversy. This is easier to override when one is working with progressively minded people who do not seek to capitalize on the ways a mental adversary can undermine you, such as people who are not opportunistic. As noted, during some periods of stress, I was subject to schizotypal thinking, unusual ideas that do not belong in the serious, objective, and engaging nature of an audit or accounting job. One example might be an improper impression you may acquire that it is most important to do your job exceedingly well, to the extent that detail is emphasized over reason, an opinion that in and of itself shows an improper mental set or attitude for such an engagement. It is imperative to have all your wits and faculties about you so that you can expertly check a client's internal controls, spot any material errors, learn their system of operations well enough to provide management advisory services when indicated, understand the particular industry, and be alert and sensitive to the personnel that you engage, including their needs and motivation.

I learned good, basic accounting principles and practices at Jackson, Thornton, & Co. that helped me to establish my own practice. I operated as a sole proprietor, like dad, and we shared expenses, which was effective and economical for us both. I purchased a very basic or rudimentary individual tax practice, set up a system for it, and developed it into a better and more profitable one by improving and increasing client services. This was accomplished by such means as educating clients on recordkeeping practices and opportunities for tax savings and investments. I had plenty of this type of work throughout the year. Dad and I purchased a computer and automated our bookkeeping services, which was an effective means to provide clients monthly financial information, a service that dad and his bookkeeper both liked. I was developing this service, which provided a steady monthly income. Some of these were corporate clients and not-for-profit entities for which I provided financial statements at the end of the year, rendering an opinion. This was often required by the funding source for the not-for-profit entity, such as United Way or the City of Montgomery, and a corporate client could present it as verification of their balance sheet and profitability. Occasionally, I did an estate or trust tax return. I reached a point at which I needed an assistant to expand and hired a full time employee in 1986, the year before I changed fields.

Pam and I married in August 1975 and divorced in January 1984. Matthew was born in March 1979. I became certified during that time and she obtained an MBA. We both worked hard as a couple, supported one another, and worked out our differences. If there was one thing that came between us, I would have to say that it was schizophrenia. I had not surfaced from its grip to become an assertive person. I was intimidated by the experience at times, such as left feeling socially inept, awkward, and out of place. There were times when I became overly preoccupied with prayer. I also went through a period of time when I was too fastidious in my work.

The schizotypal experience during a client engagement that I spoke of in chapter 14, "Accounting, My Marriage, and Another Bout With Schizophrenia" had parallels at home, when I may have been more preoccupied and self-absorbed: distant interpersonally. Events like these compromised our marital relations. I prevailed over schizophrenia most of the time, but it created a degree of insecurity that affected me socially. You sometimes have to pay the piper with schizophrenia, meaning adversaries that are lurking in your subconscious to undermine you. During that time, I did not understand schizophrenia like I do today. I was as naïve as the next person who has it. That is a definite handicap.

Pam and I did not just split up. We were in counseling for a considerable period of time. It was late fall 1982. Year-end accounting and tax planning were fast approaching. I cannot recall whether Pam had completed her MBA, during which time I had extra responsibilities at home. I do recall that it was a stressful time for me and that I became more meticulous in my work. It was like becoming more particular for ethical reasons, which led me to feel peaceful on a spiritual plane. However, I was not being practical. I was not managing my practice well, considering such things as time constraints. This culminated in my last major psychotic break. I remember shocking Pam by proclaiming that I was an apostle of Jesus Christ and capable of turning water into wine. I had some idea that I had experienced an episode of mental illness when a young Irish priest, the assistant pastor at Our Lady Queen of Mercy church and a mutual friend, who had provided me adult religious instruction for a brief period, arrived. I had assumed a catatonic posture, rather in shock. I believe that it was during this period of time that I began having auditory hallucinations on an ongoing basis.

The next day was Sunday. I was evaluated at a community psychiatric hospital by a mental health professional, June Hassell, who was supervised by a psychiatrist. I began individual therapy during the following week, which changed to marital therapy afterwards. I was back to my demanding tax practice on Monday, grateful that I was not an inpatient at a psychiatric hospital. I have had auditory hallucinations since that time. With practice, it is possible and necessary to keep them in the background by focusing keenly on an activity such as work or a conversation, so that they are not very bothersome or problematic. However, they can introduce content that can be upsetting in a number of ways if the hearer of the voice is not able to resolve whatever dilemma is created by the "voices," which can make the voice hearer feel anxious, afraid, worried, and perplexed. Under those conditions, mental opponents can penetrate the mentally ill person's cognitive integrity so that the mentally ill person feels like she no longer has good control over her thoughts and emotions. At those times, it is also difficult to engage in sound reasoning. The mentally ill person feels incompetent and awkward. Interpersonal influences are heightened, particularly if the environment is not friendly and supportive. This can be a harrowing experience, leaving the victim feeling at her wit's end. These stressful conditions tend to bring rigid personality features to the surface, placing the burden on the victim of becoming more flexible or adaptive if she does not want to face the consequences of such rigidity.

Marital therapy was very helpful. June's questions helped me to view Pam's perspective about me and our marriage in a very enlightening way. It was a great dose of reality that I needed. It helped to make me more flexible and practical. Pam and I both entered therapy with the realization that our marriage was at stake and that therapy would likely help us to decide whether we should stay together or not. It had been difficult for me to consider a divorce because of my Catholic faith and my young son, but I recognized that we were having problems and that we were not growing closer together. We communicated effectively in marital therapy until there were no problematic issues left to address, after which I continued individually for several more sessions. June made it clear to me during that period that she felt that Pam was ready to make some important changes in her life, which served as a cue to me of an impending divorce.

Change is often difficult, perhaps especially so when it involves the break up of a family, in addition to changing established patterns. However, I found my divorce to be liberating. Although I had been committed to the demands of a marital partner and a family, which is something that I wanted, I no longer had to answer to anyone but myself, aside from a healthy concern for Matthew. I soon began to run six or seven miles after work daily, which was exhilarating, began reading more, and worked longer hours when necessary to avoid a delay of services. Matthew and I visited every other weekend, which became an important part of my social life. We often brought a friend along with us and enjoyed a variety of activities together. We had a good time. I was responsible about his child support, attended any special functions that he had, and made myself available to assist Pam whenever she called on me. I also paid for part of his dental work and supported him during his college days. He is now happily married, has two beautiful children, and is a devoted father.

It is necessary for me to explain to the reader that even though religiosity or excess religious preoccupation was a feature of my mental illness, I was at the same time growing closer to God. I made a conscious decision to do so after the culmination of my first two psychotic breaks: the first when I dropped out of the University of Alabama during the fall semester of my junior year in 1972, and the second when I ran my 1966 Malibu into an oak tree in the midst of an acute psychotic episode in December 1973. I experienced his sanctifying grace during a heartfelt confession after an argument with Pam around 1979, a veritable embrace from God, and again after our divorce while renting a second floor apartment from a young couple on Thorn Place in Montgomery in 1985. I have undergone a transformation much like some of the alcoholic people do on practicing the 12 Steps of the Alcoholic Anonymous program. I would recall a mistake that I had made—a serious transgression on a worldly scale as well as a blemish on my mental life. I would ponder this event in anguish until I resolved to atone for it in some way, sometimes experiencing or re-experiencing despair and heartfelt sorrow on several occasions. Eventually, I would determine how to resolve or remedy that experience. After so much remorse, I would begin to feel liberated from this blemish on my soul. During the evenings, I would inventory my day and atone for any transgressions during prayer at night. Gradually, I was becoming a more spiritual, Christian person. I felt God's hand in my calling to psychology.

The comments that I made about my family in the first paragraph of this chapter and elsewhere may lead some people to misunderstand family life in our home. Thus, I want to emphasize, in contrast to what may seem a dim picture, my father and mother were good providers who did not neglect my material needs. They would show concern if I appeared distressed or if I approached them about a problem. They never left me out of family plans or ignored me if I had something to say. As a family, we took pride in caring for one another and helping any family member in need. Our household was a very decent place for a kid, for the most part. The outward problems we had are not uncommon to many good homes, such as an extent of periodic bickering and disagreement. But it would also be a mistake to underemphasize the subconscious struggle that prevailed.

My ability to comprehend my mental illness and thereby overcome it has been an incredible experience. It was accomplished by unraveling mysteries of the subconscious. By discipline in my work, attending to two modes of existence, and maintaining spiritual integrity so that I could discern without error, I gradually began to recognize and understand this second language that we all speak. It was a gradual experience. I remember sitting at Holy Spirit Church in Tuscaloosa, Alabama, Sunday after Sunday and being affirmed by fellow parishioners regarding all the subconscious revelations that I was acquiring, when I felt like they might be critical or envious or was just unsure about what to expect. Their affirmation helped me to move forward in conceiving this subconscious world. Many gradually revealed their personality to me through this subconscious medium: an intimacy. I have become fluent in the subconscious. It is the language of the soul, often heartfelt and not hypocritical, though it can be subjected to manipulation. It is also at times governed by spiritual laws, such as in regard to the revelations people make. I am excited to share this with the reader: to provide you these great expectations. I think that everyone will go though this process on reading the book, and, gradually, become bilingual in this special language. Let us all make a commitment to use it for the good of humanity: to use the enhanced understanding of one another to bring us closer together.

PART III:

A Vision for Humanity

CHAPTER 20:

THE EVOLUTION OF HUMANITY

I remember when I was an accountant working with dad and his secretary in1986. It must have been Holy Week: the days preceding Easter Sunday. She and I were talking about the crucifixion and Jesus' statement in the gospel of Saint Luke to one of the criminals who was crucified beside him, who rebuked the criminal who was being crucified on the other side of Jesus. He rebuked the other criminal for telling Jesus that if he truly were the Messiah, to save himself as well as them. He asked the other criminal if he did not fear God. He told the other criminal that Jesus had received the same sentence they received, but they deserved their punishment, whereas Jesus had done nothing wrong. He then turned to Jesus and said, "Jesus, remember me when you enter your reign," and Jesus replied, "I assure you: this day you will be with me in Paradise." What hounded me about that passage is that I kept thinking that it is too simple for someone who has done wrong all his life, a criminal, to enter into heaven for a momentary act of contrition.

It was during my first two years in psychological assessment services at Bryce Hospital that I tested a man who had suffered a significant closed head injury that, as can happen, made it very difficult for him to inhibit his behavior. He had a long history of anger management problems, such as angry outbursts, loss of temper, and physical aggression to others. What was also impressive is that his basic personality pattern appeared to be an Antisocial Personality Disorder (3). However, it appeared to me that over the years of suffering from the head injury, his antisocial personality characteristics were lessening in degree, and the obvious reason appeared to be that his personality could no longer support them. An antisocial personality of his type has to be able to con, manipulate, and remain in control without playing his hand and cannot show the underlying anger and rebelliousness that motivates his domineering verbal behavior, glibness, and cocky behavior. This man could not support such a personality and was slowly giving it up. For some reason, my focus turned to my idea from a review of the history that this man appeared to have been born with an antisocial personality, which did not seem right, particularly because he had later suffered a head injury and could not support it.

These deliberations began leading me to think that it must be that we have lived before. This antisocial man had not just been born that way; rather, he acquired antisocial personality characteristics as a result of his behavior over the course of another lifetime, and their manifestation in this life merely represented the progression of his personality to this point in time. That helped me to conceive that the criminal who Jesus absolved most likely had atoned for his sins and was worthy of the kingdom of God. He had not merely earned it by a sudden act of contrition; he had been somehow transformed in spirit. He must have been ready in mind and heart; he must have had the maturity to enter Paradise. Further deliberations led me to think that the head injury suffered by the fellow whom I was testing must have been a recompense for antisocial past behavior, such as wanton acts that he was now answering to because he was unable to shield his personality from erupting, regardless of the situation, which was a lesson hard learned. Of paramount importance, I noted that this person had not responded to God's just punishment with anger or disdain and sought to continue his antisocial ways, however difficult, but, rather, he seemed to have accepted his lot and was seeking to change for the better. I felt that it was due to this acceptance on his part that we had good rapport during the assessment and I was able to provide a good report on his behalf. I do not know whether he is the exception or the rule, but I do know that just because someone is afflicted, that person does not necessarily have a change of heart, which is a sad fact. We have the option of giving our misery to God and preparing for a better afterlife.

These ideas eventually led me to the full realization that our place in this life is no more than the life we have earned in a previous lifetime—that life is a progression in just that way. For example, the person who is a member of an esoteric group that uses unfair tactics, such as a coalition to undermine other people, may be born, in his next life, into a culture that lacks independence, where its members are all raised to be part of a similar class with little individuality and where it is difficult to rise above such class identification, or he might be born into a family where organized crime prevails, particularly if there was a criminal element to his behavior. The perennial uninvited mental antagonist that is a robber of insight might be a criminal who robs for a living in his next lifetime; his die has been cast to a large degree by his behavior in this lifetime, though he can make a decision to be a follower of Christ at any point in this life or the next and began his journey or transformation back to God the Father. He will be struggling in a Christian way and receive the support of the Christian community, though his degree of success in various ways may be limited. He may be a less affluent or gifted member of the body of Christ but an essential part, entitled to share ever more in his heavenly inheritance if he has the will and determination to continue along that path, to the point that God may baptize him into his body and draw him to a closer understanding of him, making him an endowed member of his flock.

I saw a documentary on the Finnish culture some years ago that described how isolated they were, or a segment of their culture, that also highlighted the popularity of outdoor public dancing, which was catching on among a people deprived of feeling for so long. They reveled in the opportunity to have this chance for socialization after years of social deprivation. Thus, a harlot or a well raised Christian who has fallen from grace due to non-virtuous living might be subjected to such a culture for a lifetime as recompense for her sins, and so on. This understanding helped me to explain why I fell prey to schizophrenia though as a young child I was indoctrinated with a strong Christian faith and sought to practice it yet encountered mental opposition that led to the disorder that we call schizophrenia. God really is the God of an eye for an eye and a tooth for a tooth. He also loves us unconditionally, always giving us the chance to turn toward him, to become a holy people, and to be truly happy. With me, it started with the simple faith of a child. We have to believe that everything is possible with God.

I usually stay away from politics. However, I feel that it might be appropriate to say a few lines about the controversial cultural issue regarding gay and lesbian marriages based on the knowledge that I have acquired from Homilies delivered by learned Catholic priests. I have come to understand that in Holy Communion, a Christian brings to the altar his representation of himself to the community over the course of the week as his offering to Jesus. We are called to be the person of Christ to a hungry world, where we have to exercise Christian virtue and principles in order to persevere in situations that can be very difficult and trying. We learn by weekly devotion to this sacrament at mass—mass being the structure and tradition by which we receive the sacrament, where we are affirmed and enlightened by the congregation of believers, and where our soul or mind is renewed amidst this joint worship and receipt of the sacrament, giving us the insight to proceed for the next week along our Christian path. We are enlightened. Our path is lit so that we know our way. This is a joyful and rewarding experience: direct knowledge of the love of Christ and the fulfillment that we are a part of a brethren—a holy community doing God's will and receiving ever more strongly the inspiration of the Holy Spirit.

Mass is the vehicle that God chose for us to use—a social gathering like the last supper or the sermon he gave to the multitudes, which were then fed by a basket of fish and loaves provided by a young boy. He wants us to come together regularly as a community in the form of the mass to receive the sacrament. This is the sacrament whereby Jesus redeemed humanity of sin, whereby he atoned for our sins and redeemed us to have a life with him. In our devotion to this sacrament, Jesus takes our soul to the father in heaven, so that we may experience his love. This sacrament is Jesus calling us to a life with him, which is the only path to true happiness. In the sacrament of Holy Communion, we are able to gain in the knowledge and the love of God, to follow his paths with greater certainty, and to enter more into this life with him. The catechism, the teaching book of our faith, explains that gay or lesbian persons are afflicted with a perverse desire that they must struggle with. They are not to be criticized or isolated in any way but, like any Christian, they have to pursue and find their spiritual path so that they can find their life with Christ. Only then can they know true happiness, like any Christian.

Open homosexuality may be condoned today socially, and it may represent a right granted a citizen. But, in acting so, the open homosexual is brandishing a perverse desire that does not belong in a social context and that is wrong, using the test that it is obstructing his spiritual calling to live a life with Christ, which is the path to true happiness. In Holy Matrimony, God calls a man and a woman to join together in spirit as a holy family. In Catholicism, we believe that a virtuous man and woman who have been chaste as they approach this sacrament will be especially consecrated by God. Their sexual intercourse represents the act that binds their spirits in heaven to become as one, receiving untold blessings and a life together of immeasurable happiness and peace. They will have grace at their table as they raise a family. A gay or lesbian relationship should not be referred to as a marriage because the spirits of a gay or lesbian couple are not joined together to become as one person in Holy Matrimony; theirs is more like a special relationship or a special friendship between two persons, and only then if they are following a correct spiritual path that is leading them closer to a life with Christ. However, to classify these relationships as a marriage with the blessings of matrimony provides us with poor models of the Holy Family. This structure to gay or lesbian relations does not provide our society with the proper direction. These marriages represent an aberration of the sacrament of Holy Matrimony.

When we consider a marriage, we consider procreation and family life to be a primary purpose. To conceive a relationship between gay or lesbian persons as a marriage would seem to provide the wrong structure and direction to society. Theirs seems more like a companionship and should be labeled as such. This is not to say that such a gay or married couple could not raise a child, because that may be appropriate or necessary at times. But the fundamental purpose of these relationships is different. As such, they should not be classified the same.

While an accountant in Montgomery, I became acquainted with a community of gay men who excelled in their work and were both considerate and witty. They did not try to hide themselves but presented themselves in a dignified way. One could grasp that they had gay attributes by their manner, including their tone, emotion, natural attraction to males, and other ways: behavioral features that had become refined in an elevated way. They were not openly gay by any means but were unmarried men who were close friends and spent time together after hours, at times living together. They were devoutly Christian, a thread that was obvious in their behavior, their manner of treating you, and direct expressions of faith, such as blessings over a meal. I have never heard more eloquent, uplifting, and faithful blessings over a meal as the ones provided by a member of this group. These men were on a happy and wholesome journey back to God. They provided models of living to the gay community or anyone.

Many of us make mistakes in living about our sexuality, not just gays, but heterosexual males and females. Society has usually been there to provide us important rules of conduct, with varying consequences for noncompliance, depending on the severity of our transgressions. These are mores that we are taught within our families, our communities, and our religious institutions. They have become traditions that have been passed down, many of which have been refined from lessons hard learned. Some are written rules of conduct, others may be relatively more unspoken, and some have the force of laws. They reflect the wisdom of our leaders, may represent spiritual guidance, and contain the bridge or the parallels between God's laws and man's laws, though we follow a secular path to governance. It seems vitally important that in being a free society that provides its members much freedom of choice to exercise their will, that we also provide those persons structure, guidance, and direction in overcoming or correcting their mistakes. That is the way to preserve and advance a society that is blessed by God and that provides its members the opportunity to thrive—to become accomplished and successful. If homosexual men and women, as chosen companions, for a time or longer, are concerned about equal economic rights, let us consider how we might make those relationship equitable from an economic standpoint. If they want to spend their lives together, so be it. If they are in a position to raise children, let us support that behavior whenever it is properly motivated. But let us not call that a marriage, in the interests of preserving and advancing a society that is blessed by our Creator. And, in the interests of all its constituents, including homosexual men and women, let us help them to structure their lives in ways that will lead them to be truly happy— to make up for past mistakes. We do not want to promote an aberration in the interest of equal rights. That will bring down our society.

CHAPTER 21:

PERSONALITY TYPES

My work in psychology has been an endeavor to understand and explain the human personality. That is the challenge of every psychological assessment: the historical review, clinical interview, and behavioral observations, sometimes complemented by testing. I have also been drawn to such understanding in everyday living, presumably due to my awakened subconscious, which is an enlightening experience that has heightened my curiosity about people and my ability to understand them. At some point in these studies, I began to recognize a phenomenon that caught my attention. I began to notice the physical likeness between people that I tested or came to know and people that I had tested before or that I already knew, such as prior friends or family members. To put it clearly, I have increasingly come to the realization that many, most, or all of us are similar in physical features to other people; thus, there may be a much more limited variety of people to the human race in that we belong to a particular personality type.

This finding became convenient in my work for this reason. If I matched a patient in my psychological work with a person that I know well or have some knowledge about, then I had a frame of reference about what that patient was like, his interests, his skills, the sort of person that he was, and so on. What I am saying is that the physical likeness that led me to identify such a personality type corresponded to the overall personality of this type that I had come to know or understand; I formed such a hypothesis and it proved to have merit. I could hardly avoid exploring this phenomenon, establishing and validating or refuting hypotheses, and similar ideas. Many people, on recognizing this subconsciously, quite obviously did not like to be compared so, and I tried not to overemphasize this finding in my research of their personality assessment. I did not want to show such bias or prejudice. However, it has gained increasing significance over time.

One finding is that some of these same types can be doing relatively well in our society or our world, or did so while living, and other types can be doing relatively poorly. For example, I have matched a successful lawyer with a psychiatric patient, deaf in one ear, mentally retarded, with a seizure disorder, and an uncontrollable temper. How do you equate the two as having a similar personality if one has achieved such success and the other has not? The comparison becomes interesting if you know their histories and recognize that the lawyer has led an unscrupulous life, obviously lacking in spiritual development, and will one day have to answer to Almighty God for his transgressions. It may be of interest to the mentally ill person that his affliction may be due to unscrupulous behavior at another time, but once he atones for his sins, he may have the ability to become someone as professionally capable as to do legal work.

Another example is provided by a scholarly friend who I have come to know better. He affirms and enlightens me spiritually at a subconscious level in such a way that I recognize his thoughtfulness and direction. Recently, I happened to run across an employee at a supermarket whose physical characteristics resembled this scholarly friend. As I was speaking to him, I realized that he had become aware of this idea of mine subconsciously and was contemplating it. My impression was that he was pondering this idea that I felt that he was like my friend, a more scholarly person than he, and my idea that we have lived before, in relation to that. It is hard for me to provide corroboration for these inferences during this brief, intimate exchange with a grocer, except to tell you that as he spoke and contemplated this idea, he embodied the gentle, easy demeanor and thoughtful contemplation that I recognized as that of my scholarly friend's personality, with whom I felt that he had a spiritual exchange. I felt this grocer not only physically was like my scholarly friend, but his personality style was similar as well. He was just a grocer, but he was able to command my respect in a similar way and let me know during that brief exchange that he had good mental capacity.

I have over time become more alert to this dual nature of communication, meaning communicating simultaneously at a conscious and subconscious level, which now happens naturally. It is not something that I do exclusively. I observe this dialogue in others, as they grope to understand those about them better. Learned persons are especially good at mediating their relations in this way, such as teachers and speakers. They are simultaneously reading the minds of listeners who have noteworthy questions and responding at a subconscious level, or sizing up their audience in this way to gain familiarity with their interests. It is the means by which we become comfortable with our social environment, only we do not recognize this subconscious life overtly, or most of us do not.

Let me emphasize these personality types as to their different presentations: I have looked at a red Chinese person and recognized the similarity of that individual to my good friend Joe, unequivocally having Joe's physical markings but in another race, and I have looked into the face of a short in stature young lady with Down's syndrome and seen my good friend Sally, with unmistakable physical attributes that make her resemble Sally, more than that to me, that identify her as that personality type. In the language that I have come to understand, you may be able to get away with your transgressions today, but remember, you are going to have to give that back to God. I have come to more clearly understand scripture that I have heard before. Statements like, "God loves us unconditionally," but also, "He is an exacting God." He loves us enough to give us a second chance, but he also loves us enough to ensure that we learn to follow his ways. He is the great behaviorist who shapes us to follow in his ways. We need to recognize his loving plan for us, so that we become more Godlike, happier as individuals and as a people: a people of God.

One revelation from chapter 20, "The Evolution of Humanity" and chapter 21, "Personality Types" is how closely connected we are as a human race. Our place on the globe today is a reflection of our spiritual journey back to God. That should motivate us all to work more closely together to make for a better planet.

David Anders, the Catholic theologian who reviewed my manuscript, related to me that my theory about reincarnation and about our lives being continuous is contrary to the catechism of the Catholic Church, which states that we only have one earthly life, after which God provides us a "time of grace and mercy" to resolve our life on earth "in keeping with his divine plan," during which our "ultimate destiny" will be determined. David also felt that Jesus repudiated the "eye for eye" doctrine, noting that the key to the Catholic doctrine of salvation is grace. Finally, David felt that the theory about personality types and personality likeness that I proposed was "deeply prejudicial...."

My response to David as a lifelong practicing Catholic in the world is that Jesus Christ, through the inspiration of the holy spirit of God, in the very ordinary medium of my psychological work, which has been my laboratory for the past 25 years, revealed the idea that we are reincarnated and that our lives are continuous, in two ways. The first came to me, as I describe in chapter 20, "The Evolution of Humanity," when I tried to understand the agony of an individual who appeared to suffer from a lifelong antisocial personality disorder and suffered a head injury that prevented him from having the cognitive integrity to support his antisocial personality. The result was repeated angry and aggressive behavior, which caused him injury, incarceration, and social alienation. In considering his plight, it dawned on me that God would not be so unfair if not for a reason. What merits a person to be born with an antisocial personality? The only plausible answer was that this man had lived before and acted in an antisocial way. Similarly, was there a divine design behind him not only being born antisocial, but also suffering the cost of an accident that prevented him from supporting those personality dynamics? The only answer that seemed plausible was God's justice.

The second revelation supporting my assertion that we are reincarnated and that our lives are continuous comes from the material in this chapter, chapter 21, "Personality Types," which complements chapter 20. We all have, over the course of our lifetimes, noticed how people favor. In my psychological work, I became more perceptive of this phenomenon, meaning that I both noticed it more frequently and in a broader way, such as observing an African American or red Chinese whose physical attributes were like those of a close friend, or noticing, unmistakably, the physical attributes of a female I knew and liked in a younger girl with very obvious markings of Down's syndrome. This was not a coincidence. This was a revelation from God from the greater perception that I acquired by means of my awakened subconscious that someone who was very much like my friend had done something in a prior lifetime that had caused her to suffer this plight.

The bible is filled with scripture about our need to make up for our transgressions in order to be worthy of God's grace and how they cost us. I mentioned the Epistle of James previously, where he asks sinners to begin mourning. I also mention that it is scriptural for us to be reconciled with a neighbor toward whom we have committed a transgression before approaching the altar to gain access to God's holy spirit. Jesus, in one of his famous parables, described the plight of the man who did not invest the coins his master left in his custody but buried them, an abstract reference to his expectations for us to invest our talents well. Finally, the revelations in chapters 20 and 21 attest to the repercussions to us of failing to follow God's plan for us.

CHAPTER 22:

THE SPIRIT WORLD, REVISITED

When I speak of the concept, "the spirit world," I am speaking in the context of humanity, and I am referring to our conscious and subconscious mind. That comprises our soul and the totality of our mental or spiritual life: our spiritual world. I believe this is a spiritual life that we have to nurture and develop in order to reach ever greater potential for thought and wisdom. This premise is supported by scripture and many of our human experiences. What is our capacity?

Recall the well known biblical scripture stating that we are made in the image of God. For me, that passage once conjured up images of Michelangelo's paintings of God on the ceiling of the Sistine Chapel in Vatican City: his inspired murals of God in human form—a muscular, handsome, stern, white-haired, elderly man. It must have been the summer or fall of 1988, when I was enrolled in school at AUM and in process of changing careers from accounting to psychology. I was leasing an apartment unit at the Country Club Apartments from the Stowers Realty Company on Fairview Avenue, which boasted some of the most beautiful patio gardens around. It was Sunday morning, and I was listening to Dr. Dale Huff, the pastor of the First Baptist Church in Montgomery, Alabama, as he delivered his homily to his congregation and television audience, which made reference to that same biblical passage: we are made in the image of God. Dr. Huff explained that the passage refers to our mental (if also our physical) self. In other words, we are meant to have the mind of God. That statement was most enlightening and broadened my view of the passage that we are created in the image of God. It then follows from our human experience and pertinent biblical references that we have to earn that spiritual capacity, for most assuredly, God has a brilliant mind.

Recall my discourse earlier about the general differences between the language ability of a member of the working class and a member of the professional class, including the studious application and hard work that would be required to make the transition from the working to the professional class. That is the path for all of us to become smarter: studious, hard work. By applying ourselves assiduously, our weaknesses today will be tomorrow's strengths. There actually is no other path to being intelligent. Thus, our capacity for higher order or any kind of reasoning and for wisdom is unlimited, given that mentally or spiritually we are created in the image of God. Furthermore, our present ability, based upon the insights derived from chapter 20, "The Evolution of Humanity," is simply the mental state and capacity that we have gained or earned to this point in our lives. In most instances, a person who is born into and raised within a working class environment would be expected to have less capacity than a person born into and raised within a professional class setting, but that is simply a presumption because we do not know God's reasons for such placement or the mental capacity which accompanies that person.

I do not like to preach to humanity. We are a tremendously diverse people. Yet, with reference to chapter 20, "The Evolution of Humanity" and chapter 21, "Personality Types," I have to say that we also have a common denominator. We are all governed by God, and with the insights provided by those chapters, we can see that we are not so different at all. The chapters hint at our need to find our way back to God and reveal that clearly if we take a close look. What is the course back to God? The Christian Bible, which Christians observe as the inspired work of the holy spirit of God, is a rich reference source for such guidance. For example, it says clearly and unequivocally that God calls us to be a holy people, a royal priesthood, a people set apart. That is the equivalent of saying that we are God's people, that we are on a journey back to God, and that we need to find our way. We can only do that by growing closer to God. To do so, we need to understand God better, which is a spiritual life that is revealed to us by means of the inspiration of the Holy Spirit or Holy Paraclete, one of the forms of

God. Our Christian teachings reveal that God made man, Jesus Christ, upon his death, out of his love for humankind, left believers the gift of the holy spirit of God so that we could have intimate communion with him and with one another. God reveals his will for us through the Holy Ghost and through intimate communication with all believers. We believers who were raised in the Christian faith identify ourselves as Christians because we are disciples of Jesus Christ. We come to know God's will for us and follow it through enlightened thought, namely the inspiration of the Holy Ghost and of other Christians. These enlightened minds are also bright minds; they are illuminated by growing closer to God. As such, they are growing in capacity for reasoned thought and wisdom.

I have been taught and believe that God loves us equally and unconditionally, regardless. I have also been taught and believe that God gives each one of us a free will, to choose and decide our course in life. Obviously, considering the insights provided in various chapters, including chapter 20, "The Evolution of Humanity," and chapter 21, "Personality Types," some of us have made poor choices. Effectively, we have led past sinful lives and carry that baggage now. We have to turn aside from sin and become more spiritual; we have to find our way or path back to God. That is the only way to true happiness, for some obvious reasons. One is that sin creates psychological conflicts for us. It impedes our ability to have unfettered thought—to reach out to the cosmos with a totally open mind and contemplate the wonders of the universe—which, I think we need to do in a disciplined way, schooled by mentors in our course of study, for example. We lose capacity for illuminating our minds in a priestly way by the dimming effects of sins or transgressions upon our souls. We cannot be enlightened by the holy spirit of God and cannot have intimate communication with other believers when our minds are encumbered by the effects of sin. Thus, we are not able to share in the happiness that comes not only from the rewards of intellectual advancement, but also from the knowledge that we are close to God and to other believers, that we are doing God's will and are growing closer to him, and that we are distancing ourselves from the undesirable effects of sin.

There is yet another reason that growing closer to God will make us happy. I have been taught and believe that as disciples of Our Lord, all doing his will, we are all members of one body: the body of Christ. Regardless of our function, how big or small, we all have a vital role. Otherwise, the body would lose functioning parts and corresponding vitality. Beyond that, I have been taught and believe that God has a special plan for each and every one of us. Thus, by growing closer to him, we are able to learn his will for us and follow it in order to fulfill the role that he would have us assume as a member of the body of Christ. Imagine the joy from knowing God through the medium of the Holy Spirit, having intimate communion with other believers, knowing that we are free of sin and doing God's will for us, and realizing our dreams. I remember that when I was still in Montgomery and married to Pam, I attended an adult education class headed by David McGuiness, a young, intellectual, inspired Irish priest at Our Lady Queen of Mercy church. He was contrasting the Fundamentalist and Catholic interpretation of the Bible message about the end of the world. Father McGuiness explained that the Catholic belief is that the resurrection of our body begins here on earth and that we are called to be a resurrected people, meaning that we can have access to heaven right here on earth.

What is the best path back to God? How do we go about finding it? As a Christian and a Catholic in the United States of America, I can tell you that the best path for me has been to become indoctrinated in biblical scripture through the inspired instruction of the Sunday homily by a learned priest at church, complemented by Catholic education led by knowledgeable sources (limited, to date), individual study (limited, to date), and contemplation of these teachings and sacred scriptures. However, indoctrination in the scriptures and applying them to one's daily life are two quite different tasks, for there is a wide gulf between acquiring knowledge and applying it in a skillful way, particularly if we do not receive further education that illustrates for us in a fairly concrete way how that knowledge is to be applied. These may be instructions that come from the Sunday homily as applied to modern times, Sunday school classes or adult education classes about our religion, and mentoring from our parents and perhaps from significant other people in our lives. I believe that many of us have had a richer culture in the indoctrination process that in the application process, the latter of which is indispensable to facilitate our Christian journey back to God. Let's consider that journey.

The Christian path is well announced biblically. There is ample scripture and direction which specify that as Christians, we must be willing to lead the life of Christ and his disciples and to be similarly persecuted for his name's sake. As Christians, we are to personify Jesus to a hungry world: a world in need of his love and compassion. This is our weekly vow in the tradition of the celebration of the mass, where we are renewed in spirit and once again called to go forth with his message to a world that may challenge our Christian faith to its core. It is within that struggle to assert ourselves as Christians where we win or lose the battle for our very lives: our souls. Being indoctrinated in our Christian religion and finding and following that path in our daily lives are quite different challenges. We can become sidetracked by a world that rejects us.

The world may seem like a rat race in our early struggle, until we achieve greater mastery over it. We may feel such a great sense of disharmony that prevailing in Christian ways seems to not quite have relevance to the environment that we live or work in. But, that is the very environment that we are called to understand, survive, master, influence, and transform with our positive energy. Along that path, as I mentioned above, we are surely to encounter elements of persecution, in a worldly sense: arrogance, prejudice, inequity, insult, jealousy, mistreatment, hatred, and the like. My mother referred to people who are hard to convert as "hard hearts"; we are likely to encounter hard hearts who oppose our ways.

I had the good fortune to belong to a peer group that nurtured and affirmed me until they left an indelible mark of Christian living upon my soul. It is my calling, and I view it as their assignment, to bring their spirit to a hungry world. This hungry world consists of people who have had less capable role models; who have been shown not consideration, but a lack of it; who have been taught to think of themselves first, at the expense of their neighbors if necessary, because that is what it takes to get ahead; who have learned to compromise their principles by forming alliances with those who might help them to get ahead, even if it means slighting other more deserving people who do not figure in their picture of success; who were treated in a mean, cruel fashion when they sought a noble path, mistreated for showing compassion; who lacked basic necessities and, thus unfortunate, are resentful of those more fortunate; whose life experiences have taught them to harbor spite, malice, disdain, jealousy, and hatred towards more fortunate others for their better lot in life or what that meant for them, because they were not selected for the finer things in living, better places at church, school, work, and other social occasions; who were raised in an alcoholic home (a home where one or both parents experienced alcoholism), where they were subjected to various forms of neglect, abuse, and exploitation; who, being raised in an alcoholic home, lacked awareness that the roles they were ascribed or assumed within those homes were improper and would lead to adjustment, emotional, psychological, and behavioral problems; and so on. How then are we as Christians to rise to this challenge against people who have acquired indelible marks of non-Christian living or non-Christian ways?

Our response will depend on our own indoctrination, such as how knowledgeable we are about Christ's precepts, about the message or lesson in biblical scripture, how close to God we have grown by following Christian ways, how we have been influenced by other Christians who have brought his message of charity, love, and peace to us, and how well we have learned to seek out his spirit as the guiding force in our lives. These are the armor and the shield that we take into battle: into our schools, our social functions, our work places, and other settings. Our work places provide us a context for the task of persevering in Christian ways amidst strife, where we may be faced with attitudes such as, "It is every man (or woman) for himself (or herself)." These may seem to be highly competitive environments where our decisions are likely to have notable impact in terms of the success that we enjoy and our mistakes may be noticeable or costly. Regardless of what is at stake as we apply our skills, we must also become adept at applying our Christian principles to make for desirable work environments, which is not an easy task for the very reason mentioned, that there is a segment of society that will reject those principles, seek to undermine them, and try to use all their cunning and wit to defeat the Christian person.

It is most important to exercise care at work and in other settings in order to get things right from the start so that we do not begin to follow unhealthy patterns. There may be institutional or systemic issues at work that are easy to overlook, including areas where we are unfamiliar that are easy to ignore and that can set the stage for being less than thoughtful. In my psychological work, this might be failing to speak assertively as a novice when the treatment team's comment about a patient incident the night before does not satisfy me, bowing to pressure to defer to those who are more experienced, and so forth. The task of the Christian and anyone who seeks to be considerate about his clients or his work is often no more difficult than keeping his eyes and ears—his senses—alert to the environment where he works and using his God-given intelligence to ask the right questions in a considerate way so that he may obtain the information needed to proceed, but he must be sure to do that. He must also be prepared to make well-placed remarks here and there in order to put other people in their place so that they do not crowd and bully him but respect him. If he does not get answers that satisfy him, it is important to follow up with someone who is more knowledgeable, such as his supervisor, until he is satisfied, and if not satisfied, to take proper action.

These events and circumstances often occur amidst the hustle and bustle of the day, when we are already faced with the challenge of our work, doing it well, and doing it timely. Such events can be pressure packed, and our priorities can become confused. These are tests of faith and challenges to our spiritual integrity, which a Christian must rise to in order to earn his place as a member of Jesus' flock. It is precisely within such a framework at work that we must demonstrate courage and be upright, demonstrate to other people that we follow a high standard because it is right and just to do so, and succeed in adhering to such standards. It is by such practices, those noble efforts, which may be very arduous and trying at first, that we are inspired, enlightened, and receive the direction that we need in an illuminated way. This is why it is so essential for us to walk up to the altar on Sunday at mass as Christians. We present Christ our prior week's struggle as our offering to him for his grace and spirit in Holy Communion that he might find our efforts worthy of his gift of the Holy Spirit to enlighten our hearts and minds and to refreshen our spirit so that we may be prepared to continue along our Christian path during the following week, showing the way to those less well endowed. To become truly Christian, we have to be smart, knowledgeable, and shrewd about worldly ways. We have to acquire social intelligence, smarts about living in the world, and the ability to lead others in order to make the world a better place in which to live. Don't underestimate God. He will fashion us in that way, if ever slowly. Christians are smart. They are successful. The biblical passage is true. Put Christ first in your life, and everything else will be granted onto you.

This is a formidable task. Among all elements of society, there are people who have forged ahead by hook or crook, forming a coalition here, using power and rank unfairly there, entering into compromising relationships, sexual liaisons, catering to subordinates with the understanding that they are the most important and to be recognized as the leader, who are anything but Christian in their approach to living. How is a Christian to succeed—to assert himself in such a work setting, amongst such a work group? We have to do this gradually by showing other people that there is a better way and convincing them that it is in theirs and everyone's best interests to follow it.

In order to achieve this end, we have to be successful in our vocational pursuits while upholding Christian principles so that we become recognized leaders who other people are willing to listen to. This is not an easy task but it is within our grasp. It is God's calling for all Christians, so that we can transform the world in which we live and make it a better place. This also means that we can count on God's support through the medium of the Holy Spirit, the intercession of saints to enlighten us and light our way, and the Christian community to which we belong. This is a winning team.

This knowledge of the Bible, the inspired scriptures wherein God speaks to us, and application of that knowledge to do God's will for us here on Earth, in our respective capacities, will gradually bring our baptism into the body of Christ, as members of his flock. We will grow closer to God in this process, to having the mind of God, to lead more inspired lives, to recognize the guidance of his holy spirit and his will for us, and to become "a resurrected people." This is a calling not just for Christians, but for all humankind, that we began the journey back to God and that we become members of his body, each doing his or her part, to transform our world into a most charismatic village, free of the snares of sin.

Father John Fallon, a former pastor of Holy Spirit Catholic Church here in Tuscaloosa, gave an inspired homily about the many scientific, technological, and practical advancements of humankind some years ago, which I previously spoke of, in order to highlight our failure to advance as a race, beyond war, negative attitudes, and emotions such as jealousy and anger, criminal behavior, and other undesirable acts, which Father Fallon referenced in his discourse about what God would have to say to us if he were to address our state of human affairs. If we could identify one area where advances or changes might help to improve our human lot, it may well be the subconscious world. The reason is that the subconscious underpins or supports all human behavior from benevolence to treachery and provides the missing link for behavior that is baffling or unexplained.

Consider a young male drug user that enters a psychiatric treatment facility for the first time. He is provided expert substance use treatment to help him in his recovery from the substance use pattern, and he is shown practical ways that can begin in the hospital to start the process of rehabilitation. Much to his therapist's disappointment, he does not seem to cooperate with his treatment very well, exhibiting behaviors such as not arising timely, failing to attend some important group activities, and talking in the therapist's class rather than contributing to the discussion. The therapist eventually realizes that this client does not seem to conform to social standards or identify well with traditional professional authority figures and eventually surmises that this client must have an alternative reinforcement system that supports his undesirable behavior. This alternative reinforcement system would be represented by those people, past and present, whom this young drug user has identified with and listens to. He has to a large extent already been indoctrinated in his pattern of behavior so that he may not need a lot of direction at this point in time, but he is also likely to continue to experience conscious and subconscious influences from this alternative group that promotes his undesirable behavior in this facility.

A thorough social history and meetings with his family could help to identify this young man's reinforcement system. It may be comprised of a range of people, some who are more central to his way of thinking than others. For example, a core group might be disenchanted youths, which includes the young man, who were not provided a good academic foundation for various reasons, such as parents who were relatively uneducated, an upbringing in a low socioeconomic environment where the family struggled to survive, and other circumstances which created a climate that was not conducive to academic achievement and intellectual advancement. The daily toil of these families amidst poverty and a perception of limited opportunity for advancement, while observing more fortunate people who have plenty, can lead to bitter feelings. These feelings can be a source of negative emotions such as anger, resentment, and discouragement. Some may find reprieve from their experience by using alcohol and drugs, which can exceed a mere uplift of the spirit to intoxication and abuse, a pattern that can become problematic. For example, the disinhibited emotional state resulting from substances can lead to promiscuous sexual behavior, rowdy behavior, fighting, impulsive and unplanned acts that include crimes to support the pattern, and other undesirable behavior. Thus, these disadvantaged families or its members appear to be at some risk of developing undesirable patterns of behavior.

Other dysfunction within the family may be evidenced by feuding between the parents, a lack of time and consideration for the lives of their children, divorce and the attendant emotional problems of parental separation, and modeling of undesirable patterns by some of the children. Some may drop out of school early and fail to develop trade skills. That is not to say that some of these low socioeconomic status or underprivileged families will not exhibit desirable norms, such as being honest and hardworking, struggling to eke out a living, and doing more in an effort to get ahead. Some may also belong to a church community that promotes desirable values, such as honesty, patience, kindness to neighbors, and diligence about opportunities to advance socially, academically, and vocationally. It is to say that children raised within a disadvantaged home environment like the one described may not feel very much a part of things in society. They may have identified with their parents and modeled them, meaning that they may harbor bitter and angry feelings towards people more fortunate than they have been and society at large. These people may recognize each other quickly, by their simple vocabulary, poor grammar, and less than precise expressions; their dress; the subject matter, music, and television they are attracted to; use of profanity; disclosure of substance use habits and disclosure of other interests; and obvious disregard for social standards and authority figures, including neglect of rules and manipulative behavior.

These disenchanted youths, who have a background and a similar experience as the young drug abuser, would represent his core group, the alternative reinforcement structure that he listens to, which is an obstacle to progress that the therapist must overcome in order to provide effective treatment to this young man so as to facilitate positive changes. There are also many variations to this core group: other people who are a part of his alternative reinforcement system. For example, if the young man were also part of a gang, then he might quickly identify with other people in the psychiatric treatment setting who were in gangs and who espouse similar norms as his gang. Similarly, there may be custodial workers and nursing assistants—young and old—who have had similar experiences as the young man or his parents and who, for that reason, may quickly pick up on his behavior and become a part of his alternative reinforcement group.

This is why it can be very difficult to produce change in a direct or linear fashion: because within the very structure of an organization, such as other clients, supporting personnel, direct care staff, and some professional staff, there may be similarly disenchanted individuals who by their manner, reactions, and attitude, in general, and their engagements with the young drug abuser, specifically, convey to him that they have a similar identification, to varying degrees, depending on their role. Likewise, by their sometimes discordant relations with other professionals, such as the young man's therapist, and a subconscious dialogue that they develop with the young man, they provide support for his undesirable patterns at a conscious and subconscious level—a bonding of sorts that makes it considerably more difficult to engender desirable changes in the young man. This is why it is most important to have a well defined structure and well defined role functions within an organization. Likewise, we need competent leaders who promote lofty principles in the work setting for specific employee roles and who discourage personality problems between its members. For example, in a mental health setting, a skilled nurse who is part of a progressive treatment team and who relates well with the professionals on her team can help the direct care staff members to develop their roles in an effective way, helping them to relate well to the other professionals and helping them to see their opportunities for advancement, which may discourage them from supporting practices that impede treatment efforts.

A thorough social history, familiarity with the patient's family, and knowledge of the patient can all help a skilled practitioner to recognize the elements or members of the young man's reinforcement system. One can see how well integrated such a system can be and the difficulty of changing the system itself, which falls within the purview of education and prevention, not just treatment. In the case in point, it would likely be difficult to change the young man's supportive cultural subgroup due to its prevalence within society. However, I would point out that self-help groups such as Alcoholics Anonymous, when the substance user has experienced sufficient problems to desire change, have been very effective in producing such changes. Similarly, a therapist who is knowledgeable, perceptive, and skilled can begin the process of change by attributes such as exhibiting a nonjudgmental attitude while introducing ideas that lead clients to recognize their opportunities and question their practices.

We are the product of our ambient culture; that is, our values are usually a reflection of the environment in which we are raised. Our behavior is an example of that social reinforcement system where we learn social behavior based on the contingencies for approval and disapproval that are established by our leaders, such as our parents, our teachers, our coaches, and other significant influences, including our good friends and their social structure. Our differences from other groups provide us information to make calculated inferences about the ambient culture of the members of that group. The behavior of each group is a reflection of the quality of their respective social reinforcement system, including their mores, traditions, and values. Similarly, their behavior provides information about the richness of their spiritual lives or subconscious dialogue.

Some 25 years ago, when I was doing my practicum work at a substance use treatment facility, I treated an alcoholic and drug addict who belonged to a family of racketeers: a ring of professional thieves. He was referred to us through the court system. I was able to piece together this information from history provided by extended family members who wanted him to change his ways. His father had experienced alcoholism and had spent much of his life behind bars. The man and his four brothers had followed in his footsteps. One of their rackets was to steal cars, transport them across state lines, dismantle them, and sell the parts or use them to rebuild other cars. They appeared to be a part of a larger, organized ring of racketeers. This man hardly ever showed any emotion and would not reveal anything about himself. Regardless of how convincingly I presented information to him in order to encourage honest disclosure, he would reply that he could not remember or provide unexplained details such as "I had an alcohol problem" without describing his circumstances or specific behavior further. Of course, this was not the route to recovery from alcoholism by AA standards, which require a commitment to identifying undesirable patterns of behavior, changing unscrupulous ways, and leading a more principled life—a process during which honest disclosure is essential. However, these recovery principles were at odds with this man's professional code of conduct and his peer group—the alternative reinforcement system guiding him—which he was not ready to give up despite significant losses. His father and mother both had died from health problems associated with alcoholism, one brother met his fate in prison, apparently at the hands of rival racketeers, and another brother was a homeless alcoholic who had obviously not fared well from a life of crime.

This man's crimes were not so atrocious, meaning that he had not committed a capital crime such as murder. Even so, his behavior was reminiscent of the stereotype of the cold-blooded criminal who can lie with a straight face without showing any emotion. He had been indoctrinated in these protective behaviors through conscious and subconscious dialogue with his ambient criminal culture in order to support his antisocial behavior and likely continued to receive that reinforcement, though the immediate ranks of his support group had thinned considerably, he was depressed, and he was experiencing worsening alcoholism. If we could have been privy to the subconscious dialogue of his primary support group, such as professional racketeers who were sworn to a code of secrecy or one of his siblings, we might have heard such person(s) provide him instructions such as, "Tell him that you don't remember," "Don't appear anxious," or "Just tell him that you had a problem with alcohol." I encouraged this man to rejoin society through the medium of the AA fellowship, a viable alternative group, pointing out the dismal failure that his practices had brought him and his family, a strategy that appeared to have had some, though limited, success.

Alcoholism itself provides an example of another unusual subgroup regarding the undesirable practices that are supported at a conscious and subconscious level by its ambient culture. I have in the past referred to alcoholics and drug addicts as strong personalities because they seem able to suppress emotions such as shame, guilt, and anxiety related to their unscrupulous ways continuously during the course of their substance use pattern. This contrasts sharply with the typical Christian or social attitude and would not occur without support from their alcoholism subculture. Typically, when upright members of society or Christian people engage in sinful ways, those ways are not supported by their social reinforcement structure. They may feel disgraced among their social group members, who, if not directly aware of their behavior, gain awareness of it at a subconscious level, which may make the perpetrator feel awkward, guilty, and lacking in spiritual harmony, if he is not already prone to do so. I also believe that when the sin is very serious, such as fornication, people who traditionally uphold and follow Christian ideals impair their customary harmonious relationship with the holy spirit of God and experience a strong sense of disgrace from that impairment—God directly bears on their mental state. Their mental state tends to create remorseful feelings and motivates them to express feelings of regret and sorrow and to seek reconciliation for their transgressions. This may become a reinforcing journey as these individuals, over time, very gradually regain the spiritual harmony that they have lost, until they reach that time of reconciliation when they can once again feel at peace with their God and with their social group.

The social structure of the alcoholic and drug addict is altogether different. For example, in a home where one of the parents is an alcoholic— say the father—the alcoholic parent, in order that he may continue in his alcoholic ways, may feel a need or seek to recruit all the family members to support his alcoholism pattern, or his spouse may do so. Typically, he may want home life to be secretive or hidden from public view, which may be necessary to sustain it because society would not condone his practices. In order to comply with his wishes, his wife and children may agree to or adopt a limited social life. These behaviors that aid and abet the alcoholism pattern tend to compromise the spiritual lives of all the family members because they lead them to become a part of the problem or the alcoholic sickness, which is referred to as co-dependence; they develop psychological or emotional problems as an outgrowth of limiting their own lives by supporting the alcoholic pattern in the home. It also may be that when the alcoholic becomes abusive to the other family members, it is due to anger from knowledge that they have violated the standard that has been set, such as attending a school social event where the wife and children acted sociably.

Alanon is the family educational arm for the non-alcoholic spouse, such as the wife, to help her learn how to detach herself and her children from the alcoholic and his alcoholism problem in a loving way instead of supporting him and becoming a part of the problem. Adult Children of Alcoholics (ACOA) is a support group that helps the adult children of an alcoholic parent(s) to address the psychological or emotional problems they developed in the alcoholic home, where they often are cast in or assume roles that may be necessary for their immediate survival but that are poorly adaptive in the long run because they lead to emotional problems and hinder the development of mature, adult roles. Some of the psychological problems these children develop can be related to "boundary issues" that may be present in these homes and emotional "enmeshment" wherein the parent tends to become so invested in his children's emotional problems that the parent has a similar experience. Effectively, the parent does not provide the children the space or autonomy to resolve their emotional problems independently, which prevents the children from achieving mature emotional development.

Dr. Susan Dudley, the leader of our Psi Chi group in my clinical psychology master's program at AUM (1988), an honors group, on the subject of incest, spoke about the irony of incest being taboo within our culture though it is thought to be so prevalent that it may occur as often as in one of every five families. Considering the boundary and enmeshment issues in an alcoholic home and the personality changes that an alcoholic parent experiences during the drinking cycle, the incidence of incest within the alcoholic home would be expected to be considerably higher than in the general population. It may well be a contributing factor to the high population rate.

There are other reasons why alcoholics and drug addicts are able to suppress feelings of guilt, shame, and anxiety related to their unscrupulous behavior other than support from their families. A number of alcoholics may themselves be children of alcoholics; as such, they may have never had a chance to experience a normal childhood and have never grown up, meaning that they remain immature and less responsible for their behavior for that reason. Some children of alcoholics may feel their use of alcohol was promoted within the family and provides relief to the alcoholic or drug-addicted parent for whom they are shouldering some of the blame, which may help them to excuse their own behavior. Indeed, their parents and siblings may support and abet their pattern. These and a number of others may become a part of a marginal social group of people who drink and use drugs and who, as a whole, may tend to be socially irresponsible.

Many of these substance abusers slowly crush their spiritual life or do considerable harm to it by being part of subgroups that do not hold them accountable for their prodigal behavior but, rather, support it. This pattern distances them from traditional society. It usually makes them feel uncomfortable in traditional social groups, where they may become very sensitive and suspicious, especially in a very pro-social or Christian group, such as a church group. The church group may begin to get a sense of their behavior from what they hear or have heard in their community about them or as a result of subconscious revelations that surface to provide a sense of the behavior of the alcoholic or drug addict. Likely as a part of the norm in the alcoholic home of keeping family activities hidden from public view, children from homes where a parent is an alcoholic are well known for presenting very well publicly so that someone who does not have a well-trained eye or specific knowledge about the family might never guess that these are children from an alcoholic home who are suppressing behavioral indiscretions and psychological or emotional problems.

I was naïve about people growing up. I think the reason was that I had a difficult time looking at them in a critical way. I can think of two reasons for this, which may be intertwined. My simple early faith understanding was that we are not supposed to be judgmental, which I had not distinguished from being interpersonally critical. Furthermore, with my burgeoning schizophrenia, my mental opponents hindered my ability to engage other people in general, such as creating distressful feelings within me if I tried to use much discernment in relations with others. Thus, in order to be nonjudgmental and to feel at peace, I was often insufficiently critical with regard to another person's comments and behavior. This attitude, which prevented me from becoming interpersonally skilled, was consonant with parental wishes.

They were not training or mentoring me in that way due to their motivation to limit my social advancement and unencumbered growth. That was a way for them to exercise some control over my life to suit their plans.

My awakening subconscious gradually changed all that. It liberated me from the hold that my opponents had upon me as I recognized their motivation. I was able to look at them critically, a very gradual and natural process that came about from the more in-depth perception of training myself to perceive both conscious and subconscious messages. For example, people may express their views consciously but also reveal an alternative motivation by their nonverbal facial and bodily expressions, including their corresponding emotional message and their very persona. They may also reveal their true motivation by the voice of their mind. Additionally, other people who are part of the conversation or who are in the vicinity can access the opponent's subconscious and provide cues about his motivation either overtly or subconsciously by the voice of their mind. People without the room who are privy to the conversation can also communicate by the voice or their mind. Although these phenomena are not always reliable, including manipulative tactics by some of those involved, over time, I have become fairly certain of another person's motivation in this way. Some of these comments may seem questionable. Many of these revelations may be more readily observed in group dynamics than a meeting between two persons only. Regardless, the subconscious dialogue, cues, and messages are an ongoing phenomenon, so that, over time, I have been able to become certain about ideas that were doubtful at first. Initially, I was daunted by this experience, which revealed another individual's personality and motivation to me, about which I had been so naïve previously. However, in time, I recognized it as a gift that I have been able to use in constructive ways, such as to avoid entanglements and promote fair play.

I have experienced parallel spiritual growth and maturity. This greater knowledge of people and their motivation has been complemented by a greater sense of responsibility to assert myself, when not to do so could prove to be detrimental to me, people I care about, people I serve, and people who are not very capable of representing their interests. I began to recognize better the leadership or supervision that I engage and the corresponding motivation of these superiors and authorities, which has helped me to negotiate my daily interactions with them. I have also been able to recognize the influence that coalitions seek to exert so as to retain my position when I have felt that it has merit, and I have been able avoid the unsettling effects of such wholesale opposition. I learned over time that we are bound by spiritual laws that promote fair play even in dire or lopsided situations. For example, my opponents frequently have had to reveal their well laid plans and motivation in order to prepare me for their undesirable actions, and I have been the recipient of further enlightenment about the human personality and rightful paths by persevering in faith and trial, so that I have been able to grow ever confident of my way.

An awakened subconscious, as I previously mentioned, made me much more perceptive about people. As a result, I begin to notice a number of group norms. One that caught my attention, which may have been partly due to my psychological studies, was an element in society that I identified as narcissism. It seemed that on a regular basis, I encountered people who promoted themselves, placed themselves above the crowd, were quick to point out their intelligence, and so on. If this were not so, or in addition to such narcissism, these people acted snobbishly, slighted those persons who they did not recognize as members of their esoteric group by putting on an air of superiority or viewing them as inferior, ignored people who did not belong to their special group, and exhibited other rude behavior.

I have not always been personally involved in these actions. I have glimpsed this behavior in the various ways that we encounter society at large, including print and television media, observation of the workings of groups, and so on. These people seem to ascribe to some of the characteristics or be-havior patterns that we think of when speaking of "yuppie" or "preppie" types among the young adult population, though the narcissism that I speak of has not been limited to a particular age group. It has at times seemed so prevalent that I have thought to myself, "A segment of our social leaders act as if they have a Narcissistic Personality Disorder" (3). When I have encoun-tered this attitude from an individual, it has immediately impressed me as unconscionable, and it has evoked scornful feelings from me because of my Catholic background. Regardless of the actual intelligence of the speaker, I have tended to view such behavior as immature behavior that should not be condoned and that needs a rebuff. Although I have usually tried not to show my feelings in these circumstances, as a student of psychology and human behavior, I have sought to understand the driving force behind it. I think that I have found the answer as a result of the many psychological cases that I have studied; from knowledge gained about these individuals, which I have followed over time; and by the special insight that my awakened subcon-scious has brought me.

Some of this subgroup of people emit a lot of aggressive energy as part of their narcissism, which may offend those people that are the object or target of their pompous behavior and upset their easy demeanor. This has the effect of providing the aggressor access to that person's insight, as previously discussed; by upsetting their target's disposition, they temporarily gain a degree of access to the target's mental state, which enhances their own. Thus, some of their pompousness is generated to upset their target's disposition in order to broaden or heighten their intellectual ability. Their mental effort changes from a rough go to a glide or from a slow pace to smooth sailing, if only for the period of time that they are able to upset the other person's mental state or constitution.

Many of these people, as I have noted, are in leadership roles. If not, they may be in a subservient position to the leader, lackeys of sorts. In group situations, they often dominate and control the conversation, often in concert with their subordinates, who are similarly motivated. Effectively, such people, working in concert or as a coalition, depict a group conscience in their efforts and seem to jointly gain access to the mental integrity of the target when he loses it by becoming flustered, angry, and so forth. If the reader has never encountered this behavior, I can attest that two, three, or more people in a group situation can very effectively frustrate another group member's efforts to make a point, particularly to make it timely without it seeming awkward or misplaced, if it is made at all. They can be so adept at this behavior, which occurs at a conscious and subconscious level, that by the time the targeted group member has a chance to say anything, his point no longer seems pertinent. Of course, one of objectives of the coalition in these circumstances is to upset the targeted individual. All that being as it may, I have formed the impression that group leaders often seem to have become more skilled than that at achieving their goals, or less clumsy.

One of the tactics of such group leaders is to stall the targeted group member's response so that the group can gain access to it subconsciously as that group member considers what to say, which may occur a number of times while the coalition is effectively preventing him from expressing his views. Their reasons for doing so appear to be multifold. One important reason is that they want to maintain their leadership role and feel threatened by someone who may introduce bright ideas. Consequently, an initial reason for delaying the targeted group member's response is to gain access to the idea, subconsciously as his mind thinks or says it, so that they can know for sure whether it is an original idea that they should be concerned about. Secondly, if it is an original idea, then they will seek to undermine it by making it conscious, perhaps in an altered way that will not be so obvious, and group leaders seem to be able to do this very effectively by eliciting this information from their subordinates (primarily) or themselves making such remarks (secondarily). Still a third tactic, perhaps a last resort, which they may implement when they feel that other tactics are ineffective, is to undermine or slight the idea by ignoring the group member who originates it, creating a distraction, becoming involved in another conversation, and other ways. This behavior further undermines the group processes.

There is a rich variety to this sort of behavior, of which the above may be a fair representation. Subconscious processes like these are not at all unusual in groups where people form coalitions that serve their interests but that do not consider the interests of all group members. My impression is that many of these people have resorted to similar behavior throughout their lives, which I refer to as mental cheating. Typically, they have a lot of mental energy and can read and absorb what they read, but their comprehension may be more like absorbing the facts without rich understanding, and they may not be very capable of applying that learning in a general way. They can be very skilled at similar situations, such as situations that require delivery of consequences to people who have acted wrongly or stern reprimands. However, they are not the most capable leaders because they lack the confidence and skills to obtain the best information available from the group at hand in order to achieve the best results. They fail to develop their subordinates so that they may one day become able leaders. They follow ineffective practices that do not nurture deserving group members. They themselves may fail to advance in leadership skills over time except for those gained from novel members to their esoteric group who may add to their skills repertoire. The novel person to their esoteric group may add to their skills repertoire but can be expected to have selfish motives and jealous feelings that will serve to undermine dedicated workers who are earning their place.

When I went through orientation at Bryce Hospital some 25 years ago, I joined several of the other professionals and perhaps some non-professionals, who had been through orientation, in a comfortable room in the main building at the end of our orientation. There must have been a group of seven or so of us led by a leader named Earle Sandy, a former social worker who had become a member of staff development, in which capacity he demonstrated exceptional skills in the treatment plans in-service where I encountered him subsequently. He and his wife Rosemary, who was also a social worker at Bryce Hospital, were also members of Holy Spirit Catholic Church. Mr. Sandy engaged us that day in higher order reasoning related to our orientation, challenges that we would face, appropriate strategies in various situations, and the like. I recall how well the conversation flowed, which was special. Mr. Sandy, apparently responding to my observation of this, as if to really emphasize this event, communicated explicitly, though at a subconscious level, "It is supposed to go around the room." This was an inference by me that lacked corroboration, and I realize that; as such, I could be wrong, although I do not think that I was. Regardless, that idea captured for me what had transpired and the intimate communion that I think we are meant to have. That is, communication by dedicated professionals in the course of their duties who have the conscience, consideration, and unselfish attitude to let the conversation flow to that person who has the most vital and pertinent words to say at the time, a phenomenon that is controlled by the group conscience.

I held a weekly group that was focused on group dynamics when I began my first job after graduating from AUM in December 1988 with a Master's degree in clinical psychology, which was at the Cadet Center, a 30-day inpatient substance abuse treatment program, one of several programs within the Chemical Addictions Program in Montgomery, Alabama, and the program where I had earlier completed my practicum as a night counselor. The group was based on material from my AUM text, An Introduction to Group Dynamics by Donelson R. Forsyth (11). Part of the discussion focused on the life and achievement of groups, noting that in the earlier stages, there is often disharmony and conflict while the structure of the group develops, such as role differentiation as different members seek to establish themselves as leaders, the capabilities of different group members are unknown, the roles of different members have not been defined, and group goals and norms have not been clearly established. This would include such particulars as the variety of relations between group members, the allocation of group resources, and the allocation of group members' time. Forsyth points out that in the most successful groups, during this process, as group members become comfortable with the qualities of the person that surfaces as the recognized leader and their own roles, members are able to defer their own individual interests in service of group goals, competition declines, and a spirit of cooperation prevails.

Forsyth also points out that these groups are able to achieve a level of cohesion and harmony that allows the achievement of the group to exceed the capabilities of its individual members. They have a group conscience that allows the information to flow freely around the room so that the unique abilities of its members are recognized in an unselfish way and individual members remain comfortable with their assigned roles, because they are also representative of their achieved or earned status. Alternatively, less successful groups are thwarted by various factors, such as more than one strong leader and coalitions that remain in competition with one another and that do not show progress towards reconciliation, perhaps because of basic differences between members of the opposing subgroups or their motivation. In these instances, the group may accomplish some of its basic goals but will not be as successful as they might be otherwise because the members are not able to proceed beyond their personal or subgroup aims to achieve a spirit of co-operation and unity. Their group conscience or subconscious motivation is not in harmony. Rather, there is prevailing competition of strong wills that results in fractious aspects to the group processes.

One of my colleagues asked me a couple of questions about mental opposition, which I answered by providing a broad-based framework regarding relationships between people and groups that is pertinent to the ideas contained in this chapter and the book as a whole, which I will include here. He asked me, "Fred, you describe the person who experiences schizophrenia as an unwilling host at a subconscious level to the minds of other people, who act as predators, and you indicate that these other minds are those of people with whom the person who experiences schizophrenia regularly associates. These statements provide a very negative connotation of interpersonal relationships. Can people disagree without being malevolent predators?"

Our mental life and our mental experiences, that part of us that is not visible except as we reveal it by our behavior (how we go about doing things in word and deed), this consciousness, represents our persona or personality—who we are. We all bring this personality to bear on everything that we do and think throughout the day and night, whether we refer to it as our consciousness, our spiritual self, our mental life, or our psychological self. It is an omnipresent aspect of our existence. It is who we are. Thus, our personality bears on every interpersonal relationship that we have. It then follows that the effectiveness of relations between two people is likely to be determined, all else being equal, by how consonant their personalities are with one another. And, it also follows that interpersonal relations are as variable as there are different personalities in this world.

Thus, relations between people and groups will be determined by the personalities involved, and it may not be difficult to guess, based on the character of these people, which relations are likely to be cordial, pleasant, and productive, and which are likely to be difficult, trying, and fractious. These are important ingredients in determining when there is likely to be disagreement in relationships that may lead to worsening relations and more intransigent problems, such as ongoing mental opposition. Other variables are also important in how relationships evolve, such as the leadership at hand, which determines the norms or standards that develop for interaction. For example, a progressive group or organization may have an unwritten norm that it is okay to agree to disagree but that argument is undesirable because it tends to be counterproductive. Without able leadership to direct and monitor relationships in a lofty way, interactions are likely to reflect the learned behavior of the group or community, which can span the full range of manner in relationships, from being neighborly and following the Golden Rule (e.g., "Do onto others as you would have them do onto you"), to people or groups who are always at odds or worse.

A predator relationship is most likely to develop when there is discord present, but, even then, there can be a group norm to respect each person's mental life. However, there may be people within that culture or subculture, as in society at large, who violate that norm. In my opinion, people who do so, from inception, are acting on a continuum with what would have to be regarded as a personality disorder. They have not learned adaptive ways to solve their problems and dilemmas, such as seeking out guidance or following right paths, to the extent that they seek to prevail by impeding another person's mental life—trying to undermine that person psychologically by unfair practices, to their gain. If this predatory behavior continues and becomes a pattern, a personality disorder, then it should have a complement in outward behavior. For example, people who are familiar with these individuals, who know them well, can likely tell you the range of behaviors that characterize their particular personality disorder: their undesirable personality characteristics.

PART IV:

Directions in Psychology

CHAPTER 23:

PREVENTION

In this chapter, I refer to social events that increase risk for psychiatric problems, including mental illness, in order to raise the public's awareness of them. These are common sense statements the public may already grasp and are not comprehensive. They should be augmented and modified, as necessary, by advice from experts in the field of education and mental health.

The family typically is our first unit of socialization. As a general rule, the better the guidance and the overall family experience is, the more likely it will be that its members will work well together, will be happy, and will be well adjusted. Conversely, if the family lacks intactness, good structure, and healthy patterns, such as a single family home, alcoholism within the family, or stepdads, stepmoms, and stepsiblings from first marriages that did not work out, there will be a greater likelihood that some of the children will have emotional or adjustment problems. These circumstances will create opportunity for unhealthy family patterns and ongoing distress by some of its members that can make them more susceptible to mental illness. This is not to undermine the tremendous will and resolve of people and families to overcome adversity and surface from these types of problems but to point out how important a unit such as the family is to the health of its members and for a society to thrive.

Strong church and school communities within all segments of our society are essential for the success of society and its members. These are bodies for exchange of information where the family has access to models, leaders, and guidance to shape proper values that will help to "bring it up." We need families and children to be active in their church and school communities, participating members who make a contribution, profit from their experiences, and achieve that all important sense of belonging. These are units of socialization to spot potential problems and take early corrective action. Usually, children are likely to do best if they fit into the structure of the school system, avoid problems that will lead to a termination from school before they complete high school, and have direction toward worthwhile, desirable future aspirations.

Children should likely have guidance and career counseling as early as elementary school or during middle school in language appropriate to their age in order to help them make the connection between academic proficiency and career opportunities. Similarly, they should regularly consider their vocational aspirations tempered with a dose of reality in way of how their aspirations match their achievement, including counseling about how they might remedy any differences or whether their capabilities or skills lie elsewhere. My personal impression for someone that is not in touch with that culture—I do not have children in school—is that children would benefit from the direction provided by having a good sense of their future and how they can shape it. Language skills are a particularly important area for application because reading and writing skills are so essential to relate effectively to those around us, in which regard digital literacy has been gaining in importance and become more vital in our contemporary culture.. Socialization skills as a complement are equally important, which is the more reason for children to be active members of their church and school communities and to be vibrant members of their peer group. This calls for vigilance on the part of parents, church, and school leaders to ensure that we nurture such development for all our children.

Children whose parents have mental or personality disorders are at risk for developing a mental disorder themselves. I discuss such factors as psychological bonding with a nurturing parent, unresolved conflict leading to assumption of a sick role, subconscious conflict between parents and children who do not meet their expectations, and other factors. These are prevention planning opportunities that could start with good case histories to identify relevant factors. Children of parents who have experienced schizophrenia could benefit from common sense advice and establishment of clear boundaries due to their potential to entertain and pursue unusual or schizotypal ideas. They may pursue those ideas unless dissuaded by effective dialogue with other people who train them in practical reasoning and help them to recognize well societal expectations.

Problems in school typically present a risk factor, such as children who do not fit well into an academic environment and drop out of school, who develop patterns of delinquent behavior that frequently bring them in contact with the juvenile justice system and require placement in an alternative school, and children who began using alcohol and drugs at an early age and become part of a marginal group whose members develop anti-establishment values. Many of these kids learn from their mistakes, make amends, and turn their lives around. However, in the process, many experience a variety of societal, legal and psychiatric problems. Consequently, families who appear to be at risk for developing these maladaptive patterns, as well as families and children in general, may benefit from good awareness of the opportunities available to the children if they remain in school and avoid delinquency and substance abuse problems.

Change, losses, and trauma increase risk of psychological or adjustment problems. These events include parental divorce, a change in schools, pregnancy out-of-wedlock, the death of a love one, or being subject to incest, rape, or physical abuse. Incest between parents and children and among siblings is a particularly problematic area. Parents should take care to familiarize their children with one another well to help them recognize proper boundaries and should remain keenly alert to their behavior. They should also recognize that as much as they may feel a need to have sexual relations with their child, which may be part of a well established family pattern, that behavior violates a trust and the sanctity of that child's mental life, including the child's dignity, and it will create personality conflicts for the child that will result in rigidity within the child's personality. Many of these conflicts surface later in life, and they are often passed on to the child's offspring. As a society, we need to be alert to these behavior patterns and seek to remedy them with great tact and consideration, each as appropriate to the given situation.

I hope these comments about preventive measures, though brief and limited, may inform us about some of the factors that influence psychological problems and mental illness and thereby prompt us to be more thoughtful in these regards. They should be placed in the context of our general attitude toward living, which affects those around us. We need to accept our lot in life, considering that it is our own motivation and effort that has brought us to it. We also need to recognize that the only lasting progress is that which we earn and, therefore, apply ourselves earnestly to become more skilled at our endeavors so that we can advance. Within that framework, we should look for the window of opportunity that our Creator provides us and capitalize on it. We need to work with our neighbors according to our capacity and not compare ourselves to them but learn from desirable behaviors which they model, recognizing that they have also earned their lot in life and are getting what they deserve. They may be more advanced, which we have to accept, recognizing that God has a good plan for us and will advance us also in due time. Our Christian community, acting in place of God through the medium of his holy spirit, will recognize those needs. We should be a part of a charismatic, loving community and not view ourselves as lowly or inferior but vibrant members who will reap what the community sows. We can rest assured that our Christian community will not forget our needs but also recognize that change occurs at "Godspeed" and, therefore, be patient and abide in faith. As members of a global village with a common ancestry, we need to extend these ideas to the world at large.

CHAPTER 24:

VARIETIES OF SCHIZOPHRENIA WITHIN THE SCHIZOPHRENIA SPECTRUM

I complement chapter 23, "Prevention," in this chapter by discussing how timely family and community intervention could have averted my experience of schizophrenia and the relevance of reference groups to George's schizophrenia. Subsequently, I expound on delusions that serve a subconscious need and medication issues, caution the mentally ill to remain prudent about their treatment in light of these new ideas, and consider how they could have influenced the course of a patient's schizophrenia. I finish the chapter with a brief reiteration of the relevance of intellectual deficiencies, personality features, and values to mental illnesses such as schizophrenia and depression.

The *Diagnostic and Statistical Manual of Mental Disorders, Fourth Edition*, (*DSM-4*), was published in 1994, about two decades ago. The *DSM-4-TR* represented its revision in the year 2000 (4).The *DSM*'s are manuals the mental health profession uses to classify mental disorders, each of which is supported by the available empirical data, such as research and clinical findings. The *DSM-4* included, for each of the diagnostic categories, a review of pertinent literature with regard to any proposed changes; collaboration among specialists about such proposals; reanalysis of the data, field trials, and other pertinent methods in order to specify the diagnoses to be included; the most pertinent criteria sets for them; and pertinent text that would help knowledgeable mental health professionals make the correct diagnosis. For schizophrenia, as for most of these disorders, the diagnosis was made by tracing the disorder to its onset, following its course, identifying significant events, such as events that may have precipitated the disorder, and the signs and symptoms of the disorder that could be identified. This information was compared to the text about a specific disorder and the criteria sets to make an informed decision about the pertinent diagnosis.

The *DSM-5* (3) was occasioned by recognition from national experts in the field that changes were necessary to this manual if it were to maintain its established eminence in the domain of mental health for educators, clinicians, and researchers. The manuals to that time had retained the ordering and grouping of disorders, which superimposed a conceptualization of them for the user, whoever that may have been. They had emphasized homogenous groupings—discreet categories that would exclude people who did not fit it—when the reality of amassed data was that some characteristics of these disorders are heterogeneous. That is, these characteristics or dimensional features are shared by other disorders within a chapter or group of disorders within the *DSM* and also other chapters and disorders. As such, it became important to recognize these spectrum characteristics (e.g., the schizophrenia spectrum) and crosscutting features (e.g., sharing of depressive characteristics) in the organization and ordering of the *DSM* disorders to enhance clinical perspectives about them and accommodate research findings.

DSM-5 was published on May 18, 2013. In regard to schizophrenia, subtype distinctions were dropped by the *DSM* group of experts because they felt that most cases did not fit neatly into a subtype but, rather, contained features of other types within the schizophrenia spectrum and also contained dimensional features that are shared by a number of other *DSM* disorders. This change was consistent with an expected gradual shift in the manual to giving greater weight to the dimensional aspect and heterogeneity of the *DSM* disorders while ensuring that its utility for clinicians was maintained. By a more correct ordering, grouping, and conceptualization of these disorders, the *DSM* group thought to engender clinicians and other users to engage in unencumbered thought that would advance clinical perspectives and to provide scientists a proper framework that could incorporate their technological advances and research findings.

My comments about the varieties of schizophrenia that follow and those comments in previous chapters, such as chapter 7, "Research on Genetics" and chapter 17, "My Brother's Schizophrenia (and other examples)" describe disorders that fall within the *DSM-4* "Schizophrenia and Other Psychotic

Disorders" section and the *DSM-5* "Schizophrenia Spectrum Disorders" section. Some include references to subtypes recognized in the *DSM-4*, such as the paranoid or disorganized type, which is information that may provide helpful distinguishing features of schizophrenia for readers. I have previously depicted my schizophrenia as reactive in nature and of a paranoid type. I have described my brother George's schizophrenia as process in nature and disorganized as to type.

My schizophrenia occurred in the context of lack of permanent bonding with significant other persons in my life and oppositional forces. These events may become more evident in the future if we gain in awareness of the process by which this occurs, such as studies of the family unit, interactions between its members, and significant events that have transpired. Even if the ideas in this book had become common knowledge during my upbringing, the earliest opportunity for mental health intervention may not have occurred before my brother George engaged in delinquent behavior that came to the public eye. At that time, family intervention in the home might have revealed a lot about the nature of the problems that we were having in the household and what to do about them. My parents, my brothers and sisters, and I could have provided a mental health professional a lot of valuable information, such as my parents' dissatisfaction regarding my failure to be more responsible about events around the house and my falling out with George. This intervention would likely fall within the purview of the local mental health center and could be carried out in the home.

My pattern of being absent from the home was in an early stage at the time, meaning that further intervention at a later date might have been necessary. It seems plausible that my activities could have been structured in a way that would have satisfied both dad and me and that I could have received counseling to better understand the differences that George and I had and how to rectify them. Subsequent monitoring by the mental health center could have tracked family and individual progress in order to determine the course of subsequent events, whether further intervention was indicated, and if there were other family dynamics that were not previously identified.

It would be hard to conceive whether such family intervention could have begun to identify and resolve the underlying family dynamics and motivation that I have discussed, such as visible components of the lack of bonding and opposition that I have mentioned. This would include the discord between me and my father, my mother's attitude regarding my relations with dad, and her tendency to put me on a pedestal before other family members. However, professional intervention could have helped various family members individually, particularly George and me, and it could have helped to structure our lives in a way that would have proven to be beneficial, especially if it would have led us to change some of our undesirable patterns. This could have also provided an opportunity to receive guidance counseling in regard to planning for college and a career, which might have been invaluable. It is conceivable that these intervention methods, such as problem identification, conflict resolution, some defined structure, and realistic planning to provide needed direction, with oversight, would have promoted mental health within our family and helped us to avert psychological problems.

My schizotypal thinking began before college and became relatively prominent during my freshman year. I am referring to initial ideas to "go off to school" in order to find out "what other people are like"; the liberal ideas of the times, which interacted with my youthful idealism to distract me from my goals; and the effects of drugs, which challenged my religious convictions and made me susceptible to mental illness. I feel certain that if my peer group and I had been better informed about the nature of schizotypal thinking, that we would have spotted it in some of my ideas, although some were typical of the times. My girlfriend was the most likely candidate to recognize my ideas as potentially troublesome. I had acquired a good bit of knowledge about the New Testament that was a guiding source for me, but the use of drugs distorted my perception to bring out a paranoid element that was like a challenge to my faith. Of course, it would have helped me if some of my friends had recognized the effects that drugs had on me and warned me about needing to stop in order to avoid psychological problems. I would also have benefitted much from religious education provided by someone schooled in religion, particularly if that education and dialogue could have helped to curb my idealism and instilled a more practical religion and more practical views. Furthermore, I might have benefitted from individual counseling at the inception of my illness if someone could have obtained a good history and helped me to understand what a schizophrenic disorder is about. Once I began to experience schizophrenia, my coping patterns were relatively good, such as getting back in school, working, and attending church. However, I should have been more selective than to spend my spare time hanging out with friends and drinking beer.

What about my brother George's schizophrenia? I believe that George's path to schizophrenia began with subconscious identification with my parents and opposition to me. I think that one way this was manifested by George was in the predicaments he put me in during our childhood, which eventually got the better of me. I think that at those times, he was identifying or aligning himself with my parents, who had begun to oppose me. I believe that this was a path that he was influenced to follow by them and which he did not change, even in the midst of the support that he needed and received from me. This pattern of our lives had many twists and turns and had many variations, because, for example, I was far from perfect and made numerous mistakes, some costly ones that I have had to aright over decades.

If we look at these events in a basic and linear way, however, what my parents were doing was not consistent with the Christian values of our Catholic heritage. As such, their actions distanced them from the Christian community and its guidance. Because George followed them, this was also true for him. For this reason, George and I did not form bonds that would have strengthened both of our character. This decision by George and my parents meant that they adopted a different reference group than Christian society, the enlightened and inspired community that receives divine direction along rightful paths. Other reference groups can vary tremendously, from people who are basically good except some faults, perhaps relatively minor faults, to people with notable undesirable or inadvisable patterns of behavior that they need to change, to evildoers. Furthermore, the reference group chosen by anyone is apt to be people with similar values. This is likely a matching-up process and would include people that you would like to have as friends and those that you would like to keep as mere acquaintances. My parents, as experienced as they were at living, likely knew full well their preferences in a reference group.

My brother George, of course, was just a child as this process unfolded. He was likely naïve about such matters, like most children. Furthermore, he did not seem to be very independent minded, but, rather, he impressed me as a person who needed support and guidance, mentoring if you will, to find the direction he needed to thrive and to avoid adjustment problems. Having chosen to listen to my parents about relations with me and in general, which is the usual path for any child, he followed their lead. He did not appear to find any middle ground that might have helped him (and me) to negotiate this complex event better, some sort of compromise between his relations with mom and dad and his relations with me, that I am aware of. This process for George and me begin during our family relations in Cuba and continued from the time of our first year in the United States, where we would have sought out a reference group like the one we had grown accustomed to in Cuba. It evolved, for better or for worse, as we gained familiarity with society in the United States.

Our reference group opportunities in Montgomery included neighborhood children, kids we met up with at Cloverdale Community Center, schoolmates, and the extended church, neighborhood, and school community, including parents, coaches, teachers, and other authority figures and community leaders. It became more diverse, with more charismatic leadership as we encountered kids from upper middle class families at Cloverdale Junior High School during grades seven, eight, and nine. And, George encountered these kids in athletics at age eleven, when he played for the Rosemont Gardens Little League baseball team, and at age thirteen while in the eighth grade, when he played basketball for the Cloverdale B team. Besides those influences, he had access to a benevolent peer group throughout junior high school and into high school. So then, what about George's reference group?

George likely knew what I stood for from an early age. I was his older brother who supported him and did not put up with anyone who wronged him. He saw my principles at work daily. I was not perfect, but I was trying to follow Christian ways. He was there daily to view the schism that developed between me on the one hand, and mom and dad on the other, including some of the motive behind our differences, though these differences or schism was subtle or less visible with regard to mom. Events such as these likely present a significant challenge for children, considering the choices at hand and what is at stake. If this were so for George, I never noticed that he experienced consternation in these regards. He seemed to follow my parents unequivocally. This posture by him, as I have inferred, sometimes meant trouble for me, and it eventually led us to have a falling out, which cost us both dearly.

Thus, based on inferences like those I have mentioned, I feel that George gradually began opposing me subconsciously, in a subtle way, because this was not usually evident outwardly. As I noted previously, he and my parents seemed to be single-minded in this regard. As a result, over time, if gradually, he began saying no to Christian direction, like my parents. He may not have been keenly aware of his actions at such an early age, because he needed mentoring, about which children rely on their parents; but he also made a decision over time to follow my parents exclusively, rather than to also recognize my mentoring. Consequently, although George may have admired the more elevated members of his peer group, considering the direction provided by my parents, he had decided not to follow them entirely or to identify with their principles. Thus, he would not have listened to them wholeheartedly. They, in turn, would have sensed this by his behavior, such as some apparent lack of receptiveness to their dialogue, influence, and direction, which would have affected their relations. Consequently, George would have chosen a different peer group over time, one that was not quite so principled.

George made a couple of blunders during his upbringing that drew notoriety—one in eighth or ninth grade and one in the 10th or 11th grade—by which time his behavior was suggestive of some adjustment problems. I feel that just as surely as George must have been keenly affected by our differences during the summer before his fifth grade of school, he had opportunities to rebound from those differences and make his own way if he had chosen to. He had enough support and diversity within his peer group. He also had caring siblings and the support and direction of his parents. His task was to find an alternative reference group that would have been acceptable to my parents, such as one that would have embodied their ideals, because he did not appear to be highly selective, as I have mentioned: he depended on them.

My impression is that the direction that George received from my parents during that time may not have been sufficiently clear and unequivocal; it may have sometimes been ambivalent and motivated to undermine me, including his blunders or mistakes. The negative social effect of his blunders and his subsequent transfer to a military academy and change of high schools could also have affected his ability to become ensconced in a well identified reference group with which he and my parents were comfortable. His adjustment problems by then were characterized by his poor response to school in the 12th grade and his camaraderie with a group of friends that were embracing the counter-cultural trends of the times, which preceded his schizophrenic episode. I feel that the regression that marked George's schizophrenia could have been a reflection of continuing ambivalence by my parents and that it would have been possible to change his course with proper mentoring and direction. His regression was also a natural consequence because George was not prepared for life. Once again, I think that measures such as family and individual intervention when George exhibited notorious delinquency around the eighth grade, guidance counseling, and continuing oversight could have had a positive impact on George and family life.

What about other examples of schizophrenia spectrum disorders and how they may be manifested? It has been established that delusions can represent a subconscious defense against psychological conflict, such as events in a person's life that are traumatic and which that person has not been able to resolve in a satisfactory way. This is a more limited syndrome or complex of behaviors than is seen in paranoid schizophrenia and why it is classified as a delusional disorder rather than as schizophrenia. These delusions can also be manifested by people who have the diagnosis of schizophrenia as part of the schizophrenic syndrome. They can be motivated by a specific need, such as a need to assume a sick role due to unresolved psychological conflict, which can create sufficient stress to precipitate this type of mental illness. I have periodically made this distinction in a psychological report: distinguishing a delusional disorder or schizophrenic symptoms that are mediated by some need from the type of schizophrenia where there is perceived adversity from opposing forces, which represent significant differences that could have implications as to the person's response to medication. Although these persons, like the disorganized type, could experience an awakened subconscious that makes them susceptible to hearing the voices of other minds, which has traditionally been an intended target of the medications, medications targeting delusional ideas that spring from unresolved subconscious conflict or for the treatment of the passive-aggressive behavior features of disorganized schizophrenia may not prevail unless they could affect the brain to alter those fundamental motivations somehow. My opinion is also that medication cannot be expected to extinguish auditory hallucinations, which are the voices of other minds.

It was early in my assessments at Bryce Hospital that I recognized the contrast in the type of delusions that I refer to in the previous paragraph—those that are bewildering and frightening to the person so affected—from those that serve a subconscious need, such as the need to assume a sick role in the hospital while seeking to resolve the source of conflict. I found support for that idea in my *Longman Dictionary of Psychology and Psychiatry* (13), from which I will quote the pertinent section: "Though logically absurd, and a symptom of psychosis, they (delusions) appear to serve such purposes and needs as emotional support, relief of anxiety or guilt, blaming others for one's failures, or counteracting feelings of inferiority or insecurity (p.209)." An example within our patient population at Bryce Hospital could be grandiose delusions to build oneself up due to self-esteem needs or due to feelings of inferiority.

The course to develop a delusional disorder as a separate syndrome or as an aspect of schizophrenia usually would be quite different than that for the paranoid-type schizophrenia that I experienced or the disorganized-type schizophrenia that George experienced, in my estimation. I attended a presentation on cognitive therapy applications across a spectrum of disorders in 1995 directed by a University of Pennsylvania Professor of Psychology in Psychiatry, Dr. Cory Newman (20). Dr. Newman presented a vignette of a therapist who was treating a patient with a delusional disorder. The patient had been a graduate student in a doctoral program of about 12 students. His delusion had come to the attention of his professor during the course of a test, which he had turned in blank. His explanation was that Russian spies were using electronic devices to read his answers, which they were trying to steal for their own use. He felt that his answers were classified and that he could not run the risk of them being stolen by Russian spies. His dilemma may have been related to stress from a rigorous doctoral program and doubts about his ability as a candidate. Presumably, if the stress is resolved, the delusion should go away.

The approach to therapy was the use of a Socratic style of questioning whereby the therapist, by means of precisely pertinent questions, helped the student to examine the evidence and consider the possibility that his ideas were not rational. A complementary goal of this cognitive-behavior therapy, which begins with building rapport, is an expeditious return to one's pattern of living. I recall that the therapist was able to convince the student to return to the doctoral program after working out arrangements with the professor for him to make up the test. At this point, I think the delusion may have been compromised but had not resolved. The continuing therapy plan likely included addressing any concerns about his candidacy in the doctoral program.

A more complex example may be represented by people who have done something offensive within their family that is unacceptable to their parents. Consider a young girl who is raised by very Christian parents who aspire for her to have a rich and abundant spiritual life. She belongs to a vibrant and nurturing peer group. However, she fails to heed her parental teachings and guidelines. She meets an older guy who she thinks is very special. Against parental wishes for her to attend college and wait on a suitor until a more mature age, she enters into a common-law relationship with this older guy for a while. Later, she realizes that she has fallen short of what she wanted in matrimony, has separated herself from a charismatic peer group, and has failed to follow the master plan for which her parents were so devoutly grooming her. She has made a major mistake, and although her parents do not shun her in any way, she cannot partake in the charismatic family life she once enjoyed until she atones for her mistake.

This young girl, upon realizing her mistake and recognizing that she cannot share in very intimate family ways, may experience a plethora of emotions in seeking to be reconciled with her parents, such as shame, guilt, anger, fury, anxiety, dejection, and trepidation. Eventually, she develops a delusional framework, which leads to hospitalization. This is not from frightening adversaries that she does not understand but the product of her own subconscious; she assumes a sick role in a hospital to give her time to resolve her psychological conflicts and gather her resources, a plan of action with which her parents could possibly have a part. The difference between her experience and mine is that hers was not the product of adversarial minds but psychological conflict produced by falling short of parental expectations along spiritual lines. It is possible that the degree of her distress and preoccupation could cause her to become psychologically overwhelmed and to experience decompensation sufficient to have an awakened subconscious, which would make her susceptible to schizophrenia, a disorder that is relatively more severe than a mere delusional disorder. Her prognosis could be better in some respects than that of someone who has not bonded with a significant other person, if that aspect of her relationship with her parents is maintained. I should add that many a young girl may rebel against her parents at an early age and later reconcile herself with them following a different course than mental illness.

Another example is provided by a man whom I treated some years ago, who had been beset with schizophrenia that included adversarial elements, such as paranoid feelings that other people in his environment meant him harm. In a paranoid moment, he stabbed his cousin in the back mortally. Subsequently, this man faced great family scorn and anger, so much so that he no longer seemed motivated to leave the hospital. He would become delusional whenever we would consider his discharge, which seemed to be motivated by his desire to assume an overtly mentally ill role because he knew that he would not be accepted by his family. It is also possible that he would become genuinely mentally ill rather than subconsciously motivated to remain in the hospital on contemplating facing the community after his outstandingly bad behavior. However, if my original assumption is correct, the medication would have to alter his subconscious motivation to remain in the hospital before it could remedy his delusion. In retrospect, if the medication were able to calm him of his distress, he might consider better how he could become reconciled with his family. Noteworthy, the ideas I have described argue for a psychological basis for his mental illness, which should lead to reconsideration of the purpose and length of use of psychotropic medication, in general.

Observations about these varieties of schizophrenia spectrum disorders and the increase in knowledge from ideas in this book may provide educational opportunities so that pertinent segments of society can institute preventive measures. They emphasize the need for good social histories so that we can better understand the situational and interpersonal events that give rise to schizophrenia and other major mental illnesses, such as bipolar disorder and major depression. One concern that I have is that some mentally ill clients may rebel against their treatment as a result of the ideas that I have presented. I acquired these various ideas or my understanding of schizophrenia very gradually. My comprehension was refined over a long period of time and often involved a change from my initial perspective. I nurtured my spiritual life throughout this process, sometimes proceeding very slowly until I had spiritual enlightenment to confirm my path as the correct one.

I was fortunate to have teachers, employers, and other educators and mentors who provided me guidance to keep me from making a serious mistake. Eventually, by means of hard work and patience, I was able to structure my life in a way that I could maintain my occupation while gaining in understanding of schizophrenia and how to manage it. In effect, what seemed to prevail was that as I grew along spiritual lines, I was able to hear and understand the source and motivation of voices more clearly, an experience of greater enlightenment that has continued to this day. I was inspired to change careers and pursue the Master of Science degree in clinical psychology. In Tuscaloosa, my church community affirmed and provided direction in my life practically every Sunday at a time when I needed a lot of support and guidance. Over the course of years, by applying myself diligently in my job, I have been inspired in my work to acquire the ideas that I share with the readers. This knowledge and skill led me back to enjoy mental health. In the process, I have become more assertive and successful in living and more proficient and skilled at my psychological work. I beseech the mentally ill not to rebel against their treatment but to act prudently.

I have confidence that the mental health community will make use of any significant findings contained in this book to chart the best path for the mentally ill, including any changes to current perspectives. This may not happen overnight, but it may not take a long time either. To illustrate my point, I treated a man a while back who had typical schizophrenic symptoms. He was hearing voices that were a running commentary of his thoughts while he lived in the community. He believed that people were keeping up with him and might ambush him at some point. He was experiencing similar adversity in the hospital. He felt that he was surrounded by foes that meant him harm and would hurt him if given the chance. I brought what cognitive-behavior therapy (CBT) for schizophrenia has to offer to the table in an illuminating way with some success in disputing his ideas, but he nevertheless held on to them to a considerable degree.

We were able to reduce the intensity of his mental experiences to the extent they were not very bothersome as he earned greater privileges, had greater access to the Bryce Hospital grounds, and had greater control over his environment. His psychiatric medications were reduced, but he felt the remainder of them was necessary to control his symptoms, which remained in a less severe form. Perhaps if he had been privy to the ideas contained in this book, he may have thought otherwise. If so, he might have benefitted from the approach of a New Hampshire group of mental health professionals providing integrated treatment for the dual disorders of mental illness and substance abuse (19). They included their clients in their ideas about medication to foster compliance. If the client wanted a change that they did not recommend, after duly advising and warning the client, they often acquiesced to the change sought, but under relatively close monitoring so that the client could have firsthand confirmation of how effective or necessary the medication was.

CBT is one talking therapy for the severe mental disorders that can help clients obtain a good understanding of them so that they feel confident in their ability to manage them and advocate for themselves in the community. The ideas presented in this book should lead to a more complete understanding of schizophrenia—and I hope the other severe mental illnesses also—as well as novel treatment methods. Such understanding, under monitoring, might be a basis to reduce reliance on medication for some people who have a diagnosis of schizophrenia. This decision should be complemented by strides these persons make in regard to rehabilitation, because there are necessary parallels between desirable standards of daily living and mental health. Some yardsticks for progress they should demonstrate include applying themselves to indicated treatment, acquiring insight, developing skills to manage their disorder, building support, and developing and implementing viable rehabilitation plans that will improve their chances for a positive community experience.

I have given coverage in this book to a variety of disorders characterized by mental illness or psychotic features, such as paranoid-type or disorganized-type schizophrenia, delusions as an aspect of schizophrenia or as a separate disorder, and dementias or neurocognitive disorders. My approach to understanding the course and development of any mental disorder has always been to obtain the pertinent history, which can be very revealing. Typically, I identify the various sources of stress that appear to precipitate these disorders, which can be very illuminating. With some, the source of stress can be fairly conclusive, such as auditory hallucinations in the context of a dementia. In these cases, the brain impairment has seemed to compromise the person's cognitive integrity to the extent that he experiences sufficient distress to awaken his subconscious mind or make it permeable to his conscious mind.

Intellect or cognitive capacity—reasoning skills, if you will—has not been a dimension that I paid particular attention to at first with regard to mental illness. However, I have witnessed how relevant it is for people with intellectual disabilities who experience mental illness in observing their behavior across environments. Some are simply not able to tolerate environments that they perceive to be unstable or violent, which can cause them to constantly experience a decompensated state, by which I mean acute mental illness. Their behavior becomes very disorganized and regressed. Some examples of their behavior would include ongoing anxiety, frequent agitation, suspicion, and fighting; inappropriate sexual behavior; and smearing feces. Their improvement can be marked as they move to an environment that is more favorable or less stressful.

Personality has been another important dimension, of course. I fell in that group that exhibits obsessive-compulsive personality features, which tend to become more rigid as a way to manage anxiety during times of stress. George, on the other hand, appeared to need structure, guidance, and support, without which he seemed to be very impressionable and to respond based on the values and direction provided by his peer group. These personality features help us to discover the nature of a person's stress, which then helps us to identify the problem they are having. Stress can also explain the nature of the mental illness, such as the example of the guy with physical problems whose behavior became disorganized in order to seek nurturance within the hospital when he lost his source of community support.

I have always paid particular attention to the values suggested by people's behavior, such as whether they are traditional or scrupulous, whether they violated established social norms, whether their values seemed absent, and so forth. I find this information pertinent because the values that someone espouses or fails to espouse provide important information about their spiritual life, which is relevant to mental health. As an example, the alcoholic path is known to lead to what the Alcoholics Anonymous groups describe as "spiritual bankruptcy" due to the alcoholic's unscrupulous behavior. In order to improve their mental or spiritual life, they work a "12-step" program that is a roadmap to greater spirituality and mental health. It entails changing their past ways by becoming more principled about their daily affairs.

Similarly, I use the information that I gather from clients, including value-laden information, to understand them better, which helps me to treat them more effectively. I usually do not get into morality specifically, but it is relevant information. For example, if a client appears to experience an endogenous depression, which is a depression that seems to emanate from within the person rather than from external factors, what insights might be gained about that person's mental life from studying his or her background? Such insights might provide a roadmap to patterns or behaviors that he might rectify to alleviate his depression.

Chapter 25:

Responding to Perceived Adversaries:

O ne of the ubiquitous behaviors of people afflicted with schizophrenia is to get angry at other people in their environment who they perceive as having ill intentions toward them. This can range from aggravation or irritation to verbal aggression, threatening behavior, and violence. This is the classical symptom picture for the initiation of commitment proceedings: an overt act due to a mental illness that jeopardizes that person's safety or the safety of other people in her environment. This is to be expected considering that it is not unusual for a person who has a diagnosis of schizophrenia to perceive adversity from people in her environment and to have a good idea who those people are.

This is probably most representative of paranoid schizophrenia, by its very nature. In households where this occurs, in familiar settings where people with a diagnosis of schizophrenia regularly engage other people, and in relatively more public settings, the person with such a diagnosis may gather information about perceived antagonists. This may be someone with whom she has a personality clash, who directly opposes her, whom she views as unjust in action towards her, or who affects her in other ways. At times, these perceptions about other people can have a corresponding emotional component from the subconscious, like a sixth sense that another's action implicates her.

These reactions are not unusual for anyone that has these perceptions about other people, some of which may be supported by a long history of conflict with those persons, as can occur within families and other settings where people suffering from schizophrenia are in regular contact with other individuals, including mental hospitals. However, such adversity and reactions usually or almost always lead to conflict for people diagnosed with schizophrenia, meaning that it is a poor coping pattern for them to exhibit such emotional turmoil. In some cases, their behavior represents the overt act that leads to hospitalization, incarceration, or criminal behavior, which can follow the person suffering from schizophrenia for a lifetime.

How should the person suffering from schizophrenia respond to these perceived adversaries? I would not presume to know this answer unequivocally, considering individual differences in regard to background, experience, and personality, which can significantly impact a person's capability to respond to a given situation and how that person responds. However, my impression is that a good response oftentimes is one I previously referred to as "detachment with love." This is an attitude that can lead to a better understanding of a perceived adversary and improved relations eventually, whereas a negative reaction is likely to perpetuate personality differences and create problems for people who experience schizophrenia. These differences usually arise from personality factors that are not easily changed. Moreover, the perceived adversary is not likely to have conscious awareness of how she affects the person suffering from schizophrenia. Thus, a constructive way for the person with a diagnosis of schizophrenia to promote desirable behavior from adversaries may be to demonstrate consideration and exhibit maturity in these relations. This may seem like trying to be assertive with someone who may try to undermine you. At best, you may be able to win her respect; but at other times, you may feel undermined and humiliated.

I have learned to be effective in similar situations by hard work, being ever prepared for whatever situation, learning to improvise, and having a good listening ear for the direction that progressive people in my environment are providing me. Using this approach, the person with a diagnosis of schizophrenia is more likely to build support and improve her interpersonal skills, which may eventually lead her to achieve greater success while helping her to avoid trouble.

One of my concerns in writing this book is that some people who experience mental illness (or anyone) may sense that another person is affecting them physically or psychologically and take retaliatory action that may become violent. I would implore and beseech anyone with such notions not to do so. One important reason regarding schizophrenia would be that in many instances, there may be a number of other adversaries who would assume the role of the former one.

Another reason it would be a mistake to respond violently to perceived adversaries is that although their presence is highly undesirable, it may help people with a diagnosis of schizophrenia to act more prudently and considerately: to become better people. This is because adversaries are prone to amplify any mistake the victim of schizophrenia makes, which will increase the victim's awareness of them and decrease the likelihood that she will commit them again. Though the victim of schizophrenia needs to be flexible, the amplification of her mistakes tends to shape her behavior to become more principled and socially skilled.

Other personalities, such as substance abusers, appear to be just the opposite. Their significant others seem to aid them in suppressing would-be traumatic material so that they can continue their substance-use pattern undeterred. That is why I have referred to substance users as strong personalities. However, I have considered this aspect of my personality a strength in terms of my spiritual life because this keen sensitivity to wrongdoing has made me into a more scrupulous person.

We must also consider that ultimately, God is in control of our lives. If we were to perceive that another person was affecting us physically or psychologically in a very oppressive or injurious way, we should look to him for our answers. Oftentimes, when we rule out a violent answer, we become more resourceful in resolving our problems adaptively over time, which is the best answer. We should also consider the reasons God has afflicted us so and pray to him to help us find the best solution to our problems, consulting with knowledgeable people who may act as Christ or God for us in our society. Recall that we are called to do priestly work—to be the face and mind of Christ in our respective trade, professional, or service capacities in this world. Do not underestimate the help or support of your neighborhood, parish, or community. If you take violent action that causes serious injury or death to someone, you will lose this opportunity to understand God's purpose for your affliction and to grow closer to him in your suffering, you will face his retribution most assuredly, and you will also face the consequences of your criminal act."

What else might be helpful? I will refer the reader to my next chapter on management of schizophrenia.

CHAPTER 26:

THE MANAGEMENT OF SCHIZOPHRENIA

The schizophrenia that I have experienced is like being at war. In order to hold your own, you have to be prepared to struggle daily. Idleness is the enemy of the person who experiences schizophrenia; it is a breeding ground for the mental state that can lead a person to experience lowered self esteem, low feelings, less confidence, and other negative emotions that can promote the mental life associated with schizophrenic symptoms. As part of my instructions to populations of people with a diagnosis of schizophrenia that I have treated, I have advocated for six practical and general strategies to help them manage schizophrenia. This is aside from specific skills to manage schizophrenia, such as those offered by cognitive-behavior therapy. The first of these is hygiene and grooming.

Schizophrenia, by its nature, such as the moderate depression that can accompany it and the debilitating effects of thought disorder, which can make it difficult for a person to order and organize his behavior, can often cause the oversight of not being prepared for the public. It is of utmost importance to dress and groom yourself appropriately if afflicted with schizophrenia because your appearance will affect the way that you feel and the way that other people greet and treat you. It is difficult enough to manage the self-esteem issues that accompany this disorder, its debilitation, and the suspicious thoughts that you can have about other people without making matters worse. If faced with opposition, an adversary can make you feel just awful when you run into someone that you would like to engage, only to re-alize during the engagement that you are not socially prepared because you just threw something on, did not bathe or shave, and your hair is dirty and uncombed. A strong personality can overcome this, probably as supported by subconscious communication; a person afflicted with schizophrenia who has not bonded mentally with a significant other person in his life cannot.

Diet is most important. A person who experiences schizophrenia needs healthy calories. Poor sources of nutrition such as vending-type snacks and sodas do not provide the stamina and mental strength to fight the constant adversity that someone afflicted with schizophrenia can face. The person ex-periencing schizophrenia may have to take in a lot more of that poor nutri-tion to accomplish his tasks and is not likely to feel as good. It is important to have well balanced meals comprised of nutritious calories and not to overeat, to eat just the right amount to have that full, satisfied feeling. If you do not eat enough, then you will have a more difficult time addressing diffi-cult problems and making decisions. Overeating will lead to weight gain, which may make the person afflicted with schizophrenia, who is sensitive to his body size, feel uncomfortable. I cut out my traditional breakfast to reduce my cholesterol. I have a cold snack such as a chicken salad sandwich and a glass of skim milk for breakfast; another cold snack such as a peanut butter, banana, and pecan sandwich for lunch; and a cooked, balanced meal for supper, such as baked chicken, fish, or a hamburger patty, rice or potatoes, and one more vegetables, such as corn, a legume, or Cole slaw.

A regular exercise program to complement a good diet is important and can add desirable structure to one's day. A heart surgeon of some renown, one of the most effective and efficient speakers that I have ever heard, told us at the professional in-service held at Bryce Hospital that a 30-minute brisk walk daily would prevent cardiovascular problems, even for people who are overweight. This exercise keeps their vessels bendable and pliable, thereby preventing nicks, cuts and lesions that can develop when the cardiovascular system is brittle and that facilitate the accumulation of plaque. Of course, exercise also helps to metabolize cholesterol that has not been utilized. It also increases wind capacity and strengthens the heart, thereby making its task of transporting oxygen, glucose, and other nutrition throughout the vas-cular system more efficient.

I found that in addition to walking or riding a bike, which are considered to be cardiovascular exercises, muscle strengthening exercises are important because they help us build body strength and structure. After some 30 years of sitting behind a desk and mostly running (jogging) or walking, my frame became sufficiently weakened that when I slept, I could not sleep on my chest because my muscular structure was no longer strong enough to prevent my heart from feeling smothered nor strong enough to support my nervous system while sleeping on my back. I would awaken some mornings with back pain and concerns about scoliosis. Consequently, I started a strengthening program and increased my muscle tone to the extent that I no longer have to worry about whether I sleep on my back or my chest and do not awaken with any significant back pain. Additionally, my extra wind capacity, strong heart, and physical strength provide me the stamina and energy that I need to tackle daily problems. Before that strengthening program, I had occasionally experienced sufficient weakness that I felt that I would not be able to manage problems at full speed but would have to proceed more slowly due to health issues, which concerned me.

Sleep hygiene is of utmost importance. It can be a very problematic issue for the person who experiences schizophrenia. The problem seems to be that mental opponents—the unwelcome guests—are able to keep the victim awake, not by the hallucinations entirely or even primarily, but from the action of these adversaries on the victim's brain. I recall that when I interviewed for doctoral programs at the University of Georgia, the University of Mississippi, and the University of Southern Mississippi, I hardly slept a wink all night, not from excitement, but from the preventive action of one or more opponents. I have gone through the basics of sleep with people diagnosed with schizophrenia: the winding down process, avoiding daytime sleeping, making their bed a place for sleep and not for other activities, refraining from stimulating activities or snacks at night, resolving problems early or putting them aside until the next day, and following a regular sleeping schedule. I have also told them not to toss and turn all night but, rather, to rouse themselves by splashing their face in order to fully awaken and then try to go back to sleep, employing such a more alert and stronger mental state. I have let them know that problems that impress them during the middle of the night should be put aside and tackled the next day after they are fully awake and have had their breakfast, by which time the problem may seem of less magnitude and easier to resolve. Many receive strong medication that put them right to sleep or can have the dose changed to hours of sleep in order to facilitate sleep. All of these are good strategies but not foolproof unless it is the strong medication. However, by being in good physical condition, one can weather nights of poor sleep much better until reaching the point of getting a good night's sleep as a result of the greater fatigue or exhaustion that occurs over sleepless nights. Also, as one understands the nature of hallucinations and other psychotic experiences and how to resolve them, their attendant stress will decline, reducing the emotional intensity that can interfere with sleep.

I am hardly bothered by hallucinations. They are not very prominent or bothersome to me because I am able to identify the source and recognize the adversary's motivation. I also regularly hear supportive, guiding voices. My understanding and skill regarding hallucinations developed over a number of years and was paralleled by spiritual growth. But I think that it is possible for people not yet so skilled to acquire a basic understanding of the schizophrenic experience and build from there, especially people who have achieved sufficient education to acquire such knowledge and understanding about schizophrenia that they can proceed in a considered way.

The schizophrenic experience is such that individuals tend to become more socially isolated over time, what we refer to as a schizoid adjustment. This is a poor coping pattern for a variety of reasons. Being part of a social group or having a social network gives us all a sense of belonging. When we become socially isolated, there is nothing or no one calling us when we arise, which is a gloomy experience. Social networks are also a means for exchange of information so that our ideas can be validated and do not become extreme. When we subject them to the marketplace, we get immediate reactions that help us to consider the criticism or feedback and align our thinking accordingly. I encourage my clients to use their ingenuity to become a part of social groups. The person who experiences schizophrenia may avoid group activities because an adversary will be present. It is important to prepare for these events and take some part, even if it is not a very visible one. With experience, the person who experiences schizophrenia may grow more comfortable amidst the adversary and learn how to be assertive in those situations. That is called fitting in, which is most important.

The last strategy to manage schizophrenia, which subsumes all the others, is a schedule of activities. Our country largely follows the Judeo-Christian work ethic mentality. That is, we apply ourselves honestly to our trade or occupation daily, serving the needs of our community, and then we worship together as a church family on Sundays, when we ask God to bless our efforts. Our trade, employment, or profession gives us identity; it defines who we are. John is an expert mechanic. Jim is a trial lawyer. Jane is an elementary school teacher, and so on. One of the most therapeutic ways for people who experience schizophrenia to insulate themselves from the effects of mental illness is to engage in a productive activity. This not only leads to positive feelings if the mentally ill have some measure of success, it also helps the mentally ill to fit into their community or church parish. Their neighbors, church parish, and community become increasingly aware of the sort of people they are. Their acceptance and support are likely to be directly related to their willingness to sincerely apply themselves to becoming contributing members of society. Mental illness presents a handicap, but it does not excuse the mentally ill from this form of responsibility. Americans go to great lengths and perform extraordinarily to survive each and every day, which means that mentally ill people must also do what they can to rightfully belong to this work ethic mentality.

The mentality ill should devote a reasonable amount of time to one or both of the two fundamental constructive or productive activities that help us all to have greater chances for success in living and to thrive: education and work. We spend the majority of our time in one or the other. For example, we engage ourselves in educational pursuits early as a training ground for our subsequent vocational pursuits, after which we are likely to require continuing education, skills training, and professional development. I ask my hospitalized mentally ill clients to focus on what they want to do in life as a starting point. A well established view in the field is that the mentally ill are often likely to fare better if they pursue what they are capable of presently rather than pursue elaborate educational or vocational plans that may not come to fruition as they experience a recurrence of mental illness and due to its handicapping effects. This view and this strategy gain in application as the length of someone's mental illness and time away from school or work increases As a practical matter, they may fare better if they settle for less lofty goals in order to have a successful rehabilitation and then, once they are well adjusted, productive members of society, consider their opportunities for upward mobility. I think this is the logic behind the "supported employment" emphasis for the disabled mentally ill population; that is, they approach vocational rehabilitation counselors and job specialists who can go to bat for them under rights promoted and protected within the structure of the Alabama Disabilities Advocacy Program (ADAP). The vocational rehabilitation counselors and job specialists seek to find them jobs they can do, at a reduced rate or level than is customary to compete for that position, if necessary, to start.

Once again, I ask my hospitalized mentally ill clients to struggle in search of the course they want to pursue in living in order that they may have a greater sense of direction, which will be a stabilizing force, in contrast to the displaced energy that they are likely to experience without such direction, which will make them more susceptible to mental illness. If they are not sure, they should seek guidance, but by all means, they should choose the best course they can determine now. Can they work competitively? If not, what about supported employment? How many hours could they devote to occupational pursuits to start? If they are not able to work competitively, can they maintain their home? If they are in a group home or living with family, what could they contribute to maintaining the home? We consider activities they could do to help their family and community appreciate them and to earn their keep, beginning with the financial means they can have in the hospital through the supported employment programs that we have here, which are also designed to help them prepare for community living. They have to start somewhere. We consider that as a minimum, they should devote at least an hour in the morning and an hour in the afternoon to constructive or productive activities and try to build from there. This sort of focus on achievement is very good therapy for mental illness, such as doing something productive that leads to better skills, more opportunity, and peace of mind from honestly applying oneself to a trade or occupation.

We also consider whether it may be a good idea for our mentally ill clients to have educational pursuits, such as learning a trade, pursuing on-the-job training like an apprentice, taking a course in school that may help prepare them for the job market, and so on. Some lack much of an education. We consider that they should pursue adult education at their level. As an example, if a Test of Basic Adult Education (TABE) places them at the second grade, four months level of reading comprehension, they can build from there. The idea is that they will be increasing their literacy, if slowly, and the attendant positive mental experience will act as a buffer against mental illness. We consider the host of educational opportunities, such as self study guided by a teacher; educational media such as an on line course, interactive learning from the Internet, a computer application, an electronic tablet, or a DVD; educational television and radio programs; print literature; and word of mouth—learning from others. Once we have established the primary activities that they will perform each day, we set out to develop a well rounded schedule.

The emphasis is on a schedule of activities that is related to their goals, if at all possible, because such a schedule would be the most rewarding and fulfilling for them. We have already mentioned exercise, which would be a good complement to their schedule. Usually, belonging to a religious community such as a church parish is a good idea because these people are more likely to have the mentally ill person's best interests at heart and are more likely to be positive influences in a mentally ill person's life. Church communities and church activities have high potential to be stabilizing influences. Entertainment is also a good complement to one's daily life. Americans work hard, but at the end of the day or on weekends, holidays, and vacations, we like to relax and enjoy a variety of entertainment. We tend to integrate the social value and social structure that can arise from entertainment and other activities into our lives, which emphasizes the importance of good choices.

Hobbies can be therapeutic. They are those things we long to do when the work is done, some of which can become profitable activities. We also discuss the typical Saturday morning and early Saturday afternoon devotion to doing household chores, integrating grocery shopping into the schedule, and the all important meal preparation. We consider their placement resources (e.g., a group home) as providing them opportunities to improve and refine their homemaking or independent living skills. Such a complete and varied schedule, to be developed and implemented over time, will occupy their time well and keep them busy, which should have a therapeutic or beneficial effect on their management of schizophrenia and the attendant effects from depression. A general philosophy that I encourage is for them to engage in activities by choice, so that instead of idleness, for example, they choose leisure, and instead of random and prolonged television viewing, they decide to relax and watch a good program. Such a considered approach can increase their alertness to how they use their time and help them to use it more constructively.

These strategies should apply very well to patients with bipolar disorder or major depression except for certain caveats. For example, bipolar patients have to be careful not to exercise too late in the day or to overdo it lest they energize themselves to the extent that they are not able to sleep. I guess it should go without saying that clients should build their exercise program gradually, seeking medical opinion when necessary, so that they do not overdo it and harm themselves.

These strategies also blend well with the psychiatric rehabilitation strategies that were advocated by a Boston group (8), which led to the original coining of the Boston Psychiatric Rehabilitation Model, a group that was retained by the Alabama Department of Mental Health (ADMH) and whose practices were implemented within the ADMH system. This is a client-centered rehabilitation model that focuses on community goals and helps clients to develop a hopeful vision of themselves. Phases of rehabilitation are a measure of a client's readiness for discharge and a rehabilitation issue is established that complements or works alongside their other problems. At Bryce Hospital, aspects of this Boston Rehabilitation Model receive emphasis in our psychiatric rehabilitation classes and are retained in our treatment or service plans.

We have "peer bridge" specialists in some of our large community mental health center programs and a peer bridge specialist at Bryce Hospital. They are people who have experienced severe mental illness and become rehabilitated, who have learned effective routes to rehabilitation and can act as friends and confidants to the mentally ill in the community while pointing the best ways to rehabilitation for them. In addition, community members can play a bigger role in the rehabilitation of the mental ill by becoming instrumental in their lives. An example would be the Compeer program that has been practiced in Tuscaloosa, where members of different churches or the community adopt a mentally ill patient, whom they engage within and outside the hospital. Compeers may maintain telephone contact, pay visits in the hospital, and take on outings their adopted patient, thereby becoming instrumental in the mentally ill person's life. This is an untapped resource that could make a significant difference in the rehabilitation of the mentally ill and the quality of their lives.

Cognitive behavior therapies for severe mental illnesses are contemporary treatment for schizophrenia, bipolar disorder, and severe depression that can provide the severe mentally ill with effective, specific strategies to manage their mental illness (20), (31). They are designed to complement rather than act as an alternative to medication. I advocate for them in the sense that if the seriously mentally ill have a symptom of mental illness and can implement a strategy to manage it, then they will likely not need additional medication to achieve psychiatric stability and could possibly rely on less medication to manage their symptoms in the long run. The latter may hold true more for schizophrenic and depressive symptoms than the manic symptoms that are seen in bipolar disorder, although cognitive-behavior strategies could make a difference in the pharmacotherapy regimen for bipolar disorder patients also. In that regard, I would also mention that some of our bipolar patients with severe personality or behavioral disorders, after remediation of such disorders following years of being subject to contingency management plans, have required less mood stabilizing medications. Contingency management plans seek desirable behavior change by consistent application of contingencies, such as rules or standards, which the subject must follow to earn the applicable reward, such as more privileges and less restriction as opposed to fewer privileges and more restriction if they continue to have problems.

We consider that well learned CBT strategies and other cognitive and behavioral interventions that have proven to be effective for specific mental disorders could help all severely mentally ill clients to effectively manage their symptoms, potentially reducing their reliance on medication and need for re-hospitalization, noting that we are talking about serious medications with notable side effects. Furthermore, confidence in their ability to manage their symptoms of severe mental illness and to communicate this to the community can help them to advocate effectively for themselves, which should help to put community members who may be aware of their mentally ill episode relatively more at ease.

CHAPTER 27:

TRANSITION

The medical model, with the advent of neuroleptic medications in the 1950's, allowed many mentally ill patients who were in inpatient facilities to become more manageable and to be placed in the community, launching the community mental health centers movement. I hope and expect that the leaders in the field of mental health, with their broad knowledge and expertise, will help point the way to incorporate the significant findings in this book to usher in a new era for the mentally ill, advancing us beyond the current medical model to place less reliance on medication. I realize that the mental health world will not be able to move forward toward a new psychology until these ideas gain acceptance by the mental health world and are put into practice. One might ask the questions, "Will they prevail?" and "How long will it take for them to become accepted?"

The marvelous subconscious world that I speak about in these pages is subliminal yet omnipresent in our daily behavior and interactions. On reading the book, I think we will start becoming bilingual right away, fascinated, and move forward toward achieving greater fluency than I know now. We will recognize how we affect one another benevolently and malevolently. The idea that we speak mind to mind is an ongoing daily phenomenon that we will validate for ourselves, probably by mere reflection after reading the book. I think this and other ideas contained in this book will validate the psychological basis for schizophrenia that I have described as we become familiar with this subject matter. Even so, we should give science the time it needs to reach consensus on these findings before we rely on them. With this in mind, presuming these ideas are not refuted, I would like to make some forward looking comments that I feel will do more good than harm in way of providing some perspective.

The process of change will need to consider the needs of established consumers and how they respond to the opportunities provided by the new knowledge as they may be particularly sensitive to changes in their established mode of treatment; the process of change will also need to consider the new consumer of services, new cases, whose course may depend a great deal on new information and how diligently we use it to develop effective new modes of treatment. This suggests that we will be in a transition state for a period of time, both keeping a watchful eye on clinical trials with the existing consumers and new consumers to identify the most effective practices. One of the most obvious areas of impact is expected to be medication needs. Hopefully, an increase in understanding of mental illness by the public and the mentally ill person will lead to less reliance and shorter trials if safety concerns can be resolved.

Existing clients that have been subject to the medical model is an area where great caution will need to be exercised in deciding those that might benefit most from advances in knowledge and ensuring that the process, which could prove very beneficial, is not harmful to them. The need for medication for new cases might be determined by the relative success or failure of early intervention efforts. Good social histories are expected to be of paramount importance so that we can gain an understanding of the family and interpersonal dynamics at play in order to target our intervention efforts accordingly. In a similar vein, we will have to find the most unobtrusive yet effective means to intervene at the level of the unit where the problem lies, such as the family.

I expect that in the future, there will be greater emphasis from the inception of these disorders on the family and community dynamics and early remediation of problems or corrective practices. Modes of treatment are likely to include individual therapy, group therapy, and family guidance, counseling, or therapy. The setting for intervention may be the home, school, church parish, mental health community, private mental health practitioner, and community hospital. Community hospitals are likely to have a continuing role for acute cases, in which regard it seems difficult to estimate how effective we may be in avoiding the trauma of acute hospitalizations by proactive, beneficial outpatient treatment. State hospital admissions for extended acute care and long-term care may lessen over time.

Within the field of schizophrenia, original cases that are related to paranoid schizophrenia may be able to forgo longer hospitalizations if the individuals can acquire insight and learn effective ways to manage their symptoms. The public's greater education about the nature of schizophrenia and effective outpatient treatment could make a significant difference in whether these people receive the services and acquire the understanding to be managed as outpatients. Those cases of patients who meet the former *DSM-4* criteria for disorganized-type schizophrenia may depend on the effectiveness of early family intervention as a means to avoid the experience of regressed states requiring extended hospitalizations. Those patients who experience delusions that serve a need, such as the need to assume a sick role while they resolve psychological conflict that brought them to that state, may require extended hospitalization if outpatient treatment providers cannot help them out of their dilemma. It may also be that with greater understanding of the nature of their disorder, we are able to find more effective means for them to express their psychological conflicts.

Cases of major depression that do not respond to outpatient treatment efforts can often be treated effectively in community hospitals and may also need extended acute and long-term care in a state psychiatric hospital, particularly when there is an underlying severe personality disorder, such as borderline personality disorder. It seems harder to make a statement about any transition effects for patients with bipolar disorder. I posit two psychological routes to this disorder based on empirical evidence: the effects from bonding to a parent with this disorder and various family situations that appear to make an individual member vulnerable, such as the death of a significant other, a dysfunctional home, a substance use pattern, traumatic family events such as incest or an extra-marital affair, and similar major events that upset the family dynamics causing members to lose family support, including emotional and mental support that acts as a stabilizing force. Pertinent literature and experience indicate that bipolar disorder can be very problematic until it is accurately diagnosed. The nature of bipolar disorder may argue for pharmacotherapy as a mainstay of the treatment regimen along with sufficient knowledge of the disorder to develop comprehensive treatment and prevention plans, such as those advocated by lay persons who have acquired proficiency in managing it (10) and cognitive behavior therapists who have developed effective treatments for it (20), (31). Regular hospitalization may be necessary for the person with bipolar disorder until such mastery or proficiency in managing it is achieved.

We have some severe cases of people with a diagnosis of bipolar disorder in the hospital who have had many unsuccessful community trials, including such poor use of judgment while the disorder has been active as to make community re-entry a daunting prospect for them. Enhanced public knowledge about bipolar disorder along with good social histories that augment our understanding of its formation may help us to provide early and effective intervention in the community as a complement to medication needs, which could facilitate desirable changes within the family and its individual members, make for a less severe course of the disorder, and perhaps reduce medication needs.

There are some special populations that have traditionally required hospitalization. These would include people with an intellectual disability and another condition, such as a seizure disorder and attendant aggressive behavior problems; people who have suffered a head injury and are no longer able to exercise behavioral control; people with an intellectual disability who experience a severe bipolar disorder and remain very symptomatic; psychiatric patients who experience physical disability that makes them more frail and less capable of managing their disorder; people with an intellectual disability and psychiatric symptoms who have committed a sexual offense; the occasional patient with a chronic catatonic schizophrenia condition; people suffering from schizophrenia who also have a neurological condition such as a seizure disorder; people with an intellectual disability from very dysfunctional families who have severe behavioral problems; and people who have a chronic schizophrenic disorder and have become hospital dependent. Many of these patients need controlled environments with a lot of structure and stimulating programs in order to be at their best psychologically and behaviorally. These programs will likely need to be staff intensive to meet their individual needs and would likely include interventions at both a group and individual level. My limited experience tells me that there are a number and a variety of these programs that serve these persons well already. We might develop a greater structure of this sort within our mental health treatment system, particularly for our adult population.

There is also the forensic population. There may be less change in the treatment of the criminally insane due to the need to exercise great care as they transition to a less restrictive environment. Thus, the current model of movement from a secure facility like THSMF to a less secure inpatient hospital followed by a forensic or special group home, if it is felt that they could be managed safely there, may continue. However, this population may similarly benefit from a better understanding of their mental disorder and how to manage it, which is a variable that is relevant to risk. Hopefully, a better educated public about the nature of schizophrenia and the treatment available for it will lead to a reduction in forensic cases.

These observations suggest that there may be greater emphasis on public education and awareness as a preventive measure and early intervention efforts in the community. If public education and early intervention efforts are effective, there may be fewer hospitalizations in the future, including fewer extended acute and long-term care hospitalizations. There may be a greater emphasis on special programs for special populations that are more staff intensive. Psychiatric medication could become more specialized and less prevalent for the treatment of schizophrenia. Hospital ward and group home populations could become smaller. Other uses of facilities, some that we have had before, may be considered, such as an adolescent unit, a substance use unit, and a crisis stabilization unit for our area.

My vision, if this book is successful, is to put aside the majority of these funds for the purpose of building a model system for the country within the State of Alabama. I would like to see the University of Alabama partner with the Alabama Department of Mental Health (ADMH), acting as our educational arm and participating in an active exchange of information with our staff at all levels (e.g., administrators, pharmacists, clinicians, direct care staff), community providers (e.g., mental health centers, group home staff), and clients as we enter a new phase in the treatment of the mentally ill. This venture should help us to have at our disposal the best information possible as we seek to treat our clients most effectively and seek to develop the best treatment for them, including creative, new approaches. Some of the relevant study and research areas might include tracking medication changes, their relative success, and risk issues; developing and disseminating new treatment approaches for schizophrenia and the other major mental illnesses; providing necessary training to staff; and relying on evidenced-based practices to determine the relative success of new treatment approaches. There should also be an emphasis on providing all staff the necessary training for them to continue to effectively carry out their roles during the transition period or as they assume new roles, when necessary.

These funds are meant to be used primarily for ADMH needs beyond those operations funded by the general fund of the State of Alabama, but a portion may be used for operation needs if there are sufficient funds and such needs become necessary. A portion may also be set aside for capital and equipment needs that are identified, practical, and feasible.

Many patients or clients within the system have deficits in academic and vocational skills that dim their outlook and prevent them from developing community vision, which is necessary for them to feel positive about their lives. These are issues that are relevant to their mental health. I would like the resources from the book, if sufficient, to be used for the purpose of developing programs that meet their individual needs, including specialized or individual interventions. The Compeer program of community volunteers that we have had in the past could be instrumental in this regard. I would also like for these individualized treatment plans to consider patient rehabilitation needs, including a continuation of psychiatric rehabilitation plans by community providers in a seamless manner, beyond the transitional setting to effect successful community re-entry as much as possible. Although these funds should not be used in place of existing programs and funding, they should be considered when necessary to meet the exigencies of specific clients. The approach as a whole should emphasize an independent attitude toward living rather than increased reliance on the mental health system.

Epilogue

I was raised Catholic. I am well indoctrinated in the Catholic faith, which has been a tremendous source of guidance and inspiration in my life. I am not a theologian. I am not altogether sure how my observations will integrate with the precepts of the Catholic Church. I remember listening to a cassette disk that a friend at church provided me in which the speaker was an inspired theologian, John Martignoni, the president of The Bible Christian Society in Pleasant Grove, Alabama—someone who was schooled in the Catholic faith—and his discourse about the Bible and science always being in agreement (18). Mr. Martignoni stated that when they are not, then someone has either got the Bible wrong or the science wrong.

God made the revelations contained in this book to me by giving me the God-given conscience that prevails during conscientious, studious work. In the words of a Baptist preacher, we are made in the image of God, which means that we are to put on the mind of God. God revealed this to me as a result of my determined struggle with schizophrenia, my further struggle to understand fully the human personality and communicate that understanding, my knowledge and understanding of Catholicism and Christianity, and my God-fearing nature, which led me to seek him out amidst adversity. This was also part of my journey back to God after serious sins that separated me from being a member of his flock. I feel that the fundamental truths that God revealed to me will not violate any basic Catholic or Christian principles.

What did God reveal to me as a result of my determined efforts and studious work, when I was enlightened about the workings of the human personality? God revealed fundamental principles about the nature of mental illness—how we as humans can affect one another physically and psychologically for the good or bad. God also revealed much about the human subconscious and how it affects our conscious world. He revealed more clearly what is meant by the communion of saints and why it is important to have a clear conscience to participate in that form of communion. He revealed many ways in which we commit earthly mistakes and spiritual sins that cost us dearly, if not in this life, then in another life. In doing this, he revealed his nature. Namely, that he loves us unconditionally and will bless our efforts if we are willing to struggle with a sincere heart and mind; at the same time, if we follow the way of sin and ignore or oppose his holy spirit—his will for us—then we will repay each sin with just due.

God also revealed a lot about heaven. It is not some vague concept about after life but a better life for us here on earth, to start with. When we hurt one another, we bring humanity down; we fail to follow God's will. Let us all work to bring humanity up by finding and following the spirit of God. That is the way to individual peace and peace in our world. There are many religions in the world, but there is only one God. And there is only one spirit of God. And let's not confuse Jesus: Jesus was God.

I feel that this book is an epiphany from God that gets at the Zeitgeist of our worldly culture and these times. I feel that God inspired me in the body of the ideas in this book to provide a framework to bring humanity forward, through revelations that should serve as a wake up call for all of us to follow his precepts and to form a world of his design, not of ours. I am humbled to act as his spokesperson.

REFERENCES

1. Alberts, B., Johnson, A., Lewis, J., Raff, M., Roberts, K., & Walter P. (2002). *Molecular biology of the cell* (4th ed.). New York: Garland Science.

2. American Heritage Dictionary (2nd College Ed.) (1982). Boston: Houghton Mifflin.

3. American Psychiatric Association (2013). *Diagnostic and statistical manual of mental disorders* (5th ed.). Washington, DC: American Psychiatric Publishing.

4. American Psychiatric Association (2000). *Diagnostic and statistical manual of mental disorders* (4th ed., text revision) (DSM-IV-TR). Arlington, VA: American Psychiatric Assn.

5. Bennett, P. (2003). *Abnormal and clinical psychology: An introductory textbook*. Philadelphia: Open University Press.

6. Carlson, N.R. (1986). *Physiology of behavior* (3rd ed.). Newton, MA: Allyn and Bacon.

7. Escamilla, M., Hare, E., Dassori, A. M., Peralta, J. M., Ontiveros, A., Nicolini, H., Raventos, H., Medina, R., Mendoza, R., Jerez, A., Munoz, R., & Almasy, L. (2009). A schizophrenia gene locus on chromosome 17q21 in a new set of families of Mexican and Central American ancestry: evidence

from the NIMH genetics of schizophrenia in Latino population study. *American Journal of Psychiatry, 166*(4), 442-449.

8. Farkas, M.D., Cohen, M.R., McNamara, S. & Nemec, P.B. (2000). *Psychiatric rehabilitation training technology: rehabilitation readiness*. Boston, MA: Center for Psychiatric Rehabilitation.

9. Farrell, M.S., Werge,T., Sklar, P., Owen, M.J., Ophoff, R.A., O'Donovan, M.C., Corvin, A., Cichon, S., & Sullivan, P.F. (2015). Evaluating historical candidate genes for schizophrenia. *Molecular Psychiatry, 20*, 555-562.

10. Fast, J.A. & Preston, J. (2006). *Take charge of bipolar disorder: A 4-step plan for you and your loved ones to manage mental illness and create lasting stability*. New York: Grand Central Life & Style.

11. Forsyth, D.R. (1983). *An introduction to group dynamics*. Monterey, CA: Brooks/Cole.

12. George Washington University Medical Center & American Pharmaceutical Association (Joint Sponsors). (2002). *Medication management considerations in schizophrenia: Special report*. Washington, D.C.: American Pharmaceutical Association.

13. Goldenson, R.M.(Ed.) (1984). *Longman dictionary of psychology and psychiatry*. New York: Longman.

14. Heston, L.L. (1966). Psychiatric disorders in foster-home-reared children of schizophrenic mothers. *British Journal of Psychiatry, 112*, 819-825.

15. Kety, S.S., Rosenthal, D., Wender, P.H., & Schulsinger, K.F. (1968). The types and prevalence of mental illness in the biological and adoptive families of adopted schizophrenics. In D. Rosenthal & S.S. Kety (Eds.), *The transmission of schizophrenia*. New York: Pergamon Press.

16. Linehan, M.M. (1993). *Skills training manual for treating borderline personality disorder*. New York: Guilford Press.

17. Lundin, R.W. (1985). *Theories and systems in psychology* (3ʳᵈ ed.). Lexington, MA: D.C. Heath.

18. Martignoni, J. (Speaker) (2009). *Catholics & the Bible (The church and biblical interpretations)*. Pleasant Grove, AL: The Bible Christian Society.

19. Mueser, K.T., Noordsy, D.L., Drake, R.E., & Fox, L. (2003). *Integrated treatments for dual disorders: A guide to effective treatment*. New York: Guilford Press.

20. Newman, C.F. (1995). *Cognitive therapy: Applications across a spectrum of disorders*. Presented in cooperation with The Department of Social Work, Bryce Hospital, The Alabama Department of Mental Health and The School of Social Work, University of Alabama. Bryant Conference Center.

21. Paul, J. II (1993). Catechism of the Catholic church (text approved and promulgated by Pope John Paul II, Latin translation into English in 1994—Internet, December, 2014). Citta del Vaticano: Libreria Editrice Vaticana.

22. Spear, P.D., Penrod, S.D., & Baker, T.B. (1988). *Psychology: Perspectives on behavior*. New York: John, Wiley, & Sons.

23. Tienari, P., Wynne, L.C., Moring, J. et al. (2000). Finnish adoptive family study: sample selection and adoptee DSM-III-R diagnoses, *Acta Psychiatrica Scandinavica, 101,* 433-443.

24. University of Utah: Health Sciences: Genetic Science Learning Center: Insights from Identical Twins (Web site: November 26, 2015).

25. Wikipedia, The Free Encyclopedia. (September, 2011). Web site: *Dopamine.*

26. Wikipedia, The Free Encyclopedia. (September, 2011). Web site: *Mesocortical pathway.*

27. Wikipedia, The Free Encyclopedia. (August, 2014). Web site: *Schizophrenia.*

28. Wikipedia, The Free Encyclopedia. (August, 2014). Web site: *The causes of schizophrenia.*

29. Wikipedia, The Free Encyclopedia. (November 2015). Web site: *Hypofrontality.*

30. Wilhelmsen, K.C., Lynch, T., Pavlou, E., Higgins, M., & Nygaard, T.G. (1994). Localization of disinhibition-dementia-parkinsonism-amyotropy complex to 17q21-22. *American Journal of Human Genetics, 55,* 1159-1165.

31. Wright, J.H., Turkington, D., Kingdon, D.G., & Ramirez, M.B. (2009). *Cognitive-behavior therapy for severe mental illness: An illustrated guide.* Washington, D.C.: American Psychiatric Publishing.

BIBLIOGRAPHY

1. Alcoholics Anonymous (2001). *Alcoholics Anonymous* (4th ed.). New York: Alcoholics Anonymous World Services.

2. Bell, S.M. & Ainsworth, M. (1972). Infant crying and maternal responsiveness. *Child Development, 43*, 1171-1190.

3. Bowlby, J. & Ainsworth, M. (1992). The origins of attachment theory. *Developmental Psychology, 28*(5), 759-775.

4. Catholic Bible Association of America (1970). *The new American Bible.* Cleveland: Catholic Press.

5. Schwartz, B., Lacey, H. (1982). *Behaviorism, science, and human nature.* New York: W. W. Norton.